Garden Harvest
COOKBOOK

Growing & Cooking Vegetables

Contributing Writers
Wayne Ambler
Carol Landa Christensen

Project Consultant
C. Colston Burrell

Contributing Consultant
Kathi Keville

Illustrators
Roberta Simonds: Herbs
Mike Wanke/Steven Edsey & Sons:
Vegetables & Herbs

PUBLICATIONS INTERNATIONAL, LTD.

Contributors:

Wayne Ambler is an active horticulturist, teacher of horticulture, and has completed a master's degree thesis in horticulture education. He has provided gardening consultation for books and periodicals.

Carol Landa Christensen graduated cum laude from the Pennsylvania School of Horticulture for Women, and went on to work at Longwood Gardens as a horticultural information specialist and as a floral designer. Her articles have appeared regularly in many newspapers and magazines, including *Plants Alive* and *Gurney's Gardening News.*

C. Colston Burrell has an M.S. in horticulture; is a garden designer, writer, consultant; and is horticulture editor of *Landscape Architecture Magazine.* He coauthored the *Illustrated Encyclopedia of Perennials*, contributed to both the *New Encyclopedia of Organic Gardening* and *Landscaping with Nature,* and has served as a consultant to many other gardening books. He is a member of the American Association of Botanic Gardens and Arboreta and the Perennial Plant Association; he is also proprietor of Native Landscapes Design and Restoration Ltd.

Kathi Keville is the author of *American Country Living: Herbs* and *An Illustrated Encyclopedia of Herbs* and has served as the editor of the *American Herb Association's Quarterly Newsletter*. She has also written numerous articles on herbs for national magazines.

Nutritional Analysis: In the case of multiple choices, the first ingredient, the lowest amount, and the lowest serving yield are used to calculate the nutritional analysis. "Serve with" suggestions, garnishes, decorations, and items for "dipping" or "serving" are not included unless otherwise stated.

Photo credits:

Front and back cover photography: Sanders Studio, Inc., Chicago

Pictured on the front and back cover *(clockwise from top left)*: Mediterranean Sandwiches (page 176), Oriental Chicken Kabobs (page 144), and Salad Primavera (page 129).

Photo credits:
Bill Beatty; Jeffery A. Brown; Crandall & Crandall Photography; Heather Angel Photography; David Liebman/Quality Nature Photography; M.Claude; Jerry Pavia; Joanne Pavia; Ann Reilly/Photo/Nats, Inc.; Lise Servant.

The publishers would like to thank the following organizations for the use of their recipes in this publication: Almond Board of California; California Tree Fruit Agreement; Canned Food Information Council; Florida Department of Citrus; National Cattlemen's Beef Association; National Turkey Federation; The Sugar Association, Inc.

CONTENTS

INTRODUCTION 6

GARDEN BASICS 9

Chapter 1
Planning Your Garden 10

Climate 12
Getting Your Garden Started 14
Getting Your Garden on Paper 16
Gardening Tools 18

Chapter 2
Preparing the Soil 22

Improving Your Garden Soil 24
Fertilizing: How & Why to Do It 26
The Gardener's Recycling Plan 28

Chapter 3
Planting Your Garden 30

Starting Transplants Indoors 32
Caring for Seedlings 34
Direct-seeding in the Garden 36
Starting New Plants from Parts 40

Chapter 4
Caring for Your Garden   44

Staking & Plant Support   46
Weeding: Keep Out Intruders   48
Mulches   49
Water for Your Garden   52
Preparing for Winter   54

Chapter 5
Garden Health   56

Controlling Insect Pests   58
Nonchemical Pest Control   59
Pests & Other Problems   61

Chapter 6
Herbs in Your Garden   66

Growing Your Own Herbs   68

Chapter 7
Encyclopedia of
Vegetables & Herbs   72

Vegetables   74
Herbs   96

GARDEN BOUNTY   106

Vegetables   107
Herbs   164

INDEX   189

INTRODUCTION

Have you ever tasted a sweet, tender tomato plucked straight from the vine? How about the zing of fresh cilantro in homemade salsa? Have you enjoyed a delicious salad made with vegetables hand-picked from your own garden? Well, if not, then you're missing out on the joys of home gardening.

What's the difference between home-grown and store-bought vegetables? A tomato's a tomato, right? Wrong. Supermarkets carry vegetables that are grown for their durability, not their flavor. They have to, but you don't. Did you know that there are more than a hundred varieties of tomatoes? They can be red, yellow, green, round, or pear-shaped, and vary in size from less than an ounce to more than a pound. But your grocery can't stock them all. They decide which types to carry, not you. Sure, there are specialty grocers that may carry some gourmet choices—at gourmet prices. And who knows what kind of chemicals or pesticides they used?

Growing your own vegetables and herbs is the only way to guarantee you'll have exactly what you want. You'll not only have more flavorful meals, you'll also feel the difference in your pocketbook. That sounds great, but where do you start? How do you decide where to put a garden? What plants grow best in your climate? And what can you do with your edible treasures once you've grown them? This book was created to give you the answers.

Garden Harvest Cookbook is really two books in one—a gardening guide and a cookbook. The first part will take you, step-by-step, through everything you need to know to grow your own vegetables and herbs. From recognizing healthy plants to fighting pests and disease, you'll learn just how easy it is to maintain a productive garden. Whether you're a novice or seasoned gardener, you'll find practical advice and time-saving hints to get the most from your space—and from your plants. There's also a convenient directory of vegetables and herbs from artichokes to watermelons. Each entry gives you growing tips, uses, and a list of some of the popular varieties available.

The second section of this book is filled with more than 80 delicious recipes, specifically chosen to make the most of your harvest. You'll find it all: savory soups, salads, appetizers, side dishes, and hearty main dishes. The easy-to-follow recipes are organized alphabetically by vegetable for handy reference. And even if you don't have a garden, you can enjoy creating these taste-tempting meals!

We've taken the guesswork out of growing and cooking your own vegetables and herbs. It's easier than you think, and you'll taste the difference.

GARDEN BASICS

Nothing adds more to your meals than fresh
vegetables and herbs. And with the right planning,
you can enjoy a new crop of tasty favorites every week
of the growing season. This section will show
you the simple secrets to having a
healthy and productive garden.

A well-planned garden can produce vegetables from early summer to late fall. This garden—bearing tasty lettuce, beets, and beans—had its start with a plan thought out during the winter months.

PLANNING YOUR GARDEN

W hether it's a garden-fresh tomato on a sandwich or corn on the cob direct from the garden to the stove, you know it's true: The tastiest vegetables come from the home garden. Much enjoyment comes from producing your own crisp vegetables, and it's an activity where everyone in the family can contribute—even the very young.

The best gardens come from careful planning. Winter is a good time to plan your garden. Few things are more enjoyable on a cold winter evening than thumbing through seed catalogs while awaiting spring's arrival. But whether you plan to plant a large garden or just a few containers of vegetables on the patio, gardening is more than just planting seeds. There are many elements to consider for a successful harvest.

The first step is deciding which vegetables to grow. Which vegetables do you and your family like? Can those vegetables grow in your climate? Do you want to freeze or can some of your crop? These questions should be considered before you start planting.

We'll give you information about the essentials of planning a successful vegetable garden: site selection, varieties of vegetables and how much to grow, making a layout plan, and gardening tools. Brought together, these elements can provide you with a rewarding gardening experience.

Climate

The growing season is the length of time that your area has the conditions plants need to reach maturity and produce a crop. The growing season is measured in terms of the number of days between the last frost in spring and the first frost in fall. In general terms, these two dates mark the beginning and end of the time in which plants grow from seed to maturity. Some areas never have frost; instead, their dry season serves as "winter." The length of your growing season is totally dependent on your local climate.

The dates a certain area can expect to have the last spring frost and the first fall frost are called the "average date of last frost" and the "average date of first frost" respectively. These dates are used as reference points for planning and planting vegetables, but they're not infallible. The dates do, however, give you a fairly accurate guide as to which vegetables will do the best in your area. For last and first average frost dates in your area, call your county Cooperative Extension office or check with your local gardening center.

The average date of last frost is not the only reference point used to determine when to plant a garden. The small maps found on the back of seed packages are hardiness zone maps, dividing the United States into areas with fairly similar climates.

The term "hardiness" is specifically used to indicate how well a plant tolerates cold. Vegetables grown in a home garden fall into one of four hardiness categories: very hardy, hardy, tender, and very tender. The date on which you can safely plant each vegetable in your garden depends on its hardiness category.

Very hardy vegetables can tolerate cold and frost and can be planted in the garden four to six weeks before the average date of last frost. Hardy vegetables can handle some cold and frost and can be planted two to three weeks before the average date of last frost. Tender vegetables don't like cold weather. They can be planted on the average date of last frost, but you will need to protect them in some way if there's a late frost. Very tender vegetables will not survive any frost and must be planted after the soil has warmed up in the spring. They can be planted two to three weeks after the average date of last frost.

Vegetables have different temperature preferences and tolerances and are usually classified as either cool-season crops or warm-season crops. Cool-season crops, such as cabbages, lettuce, and peas, must have time to mature before the weather gets too warm; otherwise, they will wilt, die, or go to seed prematurely. These vegetables can be started in warm weather only if there will be a long enough stretch of cool weather in the fall to allow the crop to mature before the first freeze. Warm-season crops, such as peppers, cucumbers, and melons, can't tolerate frost. If the weather gets too cool, their yields will be reduced or they may not grow at all.

Climatic factors, such as sunlight, affect which vegetables to grow and when to plant them.

A coldframe is an outside glass-enclosed growing area used to get a jump on the growing season. The coldframe shelters the plants from wind and cold and warms easily on winter and spring days. Hardy vegetables can be grown in a coldframe during most of the year if you live in a mild climate.

Whether you sow seeds directly or use the coldframe to harden-off containerized transplants, you'll have to water the plants regularly. Coldframes dry out easily, so they need plenty of water. However, the soil in the coldframe must be amended and well drained to prevent seedlings from rotting. Use gravel or sandy soil; plants must not be in standing water.

Light is another important factor to consider when you plan your garden. Sunlight—or some type of light—provides the energy that plants need to turn water and carbon dioxide into the sugar they use for food. If light is limited, even a plant that looks green and healthy may never produce flowers or fruit. This can be a problem with such vegetables as tomatoes, where you want to eat the fruit. With lettuce, where you're only interested in the leaves, light is not as much an issue.

Vegetables grown for their fruit need a minimum of six to eight hours of direct light each day. Root crops, such as beets, carrots, radishes, and turnips, store up energy before they flower and do rather well in partial shade. Plants that are grown for their leaves, such as lettuce and spinach, are most tolerant of shade; in fact, where the sun is hot and bright, they may need some shade for protection.

Light for Your Garden

If you have a choice of where to grow your vegetable garden, don't put it in the shade of buildings, trees, or shrubs. Also remember that trees and shrubs, as well as shading an area, have roots that may extend well beyond the reach of their branches. These roots will compete with the vegetable plants for water and nutrients.

Extending the Season with a Coldframe

A coldframe uses solar heat. Built of simple materials—scrap lumber and old storm windows—it's easy to construct. Make the back about 12 inches higher than the front and face the window sash south with hinges on the higher side. During sunny days the sash can be propped open with a stick to prevent overheating the plants. If the sun is bright, temperatures can reach 85 degrees Fahrenheit even when the temperature outside is freezing. Close the frame at night and during cold weather to protect young plants.

Getting Your Garden Started

Several varieties of the same vegetable meet different cultural needs and have different characteristics.

Most vegetables come in many varieties. After giving thought to the types of vegetables you want to grow, you're ready to decide which varieties to grow. Seed catalogs, for instance, offer a selection of tomatoes that is totally bewildering: big ones, little ones, cherry ones, green ones, canning ones. Some are disease resistant, some are not; some ripen early, some late.

It's worth taking the time to consider why there are so many varieties of one vegetable. A variety is simply a botanical change in the original plant. These changes may be as obvious as a change in the color, size, or shape of the fruit. Other changes, such as improved disease resistance, better flavor, or compact growth, may be less obvious. Hybrids are bred for success. A hybrid may be the result of breeding two different pure lines. A pure line is a plant that has been selected and bred for a certain desirable characteristic, such as the size of its fruit or its ability to resist disease.

With so many varieties available, it can be difficult to choose the right one. The vegetable and herb directory (see page 72) describes many individual vegetables and their cultural requirements; this list includes some of the best and most commonly used varieties. Information on varieties may also be obtained from seed catalog descriptions or from your local Cooperative Extension office. Another indication of the most reliable varieties for your area is All-America Selections. This nonprofit organization develops and promotes new varieties of vegetables and flowers. If a variety is listed in your seed catalog as an All-America Selection, it has been tested by growers all over the country; you can be sure it's a good bet for your garden.

Each vegetable variety has its "days to maturity" listed in the seed catalog or on the seed packet. This number indicates the average number of days needed from germination or transplanting to harvest. Using a calendar, see how the dates fall for the crops you're thinking of growing. Deciding when to plant involves more than just avoiding killing frosts. It also means pacing your planting so you get the maximum yield from a limited space. This takes careful planning. Some crops can be harvested gradually, others mature all at once.

Pace Your Planting

One way to pace your harvest is to plant several varieties of the same vegetable that will mature at different rates. For instance, two or three weeks before the average date of last frost plant three different varieties of carrot. This can extend your production period over two to three months. Or plant at 2–3 week intervals to achieve the same pacing.

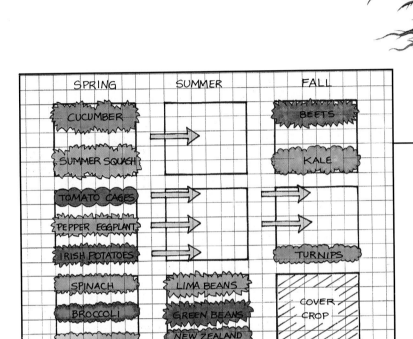

Succession planting

You can save garden space and get two or more harvests from the same spot through succession planting. After early maturing crops are harvested, replant the space with a new crop. Early cool-season crops can be replaced with warm-season crops. Start off with a fast-growing, cool-season crop that can be planted early: lettuce, spinach, and cabbage are good examples. Warm-weather crops, such as New Zealand spinach, chard, corn, and squash, can then replace the earlier plants. Finally, in the fall make a planting of cole crops (for example, cabbage, broccoli, or cauliflower) or put in root crops such as turnips or beets.

Companion planting

Another way to increase the use of your planting space is through companion planting. This is done by planting short-term crops between plants that will take a longer time to mature. The short-term crops are harvested by the time the long-term crops need the extra room. A good example of this is radishes or lettuce planted between rows of tomatoes or peppers. By the time the tomatoes and peppers need the space, the radishes and lettuce will have been harvested.

Getting Your Garden on Paper

Stakes and raised beds are just two of the items to consider when designing your garden.

You've put a lot of thought into your garden plan. You also know some vital information and dates: The names of the varieties you're going to plant as well as planting and harvest dates. Now comes some substantial paperwork.

The size of your garden depends on your interest in gardening and how much time you'll be able to give to the garden. Some gardeners use every available inch of space; others use a small corner of their property. Some don't have much choice; this may be your case if you have a small garden to begin with or if you're gardening on a patio or balcony. The larger your garden, the more time and work it's going to need. Unless you're already hooked on gardening, it's probably better to start small and let garden size increase as your interest in gardening and confidence in your ability develop.

Before deciding the exact dimensions of your garden, check the list of vegetables you've chosen and the amount you're going to grow for each one. Then calculate if all the vegetables will fit into the allotted space. To determine how much space each plant or row will consume, refer to the chart on pages 42 and 43.

Keep in mind that you'll probably map out successive plantings. Arrange your plantings to make the best use of your available space. Some vegetables (for example, cucumbers) sprawl, taking up much space in the garden. You can make use of vertical space, however, by training vines to grow on a trellis; this will free up usable planting ground.

Drawing the plot plan is the pencil-and-paper stage of planning. If you use graph paper, it will be easier to work to scale. A commonly used scale is one inch of paper to two feet of garden space, but you can adapt the scale to whatever is easiest for you. Draw up a simple plot plan with your garden's measurements in all directions. Remember, no law requires a garden to be square or rectangular. Your garden can be round, curved, or any shape that fits your landscape.

Sketch circles for individual transplants, and rows for directly sown seeds. Take care in placing the vegetables. Place taller plants in the north or northeast area of the garden so they won't shade other plants as they grow. If you're going to use a rototiller, make sure the rows are wide. In smaller gardens it's more space-efficient to plant in wide rows or in solid blocks four to five feet wide. You must be able to reach the center of a wide row comfortably from either side.

If you're serious about gardening, you should keep records. Planning your records should be part of planning your garden. Build your records the same way you build your garden; profit from past mistakes and incorporate new ideas. Keep a daily record, noting such things as soil preparation, planting, weeding, fertilizing, bloomtime, date crops ripen, and growing results. Also note any problems with weeds, bugs, or rainfall, and whether the harvest of each item was sufficient, too much, or not enough. At the end of the growing season, you'll have a complete record of what you did, and this information will give you the basics for planning next year's garden.

Drawing the Plot Plan

Measure your garden space and plot it on graph paper using a scale that suits the size. Keeping taller vegetables on the north or northeast side, start the plan by sketching in the cool-season varieties. Calculate when those varieties will mature so you can replace them with warm-season crops.

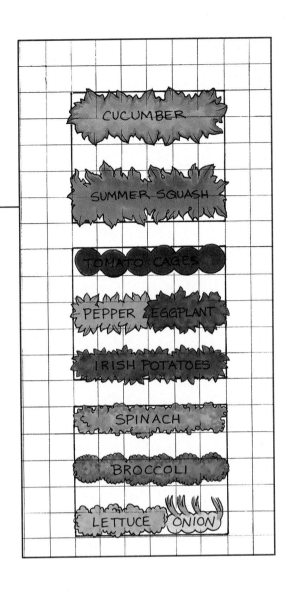

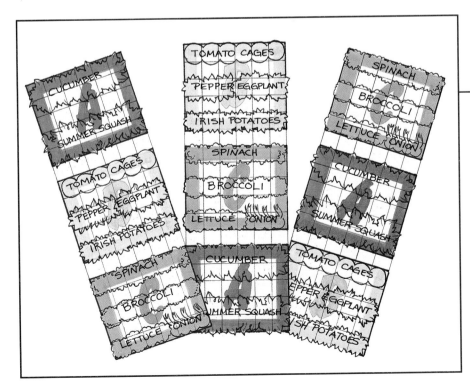

Rotate Your Crops

Do not grow the same plant family in the same spot year after year. Repetition of the same crop gives diseases a chance to build up strength. There are three major vegetable families:

- Cole crops (cabbage family): broccoli, brussels sprouts, cabbage, cauliflower, kohlrabi, rutabaga, and turnip;
- Cucurbits (cucumber family): cucumber, gourd, muskmelon, pumpkin, summer and winter squash, and watermelon;
- Solanaceous plants (tomato and pepper family): eggplant, Irish potato, pepper, and tomato.

After growing a crop from one of these families one year, choose a variety from a different family to plant in the same spot the following season.

17

Gardening Tools

Gardening tools—such as the watering can shown here—are essential for good vegetable production.

There are a great many garden tools on the market. Some are mandatory, while others are helpful but not necessary. Consider the type and amount of gardening you do and choose the implements that best suit your needs. When you decide which tools you need, buy the best you can find and take good care of them. High-quality tools work better and last longer than economy tools that may not have much durability. When you're shopping for a tool, pick it up and see how well it fits in your hands. The weight and length of the handle should balance with the weight of the blade. Garden tools come in different sizes and weights; you and your equipment should be compatible.

In caring for your tools, follow these basic guidelines:

- Clean your tools before putting them away. If you're storing them for the winter, a thin coat of motor oil will help prevent rusting. Use a file to keep your hoe and spade sharp.
- Have a regular storage area for your tools that is protected from the weather.
- Use each tool the way it was meant to be used. For instance, a rake—even a good quality rake—won't last long if you constantly use it to dig holes or turn soil.

Spade and Shovel—A shovel has a curved scoop and a handle with or without a handgrip. It's used for lifting, turning, and moving soil. A spade is a sturdy tool with a thick handle, a handgrip, and a heavy blade that you press into the ground with your foot. The blade is usually flatter and sharper than a shovel's and usually squared off at the bottom. A spade is for hard digging work; it should be strong but light enough to handle comfortably.

Spading Fork—A spading fork is used for heavy digging. Its prongs make it the best tool for breaking up compacted soil, lifting root vegetables, and digging weeds. The handle is sturdy and has a handgrip; your foot presses the prongs into the ground.

Hoe—The hoe is a tool with a flat blade attached at a right angle to a long handle. It's used for mounding the soil, making rows, cultivating, and cutting off weeds. It is one of the gardener's most necessary tools.

Trowel—This is a hand-held, short-handled tool with a pointed scoop-shaped blade. It's used as a small shovel and is helpful when transplanting young plants into the garden.

Garden Rake—A rake with a long handle and short sturdy metal prongs is used for leveling and grading soil and for removing rocks, soil clods, and shallow-rooted weeds.

Basic Tools

To be successful, every gardener needs some basic tools for starting and maintaining the garden. Buy high-quality tools; you'll save money in the end.

Trowel

Spade **Shovel** **Spading Fork** **Hoe** **Garden Rake**

Wheelbarrow

A wheelbarrow or garden cart is useful for moving tools, soil amendments, fertilizer, plants, and supplies to and from the garden. Available in metal, wood, and plastic, a wheelbarrow or cart can save you a lot of time and backache. It's essential if you have a large garden.

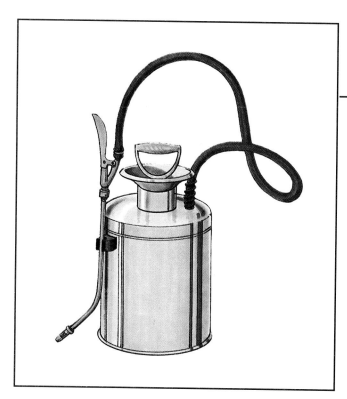

Sprayers

Sprayers are used for applying pesticides evenly to plants or other surfaces. There are two kinds of sprayers for the home garden. A hose-attachment jar sprayer has a container (usually a quart) with a screw-on lid and a nozzle that attaches to the end of your garden hose. It uses the pressure of the hose to mix the concentrated pesticide with water and then spray the pesticide. This type of sprayer is inexpensive but may not dispense an accurate dose. A hand-pump sprayer—either a backpack or a cylinder type—applies the pesticide manually by means of a pump. The backpack can hold anywhere from one to five gallons of pesticide; a cylinder type can hold one pint to one quart. Choose the size that best fits your needs.

Hand Spreader

You can use a hand spreader either to spread dry granule fertilizer or to sow seeds. It's a small box with a handle that you crank; a fan attached to the crank throws out the contents as you walk. It's effective for spreading an even layer of fertilizer or for planting a cover crop in the fall.

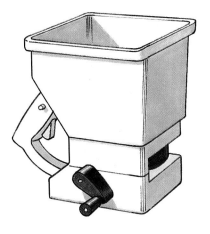

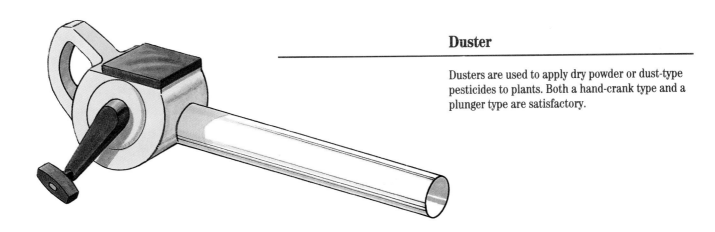

Duster

Dusters are used to apply dry powder or dust-type pesticides to plants. Both a hand-crank type and a plunger type are satisfactory.

Rototiller

A rototiller, usually gas-powered, uses multiple blades to turn soil in preparation for planting or to cultivate between rows. There are rear-type and front-type rototillers. Rear-type tillers are generally larger, more powerful, and easier to operate because they are self-propelled. However, they cost more and are less convenient to move around. Consider renting a rototiller the first year to determine your needs before making the investment.

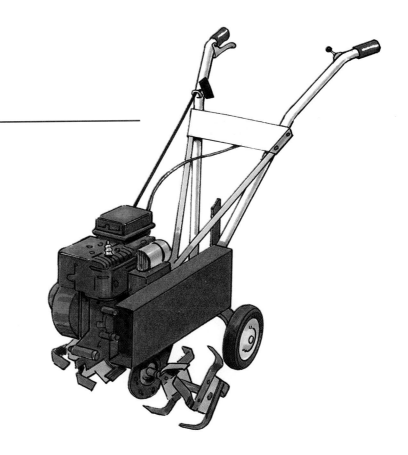

All vegetables do better in a good, rich, deep soil, making gardening easy and fun. Your vegetable garden will be more productive after adding amendments to improve the pH and organic content.

CHAPTER 2

PREPARING THE SOIL

Count your blessings if you're lucky enough to have a garden with rich fertile loam, which is deep and easy to work. Soil is often too heavy with clay or is too dry and sandy, and most beginning gardeners soon realize they must improve on one or more conditions of their soil.

The function of the soil is fourfold: It must supply water; it must supply nutrients; it must supply air to the roots; and it must be firm enough to support the plant securely. The ideal soil is a middle-of-the-road mixture, holding moisture and nutrients while letting excess water drain away to make room for air.

Vegetables can survive in a wide variety of soil types, but by making some simple preparatory changes, your garden soil can become as easy to use and productive as you'd like. Good soil must be guarded by proper management, involving cultivation, use of organic matter, and maintenance of fertility.

This chapter will take you step-by-step through a soil-improvement program. You'll learn how to test your soil for texture and fertility. Then you will see how to improve soil deficiencies. There's no need to worry if you're not satisfied with the results of your testing. Improving your garden soil is easily accomplished and is a regular part of gardening. Also, the soil-improving process doesn't have to all happen in the first year of gardening. Take time working with your soil, and you'll reap the benefits of many years of fruitful production.

Improving Your Garden Soil

Good soil is a key to healthy vegetable plants.

Good soil is 50 percent solids and 50 percent porous space, which provides room for water, air, and plant roots. The solids are inorganic matter (fine rock particles) and organic matter (decaying plant matter). The inorganic portion of the soil can be divided into three categories based on the size of the particles it contains. Clay has the smallest soil particles; silt has medium-size particles; and sand has the coarsest particles. The amount of clay, silt, and sand in a soil determine its texture. Loam, the ideal garden soil, is a mixture of 20 percent clay, 40 percent silt, and 40 percent sand.

The first step in your soil-improvement program is to have the soil tested for nutrient levels. The local county Cooperative Extension office can advise you on testing the soil in your area. Your soil sample will be sent to a laboratory to determine any deficiencies of the necessary nutrients needed for successful plant growth. The test will also tell you the kind of soil you have, such as sandy loam.

Be sure to tell the laboratory that the samples came from a vegetable garden plot. The test report will recommend the amount and kind of fertilizer needed for a home garden. Follow the laboratory's recommendations as closely as possible during the first growing season. Also see "Fertilizing: How & Why To Do It" on page 26.

The necessary nutrient levels are relative to the soil type and the crop being grown. Although different vegetable plants have varying requirements, the soil test institution calculates an optimum average for fertilizer and lime recommendations.

The results of the soil test will indicate the pH (acid-alkaline balance) of the soil as well as the nitrogen content, phosphorus content, and potassium content. The pH is measured on a scale of 1 (most acid or sour) to 14 (most alkaline or sweet), with 7 representing neutral. Most vegetable plants produce best in a soil that has a pH between 5.5 and 7.5.

The pH number is important because it affects the availability of most of the essential nutrients in the soil. The soil lab will consider the type of soil you have, the pH level, and the crops you intend to produce and make a recommendation for pH adjustment.

Phosphorus (P) and potassium (K) levels will be indicated by a "Low," "Medium," or "High" level. High is the desired level for vegetable gardens for both nutrients. If your test results show other than High, a recommendation of type and amount of fertilizer will be made.

Although nitrogen (N) is also needed in large amounts by plants, the soil nitrates level is not usually routinely tested because rainfall leaches nitrates from the soil, which easily results in low levels. Additional nitrogen through the use of a complete fertilizer is almost always recommended.

Tests for other elements are available on request but are needed only under special circumstances.

In the interest of harvesting a bigger and better crop of vegetables, you'll want to improve the texture of your soil. This improvement, whether to make the soil drain better or hold more water, can be accomplished quite easily by the addition of organic matter.

Organic matter is material that was once living but is now dead and decaying. You can use such materials as ground corncobs, sawdust, bark chips, straw, hay, peat moss, grass clippings, and cover crops to serve as organic matter. Your own compost pile can supply you with excellent organic matter to enrich the soil.

Each spring, as you prepare the garden for planting, incorporate organic matter into the soil by tilling or turning it under with a spade. If noncomposted materials are used, the microorganisms that break down the materials will use nitrogen from the soil. To compensate for this nitrogen loss, increase the amount of nitrogen fertilizer that you incorporate into the soil.

SOIL TEST REPORT

Sample No.	NO. OE. AC.	Soil Type	Slope	Soil Prod. Group	Last Crop		Last Crops Fertilization, lb/A			Last Lime Application	
					Name	Yield	N	P_2O_5	K_2O	Mo. Prev.	T/A
Dirty		Clayey			None Applied						1-5 Lb/100

Soil pH	P lb/A	K lb/A	Ca lb/A	Mg lb/A	OM %	SS ppm	NO_3-N ppm	Zn ppm	Mn ppm	Cu ppm	Fe ppm	B ppm
7.5	120 VH	314 VH	2400 VH	240 VH				6.1	16.1	0.7	9.4	1.6

Crop: Vegetable garden

*223.   Fertilizer recommendations: Apply 2 lbs of 10-10-10 per square foot. For additional information on fertilization, see note 19 (enclosed).

*619.   Lime recommendations: None needed.

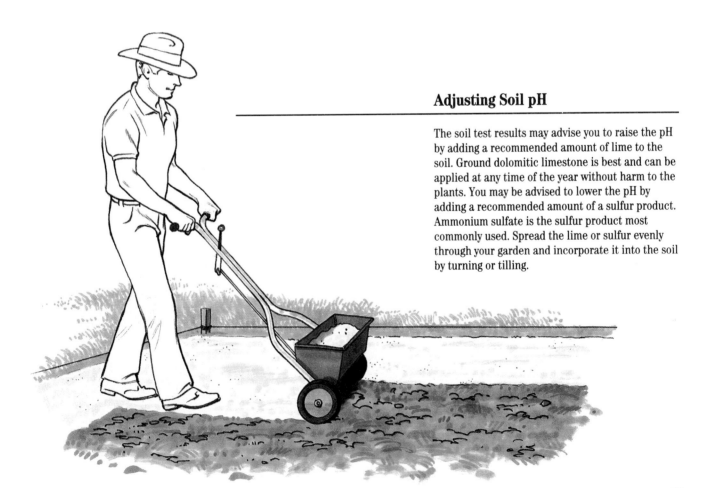

Adjusting Soil pH

The soil test results may advise you to raise the pH by adding a recommended amount of lime to the soil. Ground dolomitic limestone is best and can be applied at any time of the year without harm to the plants. You may be advised to lower the pH by adding a recommended amount of a sulfur product. Ammonium sulfate is the sulfur product most commonly used. Spread the lime or sulfur evenly through your garden and incorporate it into the soil by turning or tilling.

Fertilizing: How & Why to Do It

These golden beets need plenty of nutrients in the form of fertilizer.

Many inexperienced gardeners think that since their vegetables have done fine so far without fertilizer, they'll continue to do fine without fertilizer next year. But it's not quite that simple. Although your plants will probably provide you with vegetables without using fertilizer, you won't be getting their best effort. Properly fertilized vegetable plants will be healthier and better able to resist disease and attacks from pests. Your soil test will tell you how much fertilizer is necessary. Add only those nutrients that are needed.

There are two types of fertilizers: organic and inorganic. Both contain the same nutrients, but their composition and action differ in several ways. It makes no difference to the plant whether nutrients come from an organic or an inorganic source as long as the nutrients are available.

Organic fertilizers come from plants and animals. The nutrients in organic fertilizers must be broken down over a period of time by microorganisms in the soil before they become available to the plants. Therefore, organic fertilizers don't offer instant solutions to nutrient deficiencies in the soil. Dried blood, kelp, and bone meal are types of organic fertilizers.

Manures are also organic. They are bulkier and contain lower percentages of nutrients than other natural fertilizers. However, they offer the advantage of immediately improving the texture of the soil by raising the level of organic matter.

Because organic fertilizers are generally not well-balanced in nutrient content, you'll probably need to use a mixture of them to ensure a balanced nutrient content. The table below, as well as the directions on the package, may be used as a guide to making your own mixture. Incorporate the mixture into the soil while preparing your spring garden. Apply it again as a side-dressing midway through the growing season.

When you fertilize with an inorganic fertilizer, nutrients are immediately available for the plant's use. Any container of fertilizer has three numbers printed on it, such as 5-10-20, to indicate the percentage of major nutrients it contains. Nitrogen is represented by the first number (5 percent in this example); phosphorus is represented by the second number (10 percent); and potassium by the third (20 percent). The remaining 65 percent is a mixture of other nutrients and inert filler. A well-balanced complete fertilizer consists of all three major nutrients in somewhat even proportions. A complete fertilizer is recommended for vegetable garden use as long as the nitrogen content isn't more than 20 percent. A typical fertilizer used in vegetable gardens is 10-10-10.

ANALYSIS OF ORGANIC FERTILIZERS

Fertilizer	N-P-K*
Dried Blood	13–1.5–0
Kelp	3–22–0
Cottonseed Meal	6–2.6–2
Cattle Manure	0.5–0.3–0.5
Horse Manure	0.6–0.3–0.5
Chicken Manure	0.9–0.5–0.8

* (N = Nitrogen, P = Phosphorus, K = Potassium)

Fertilizing Your Garden: A Two-Stage Program

1 **Broadcast Fertilizing**—When you're preparing the bed for spring planting, apply a complete fertilizer—such as 10-10-10—evenly to the entire garden according to the soil test recommendations. Do not overfertilize. A hand spreader helps keep the job neat as it distributes the granules. Turn the fertilizer into the soil with a hand spade or tiller and smooth out the surface to prepare for planting. This first fertilizing step will see most of your vegetables through their initial period of growth. Halfway through the growing season, the plants will have used up a lot of the nutrients in the soil, and you'll have to replace these nutrients.

2 **Sidedressing**—As the nutrients are used up by the plants, a second boost of fertilizer will be needed to supply the plants with essential elements through the remainder of the growing season. Use the same complete fertilizer at the same rate as used in the spring, but this time apply it as a sidedressing to the plants.

With a hoe, make a four-inch deep trench along one side of the row, taking care not to disturb the plant's roots. Apply the fertilizer in the trench and then cover the trench with the soil you removed. Rain and irrigation will work the fertilizer into the soil, becoming available to the plants.

Sidedressing Individual Plants

When long-season vegetables such as tomatoes, eggplant, and peppers need a second application of fertilizer, there's no need to trench an entire row. Cut a four-inch-deep collar-trench around the plant 12 to 18 inches from the stem. Spread about ½ cup of the same fertilizer used in the spring around each plant and cover it with soil. Water the garden well after fertilizing.

The Gardener's Recycling Plan

This compost pile will serve many uses in the vegetable garden.

The backyard compost pile is the ideal way to reuse most of your garden and kitchen waste and get benefits galore. Composting is essentially a way of speeding up the natural process of decomposition by which organic materials are broken down and their components returned to the soil. The decaying process happens naturally but slowly. The proximity, moisture, and air circulation of a compost pile encourages this process. Composting converts plant and other organic wastes into a loose, peatlike humus that provides nutrients to growing plants and increases the soil's ability to control water.

Composting can save money you would otherwise spend on soil conditioners and fertilizer. It can save time, too, since it gives you a place to dispose of grass clippings, weeds, and other garden debris.

Garden waste can be turned into good compost in less than a year if the pile is properly managed. When the compost is ready—coarse, dark brown, peatlike material—it can be used for many purposes. Compost can be added to potting soil for starting garden seeds indoors. It can also be used as a mulch to protect a plant's roots from the hot, dry summer sun. Compost is also an excellent material to incorporate into garden soil to help control moisture: either increasing the water-holding capacity in sandy soils or improving drainage in heavy clay soils. The more organic matter you add, the more you improve the texture of the soil. Blend the compost into the soil to a depth of 12 inches, making sure it is evenly dispersed through the entire planting area. When compost is added to the soil, it will absorb some of the soil's nitrogen. To compensate for this, add two handfuls of complete fertilizer (10-10-10) for each bushel of compost, working the fertilizer thoroughly into the soil.

Except for diseased and pest-laden materials or materials that have been treated with herbicides, almost any type of garden waste can be composted. You can also use such kitchen leftovers as vegetable and fruit peels, vegetable tops, coffee grounds, tea leaves, and eggshells. Don't use meat products or greasy foods, which tend to smell bad and attract animals. Composting material should be kept moist but not soggy, and it should be supplied with a nitrogen fertilizer (manure, dried blood, bone meal, or commercial fertilizer) to keep the microorganisms active for faster decay.

Compost forms as organic wastes are broken down by microorganisms in the soil. These microorganisms don't create nutrients; they just break down complex materials into simple ones that the plant can use. Soil microorganisms are most active when soil temperatures are above 60 degrees Fahrenheit, and most of them work best in a moist, slightly alkaline environment. Microorganisms work fastest on small pieces of organic material.

There are two basic types of microorganisms: those that need air to work (aerobic) and those that don't need air (anaerobic). It's possible to compost in an airtight container, thanks to the microorganisms that don't need air. A tightly covered plastic trash can will convert an enormous amount of organic kitchen waste into compost in the course of a winter. The classic outdoor compost pile should be turned regularly (about once every two weeks) with a pitchfork to provide air for the microorganisms that need it.

There are several handy composting devices on the market. Each has its own advantages, but a compost pile need not be fancy to work well. A simple bin made with old cinder blocks, lumber, or fencing material can be used. Tucked aside, but not too far from the garden, the bin can be square, rectangular, or round. It should be four to five feet across and about three feet high.

There are almost as many different methods of composting as there are gardeners. Follow the basic steps of composting on the next page, and your final product is sure to be a success.

How to Start a Compost Pile

1 Start with either a one- to two-foot pile of leaves or 6 to 12 inches or more of compact material, such as grass clippings or sawdust. You can compost hay, straw, hulls, nutshells, and tree trimmings (except walnut). However, unless they're shredded, they'll take a long time to decompose. Use any organic garden or kitchen waste (except meat scraps), as long as it contains no pesticides or diseases.

2 Over this initial pile spread a layer of fertilizer. The nitrogen will help activate the microorganisms, which in turn will speed the decay of the organic materials. Add about ½ cup of ground limestone (most microorganisms like their environment sweet). Then add several shovelfuls of garden soil, which will provide a starter colony of microorganisms. It's handy to have a small pile of soil nearby when you start the compost pile.

3 Water the pile well. The pile should be kept moist, like a squeezed sponge. Keep adding garden waste to the top of the pile as it becomes available. As the layers become thickened and compacted, repeat the layers of fertilizer, lime, and soil.

4 About once every two weeks, turn and mix the pile with a pitch fork or digging fork. This will ensure that all the components of the pile, not just the center, will heat up. As the temperature in the compost pile increases, weed seeds and harmful disease organisms are killed, and the decay process will not be delayed.

1.

2.

3.

4.

Many gardeners enjoy planting time the most of all seasons. Vegetables finally start growing, and other garden adornments, such as this scarecrow, add amusement as well as protection.

PLANTING YOUR GARDEN

P lanning and soil preparation both lead to the same purpose—getting the garden planted. Most experienced gardeners will agree: Planting time is their favorite season of the year.

If you're anxious to get your garden started, read on. You'll find useful tips and ideas that will make your garden a success, even if you've never gardened before. It goes without saying that thoughtful planning and carefully prepared soil are essential tasks for successful gardening, but the real fun starts with actually planting. You'll feel a great sense of achievement when you've cared for the tender seedlings through periods of inclement weather: frosty nights, scorching sun, and drought.

There are a number of questions you should consider before you start planting. For one thing, should you be planting seeds or should you be using transplants (seedlings that you have started indoors or have purchased)? Some vegetables are not started from seed at all; new plants can be started from old plants. How should the plants be spaced: single rows, wide rows, or inverted hills? As in every other stage of growing a vegetable garden, planting poses many questions. In the following pages you'll learn which vegetables grow best from seed sown in the garden and which vegetables are best started from transplants.

Starting Transplants Indoors

Plants started indoors may need the protection of a coldframe after being moved outdoors.

Earlier harvest, extended season, and increased varietal choice are some of the reasons you may want to start your own vegetable transplants indoors. Although many vegetable plants are available at garden centers each spring, it is sometimes difficult to find the exact variety that you're looking for. By starting your own transplants, you can plan for a supply of what you want when you want it.

Your first consideration is when to plant. If you plant too early, seedlings will become weak and leggy, which is not much of a start for a productive garden. Use the average date of last frost as a reference point for when to plant each vegetable in the garden. Remember, some vegetables will be planted in the garden several weeks before this date, others near or on this date, and yet others a few weeks after this date. From the planting date, count back six to eight weeks; as a general rule, you can sow seeds indoors on this date. Large-seeded varieties, such as squash and watermelon, should be started only four weeks prior to garden planting.

Although you'll gain confidence with experience, it's best to start with just a few varieties the first year. Taking care of seedlings indoors takes time, the proper conditions, and common sense. It is imperative to provide the plants with the necessary environment for strong, healthy growth. Light, temperature, moisture, and cleanliness are just some of the elements that contribute to the healthy development of your plants.

Light—You'll need a place to start seedlings that gets several hours of light each day. Even close to a window, seedlings often stretch, trying to reach toward the light. If artificial lights are used, the bulbs must not produce too much heat. Fluorescent lights or special plant lights produce plenty of light without excessive heat.

Heat/Temperature—Different varieties of vegetables require different temperatures to germinate. Most seeds will germinate well at 70 to 75 degrees Fahrenheit. Some varieties require cooler temperatures; the seed packet will tell you the precise temperature required. Heating pads are available through garden centers and gardening supply mail-order companies, but a warm spot in the room can often be used.

Water—Since many seeds are small and easily displaced in the soil, it's best to soak the seedling tray in water to absorb water from the bottom drainage holes. Seeds will die if they are allowed to dry out after they have started to germinate.

Planting Medium—The soil you sow seeds and grow young plants in must be light and sterile to prevent a deadly seedling disease called damping-off. It's best to purchase a seed-starter medium from a reputable garden center. Garden soil is too heavy and may contain weed seeds or disease organisms.

Containers—Containers can be store-bought seedling trays or pots or items such as aluminum trays, paper cups, or other kitchen items as long as they can hold the medium and contain adequate drainage holes. Small-seeded varieties may be started in trays and later separated and transplanted to individual containers. Large-seeded varieties should be started in individual containers from the start; their roots do not appreciate being disturbed while being separated. Plantable containers such as peat-pots are handy. These are made of compressed peat, and the pot can be planted in the garden.

VEGETABLES TO START INDOORS

Broccoli	Eggplant
Brussels Sprouts	Lettuce
Cabbage	Onion
Cauliflower	Pepper
Celery	Squash*
Chard	Tomato
Cucumber*	Watermelon*

* Start in individual containers so their root systems are not disturbed.

Starting Seeds Indoors

Containers and medium should be selected to suit the needs of the varieties that you will grow. Commercially available flats, seed-starter trays, cell-packs, peat-pots, and flower pots as well as plastic-foam or paper cups and aluminum baking trays are typical containers. Be sure each container has adequate drainage. If containers have been used previously, be sure to clean them with a mild bleach solution to prevent the spread of plant diseases. Choose a light-weight sterile seedling mix to start your seeds. Mix the medium with enough water to moisten the mix well. Fill the container with two to three inches of medium and firm the mix lightly.

Sowing the Seeds

Small vegetable seeds should be sown in rows at a rate of eight to ten seeds per inch. Make row indentations about ¼-inch deep with a label or pencil and sprinkle the seeds evenly in the rows. Cover the seeds with the potting mix and press lightly to ensure contact between the seeds and the medium. If you're using individual containers, sprinkle two to three seeds on the surface. Press them about ¼-inch into the mix and cover. If all three seeds germinate, cut two seedlings off at soil level, leaving the strongest plant.

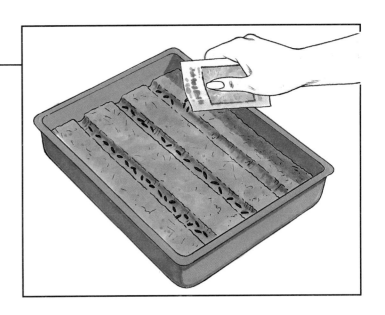

Transplanting to Individual Containers

Seeds grown in flats must be transplanted into individual containers before planting outdoors. Do this after they've developed a couple of "true leaves." The first leaves that appear are seed leaves; the next set of leaves are the true leaves. Gently lift the healthiest looking plants from the seed bed from underneath using a knife or spatula. Hold them by their true leaves and separate them from neighboring plants. Make a hole in the new planting medium deep enough to accept the roots without curling or crowding them. Press the soil firmly around the roots. Water the new plants thoroughly.

Caring for Seedlings

A little care and attention to seedlings will go a long way toward healthy, mature plants.

Young seedlings, at this stage of their development, have definite requirements. They need temperatures a little on the cool side. For most vegetables, a nighttime low of 55 degrees Fahrenheit and a daytime high of 70 degrees Fahrenheit is about right. If it's cooler, disease problems may develop; if it's warmer, the plants will become tall and spindly. It's also important that the seedlings get plenty of light: at least eight hours of bright light a day. If your indoor space can't provide enough natural light for your seedlings, use artificial light. The best artificial lights are plant growth lights. They emit high levels of blue light, which encourages good, stocky vegetative growth. Ideally, the lights should be about six to eight inches away from the leaves of the plants. Keep the lights on for about 12 hours a day.

New seedlings will need a dose of starter fertilizer to supply them with nutrients for sturdy growth. Seeds don't need fertilizer to germinate; therefore, seedling starter medium is often low in nutrients. A soluble fertilizer is best as a starter solution. Use a complete fertilizer (N-P-K) mixed with water at half strength for new seedlings. An application every two weeks—more often if leaves become pale or reddish—will be adequate to develop strong stems and foliage.

Tender seedlings will die of shock if you take them straight from the protected indoors to the garden. Cold night temperatures, wind, and rain can be detrimental to tender seedlings. You have to prepare them for the change in the environment, a process known in horticultural terms as "hardening off." You do this by taking the plants outside during the day and bringing them back in at night for at least two weeks. Keep them in, though, if there's likely to be a frost. You can also put them outside in a protected place such as a coldframe or a large box that can be covered at night. This treatment will prepare the plants for their final placement in the garden.

You may decide that buying transplants from a nursery or garden center is the easiest way to start your vegetable garden. You'll get high-quality transplants and fewer problems. But it's more expensive to buy transplants, and you'll have fewer varieties to choose from. Apply the same principles in choosing the vegetables you buy as transplants as you would if you were going to grow your own plants from seed. Base your decision on the length of the growing season and the flexibility of the plant variety. Buy your transplants from a reputable nursery or garden center so you'll know the plants have been grown with care. You'll also be able to ask for advice about choosing the best varieties. Look for plants that have strong stems, dark green leaves, and a healthy root system. You can slip a plant out of its container to make sure the roots are white and healthy. Don't forget to find out if the plants have been hardened off.

Planting Tomato Seedlings

Tomato seedlings often become tall and leggy while sitting in the garden center or on your windowsill. Long-stemmed tomato seedlings can be planted deeply or on their side so they won't become top-heavy. Tomatoes will develop roots along the buried stem that will help support the new growth. Remove the leaves from the part of the stem that will be planted, and dig a hole deep enough for the stem to comfortably support the part of the plant that will remain above ground. Another option is to plant seedlings in a trench on a slant. The tip of the stem will eventually curve upward and grow straight. When you've planted each seedling and firmed the soil, give each plant a boost of starter fertilizer to stimulate root growth.

Moving Transplants into the Garden

When your transplants are ready for planting in the garden, arrange them on the prepared soil bed to judge the correct spacing. Set two stakes with a string to ensure straight rows and use a tape measure if you'd like accurate spacing. Dig a hole for each plant as you're ready to set it in the ground, then gently slip the plant out of its container. If you have to handle the plant, hold it by the leaves so the stem does not become damaged. The top rim of plantable containers should be broken off so it will not stick up out of the garden soil: It will act as a wick and draw moisture out of the root zone. If the roots have become tightly compacted and intertwined, gently pinch off the bottom to initiate new growth. Set each transplant in the soil, and tamp the soil around it firmly with your hands. Don't plant transplants too deep; set them at the same depth they were in the container.

Direct-seeding in the Garden

Direct-seeding is often the beginning of many vegetable gardens.

Seeding directly into the garden is the easiest and least expensive way to grow vegetables. However, you may not have the climate that will let you direct-seed some vegetables: The seedlings may take longer to grow, making them more susceptible to weather conditions than transplants grown indoors. The vegetables to grow from seed are those that will mature within the span of your growing season and those that don't like to be transplanted.

The key to successful planting is proper soil preparation. When the soil is neither too wet nor too dry, turn the soil to a depth of 8 to 12 inches while adding organic matter. You should also apply a complete fertilizer, working it evenly into the soil. As you're preparing the soil, remove all stones, rocks, lumps, and the assorted debris that accumulated over the winter.

The depth you plant your seeds depends on their size. They only need enough soil to cover them and supply moisture for germination. Seeds buried too deep may not be able to struggle through the soil to the surface. The planting guide at the end of this chapter tells you exactly how deep to plant seeds of each type of vegetable. As a rule of thumb, seeds should be covered up to twice their diameter at their largest point. After you've set the seeds at the correct depth, firm the soil by tamping it with your hands or the end of your garden rake. This will improve contact between the seeds and the moist soil.

Seed spacing is also critical: If plants are forced to grow too close together, they may produce little or no yield. If seeds are large enough to handle, such as beans and corn, it's fairly easy to space them correctly. But with tiny seeds, spacing can be tricky. Take your time in spacing while planting, but you'll still probably have to thin seedlings soon after germination. The planting guide at the end of this chapter details the amount of space each plant needs for best growth.

Decide whether you'll sow seeds in a single row or a wide row. Vegetables such as beets, carrots, collards, kale, leaf lettuce, mustard, radishes, and spinach will produce nicely in wide rows while conserving space and water. The rows should be no wider than about 36 inches, making it easy to maintain and harvest vegetables. Prepare the row by loosely raking the soil, leaving the indentations made by the rake. Sprinkle the seeds evenly over the soil, and use the rake to press them into the soil. Cover the row with a thin layer of soil, straw, or loose compost to help keep the soil moist.

Planting in a single row is the most commonly used seeding arrangement. It's the easiest to maintain because you can com-

fortably cultivate between rows, but it's the least economical. Plants dry out faster, and there is more unused garden space.

Plants such as cucumbers and squash and other trailing vegetables benefit from planting in inverted hills: a shallow depression made by removing an inch of soil from a circle about a foot across and using the soil you've removed to form a rim around the circle. The inverted hill catches and holds extra moisture. During a heavy rain the outer rim of the soil, instead of being washed away, falls in toward the plants, providing extra anchorage for shallow-rooted plants.

Planting Depth for Direct-Seeding

Seeds should be covered no more than twice their diameter at their largest point.

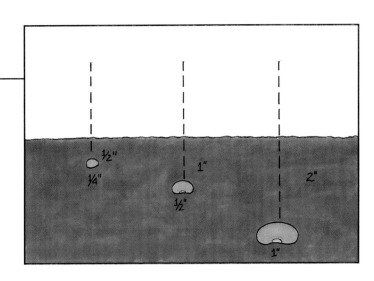

Single-row Planting

Once the soil has been properly prepared and the timing is right, you're ready to plant. Use a planting guide—a string and two stakes—to mark your row. Then with a hoe or the end of a rake handle, follow the string and cut a depression into the soil to a depth twice the seed's diameter. Sprinkle the seeds directly from the package or take a pinch of small seeds from the palm of your hand.

Wide-row Planting

Properly cared for wide-rows will produce higher yields per square foot than single-row planting. Prepare the soil and mark the width of the row with string or a rake depression. If small-seeded varieties are being sown, loosen the soil with the rake and sprinkle seeds on top of the soil. Use the back of the rake to press the seeds into the soil; cover them with a thin layer of soil, straw, or compost. To plant large-seeded varieties, rake one inch of soil from the row to the side and sprinkle the seeds. Cover the seeds with the soil you removed earlier and gently tamp the soil with the rake.

Inverted Hills

Trailing vegetables that sprawl over the garden are well-suited to inverted hills. Use a hoe or rake to pull soil into a mound. Hollow out the hill to form a bowl-like depression. Plant five or six seeds at the correct depth inside the circle. When the seedlings have developed two true leaves, thin them out, leaving the two or three strongest plants.

Thinning Garden Seedlings

Thinning is an essential task in the early stages of a seedling's development. When seeds germinate, seedlings are sometimes close and overplanted. When planting in inverted hills, extra seeds are deliberately planted because not all the seeds will germinate and some seeds will produce weak plants. Thinning must be done early, before plants are weakened by overcrowding. Use a scissors to cut at soil level all seedlings that should be thinned. If you pull seedlings from the soil, you risk damaging the roots of the remaining plants. Sometimes it is necessary to cut back growth in order to keep the plant from becoming leggy or from crowding neighboring plants. Always trim leaves or branches back to their growth shoot.

Protect Young Plants

Extreme weather conditions pose a threat to tender young plants. If hot sun threatens to dry the topsoil where the roots are developing, shade the plants with a board, a basket, or a layer of burlap. Provide this shade on windy days as well as sunny days until the transplants become established. If there is any risk of frost, cover the seedlings with a type of homemade hot cap: A light covering of straw, bottomless plastic jugs, flower pots, and buckets work well as temporary protection.

Water Seedlings

Don't let seedlings die of thirst. Adequate watering is essential to young plants in their early stages of growth. Water to a depth of six to eight inches to encourage deep rooting and stronger growth. If watering is not deep, shallow roots will develop, making the plant weak and susceptible during dry periods. Using a soaker hose, sprinkler, or spray nozzle, apply water long enough to soak the soil but gently enough that seedlings will not be displaced.

Starting New Plants from Parts

Rhubarb is an excellent candidate for division.

Seeds and transplants, while the forms you'll use most often, are not the only methods to raise new plants. Some vegetables are started from other plant parts: suckers, tubers, slips, crowns, sets, cloves, divisions, or cuttings. In some cases plants can be grown either by seed or from plant parts. Onions, for instance, take a very long time to germinate from seed, so it usually makes more sense to grow them from sets. Other plants grow best from plant parts.

Suckers, or offshoots, are plants that grow or shoot up from the root system of a mature plant. These suckers can be dug up and divided from the mother plant, and then transplanted to mature into new plants. Globe artichoke is usually the only vegetable grown from suckers.

Tubers are specialized swollen underground stems capable of producing roots, stems, and leaves. Irish potatoes and Jerusalem artichokes are usually grown from tubers. When the plants are cut up for planting, as in the case of Irish potatoes, they are called seed pieces.

Slips are young, tender, rooted cuttings or sprouts grown from vegetable roots. Sweet potatoes are the only vegetable commonly grown from slips.

Crowns are compressed stems near the soil surface that are capable of producing leaves and roots. Crowns that are planted with the roots attached are referred to as "roots." Crowns are divided from the mother plant when the plant is dormant. Asparagus is grown from crowns.

Sets are one-year-old onion seedlings that were pulled when the bulbs were young. The bulbs are air-dried, stored for the winter, and planted next spring.

Cloves are the segmented parts of bulbs. Garlic is the only vegetable commonly grown from cloves. Each garlic bulb is made up of a dozen or more cloves, and each clove is planted separately. For the highest yield, separate the cloves as you plant.

Divisions occur naturally in the form of small, rooted plants or bulbs that grow from the mother plant. You separate or divide them off to grow as individual plants. Dig up the mother plant, separate the small new shoots, and replant each new unit. Horseradish and rhubarb are grown from divisions. You can divide plants in the spring or the fall. Fall is preferable because the cool, moist weather helps the plants become well-established.

Cuttings are started by cutting a piece of stem from the plant at the node—the lumpy place on the stem where leaves are attached—and forcing it to develop new roots. This is best done in early summer, when the stems are actively growing. Treat the cut end of the stem with a commercially prepared rooting hormone and stick the cutting in moist soil away from direct sunlight. New roots will form in a few weeks, and the new plant can be placed in the garden. Tomato shoots are often rooted for a late crop.

1 Dividing Perennial Vegetables

You can turn a well-established rhubarb plant into six or eight new plants by simple division. Rhubarb is best divided in the fall or early spring. Choose a specimen with thick, long stalks. Use a spade or digging fork to dig the plant up, keeping intact as much of the root system as possible. After lifting the plant from the hole, shake excess soil from the roots to determine the best natural divisions that can be made.

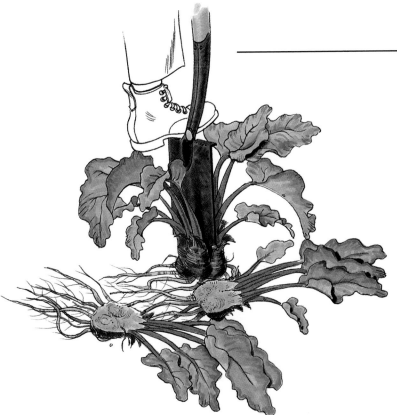

With a sharp knife or spade, slice the fleshy root into as many sections as there are crowns (the part of the plant from which new shoots develop). Each new division should contain a crown and roots. Divisions that have a strong crown and strong roots will easily become established as new plants. Cut off any roots that have become damaged and replant the divisions in their new sites. **2**

PLANTING GUIDE: SPACING

Vegetable	Inches between plants	Inches between rows	Depth of seed (inches)
Artichoke, Globe	36–48	48–60	1–1½
Artichoke, Jerusalem	12–18	24–36	
Asparagus	12–18	36–48	1–1½
Beans, Broad	8–10	36–48	1–2
Beans, Dry	4–6	18–24	1–1½
Beans, Lima			
bush	2–3	18–24	1–1½
pole	4–6	30–36	1–1½
Beans, Snap or Green			
bush	2–3	18–24	1–1½
pole	4–6	30–36	1–1½
Beets	2–3	12–18	1
Broccoli	3	24–36	½
Brussels Sprouts	24	24–36	½
Cabbage	18–24	24–36	½
Cardoon	18–24	36–48	½
Carrot	2–4	12–24	¼
Cauliflower	18–24	24–36	½
Celeriac	6–8	24–30	¼
Celery	8–10	24–30	¼
Chard	9–12	18–24	1
Chayote	24–30	60	
Chick pea	6–8	12–18	½
Chicory	12–18	24–36	1
Chinese Cabbage	8–12	18–30	½
Collards	12	18–24	½
Corn	2–4	12–18	1–1½
Cress	1–2	18–24	¼
Cucumber*†	12	18–72	½
Dandelion	6–8	12–18	¼
Eggplant	18–24	24–36	¼
Endive	9–12	18–24	⅛
Horseradish	24	18–24	¼
Kale	8–12	18–24	½

PLANTING GUIDE: SPACING

Vegetable	Inches between plants	Inches between rows	Depth of seed (inches)
Kohlrabi	5–6	18–24	1/4
Leek	6–9	12–18	1/8
Lettuce	6–12	12–18	1/8
Muskmelon*†	18–24	60–96	1
Mustard	6–12	12–24	1/2
Okra	12–18	24–36	1/2–1
Onion			
sets	2–3	12–18	1–2
seeds	1–2	12–18	1/4
Parsnip	2–4	18–24	1/2
Pea, Black–eyed	8–12	12–18	1/2
Pea, Shelling	1–2	18–24	2
Peanut	6–8	12–18	1
Pepper	18–24	24–36	1/2
Potato, Irish	12–18	24–36	4
Sweet Potato	12–18	36–48	3–5
Pumpkin*‡	24–48	60–120	1
Radish	1–6	12–18	1/2
Rhubarb	30–36	36–48	
Rutabaga	6–8	18–24	1/2
Salsify	2–4	18–24	1/2
Shallot	6–8	12–18	1/4
Sorrel	12–18	18–24	1/2
Soybean	1½–2	24–30	1/2–1
Spinach	2–4	12–24	1/2
Spinach, New Zealand	12	24–36	1/2
Squash, Summer*§	24–36	18–48	1
Squash, Winter*‡	24–48	60–120	1
Tomato	18–36	24–48	1/2
Turnip			
greens	2–3	12–24	1/2
roots	3–4	12–24	1/2
Watermelon*‡	24–72	60–120	1

*Note: Plants in inverted hills should be thinned to three plants in each hill.
† Hills should be 36 inches apart.
‡ Hills should be 72 inches apart.
§ Hills should be 48 inches apart.

A rich harvest of fresh vegetables awaits those who take the time to care for a garden. These carrots, tomatoes, and zucchini will perk up any meal.

CARING FOR YOUR GARDEN

You can get a great sense of achievement from planting your garden, but keep in mind that your labors are by no means over when the seeds are in the ground. Even a small garden of tomatoes and squash requires a certain amount of time and care.

Besides well-prepared soil and proper planting, plants need water, and since nature is not always cooperative, you may want to devise an easy way to supplement your rainfall through simple irrigation. A watering plan should be designed according to the size of your garden. Your options range from a simple watering can to a sophisticated drip system. You'll even see how low-pressure ooze watering can save you water.

The benefits of a well-maintained, weed-free garden are immeasurable. Vegetables that have to compete with weeds for water and nutrients become frail and sickly; weeds can also harbor diseases and insect pests. We'll show you several time-saving ways to help control these garden invaders, including cover crops that prevent weed growth and the use of mulches to conserve water and inhibit weeds. In addition, end-of-season garden care can save you time. Preparing the soil in winter will save you a great deal of work with wet soil when you plant your early spring crops. These techniques will help you maintain a clean, healthy garden. The end result will be great vegetables as well as a feeling of accomplishment.

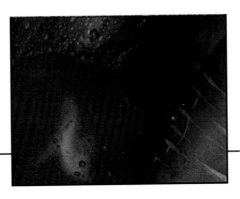

Staking & Plant Support

Many plants, as they mature, need support to help them grow. This is especially true of tomato plants and such climbing plants as beans, cucumbers, and winter squash.

As tomato plants mature, they begin to sprawl along the ground because they become heavy with fruit. If left to grow without training, the fruit is exposed to sunscald and inclined to rot. An effective way to prevent these problems is to train the plants to grow vertically by staking the plants. Another simple training method is to build tomato cages. As the vine grows, guide the stems into the cage.

You can use your vertical space by designing a trellis system to support twining and climbing plants. An important consideration is sturdiness. Vines and wind will be tugging on it for several months, so build the trellis well. The stems of bean plants will twine around the trellis for support; with a little bit of guidance, cucurbits will grab the trellis with their tendrils.

Staking helps keep disease and other plant maladies at bay.

Tomato Stakes

Use strong stakes for tomato plants: 2 inches by 2 inches, about eight feet long and driven 24 inches to 30 inches deep will support most tomatoes. Drive in the stake before setting the transplant, so you won't disturb the growing roots. As the vine grows, tie it to the stake with twine or plastic tape.

Tomato Cage

Use 60-inch, 6 × 6-inch welded concrete reinforcement wire to build tomato cages. Regular fence wire won't work because the openings aren't large enough to harvest the fruit. Cut a five- to six-foot section of wire, leaving prongs so the wire can be bent into a cylinder and clamped together with the prongs. Cut off the bottom rim with heavy wire cutters so the bottom spikes can be pushed into the soil around the tomato plant.

Using a Trellis System

Your trellis system will need some kind of support: 4 × 4-inch posts driven into the ground or a tee-pee design that supports itself are typical solutions. From tower to tower, lace heavy twine or wire and pattern string from top to bottom to support the crop.

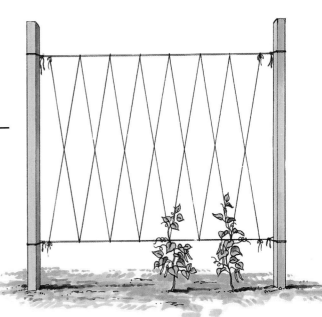

Weeding: Keep Out Intruders

Weeds, such as this dandelion, should be controlled early in the season.

Cultivating, or weeding, is probably going to be your most demanding task as garden caretaker. Weeds are both resilient and persistent. At times, you'll probably feel that if your vegetables grew as well and as fast as your weeds, gardening would be child's play. It's important to keep down the weeds in your vegetable garden. They steal light, water, and nutrients from the vegetables, and they shelter insects and disease.

To successfully control the weeds in your garden, you have to learn to recognize them when they are young. It helps to understand how and when weeds grow to keep the garden clean and weed free. When weeds are small, regular cultivation will control them easily. If you let them become established, getting rid of weeds will be a struggle.

Annual weeds are like many of the vegetable varieties. There are cool-season annual weeds, and there are warm-season annual weeds. Cool-season weeds, such as chickweed, generally germinate during fall and winter in the garden. They produce flowers and seeds in the spring. Although the weeds disappear, the seeds lie dormant in your soil through the summer. If these weeds are allowed to produce seeds, you'll have the same problem the following season. Warm-season annuals are much the same, but their growing season is spring through fall.

Perennial weeds persist year after year, some with deep taproots, others with a long-spreading network of roots. Some perennial weeds will spread through the garden like wildfire; don't wait for this to happen.

Weed seeds will germinate wherever the ground is bare, especially where you have supplied the soil with organic matter, fertilizer, and water. Many weeds are stimulated to germinate by light. To help prevent weed germination, try to keep the garden covered with mulch or a cover crop. This method isn't always practical when you're waiting for a row of vegetables to germinate, but it will help keep out many weeds.

The best way to control weeds is to chop them off at ground level with a sharp hoe. If a weed is close to your vegetables, don't try to dig out the whole root system of the weed; you may also damage the root systems of neighboring vegetables in the process. Instead, just remove the top of the weed. Persistent weeds, such as dandelions, may have to be cut down several times, but eventually they will die.

Herbicides can be useful in controlling weeds under certain conditions, but these conditions are usually not encountered in the small home garden. In addition, herbicides require such careful handling that the home gardener would be well advised not to use them more than absolutely necessary.

COMMON WEEDS	
Annuals	*Perennials*
Bindweed	Burdock
Chickweed	Canada Thistle
Ground Ivy	Dandelion
Lambs-quarters	Plantain
Pigweed	Poison Ivy
Purslane	Giant Ragweed
	Common Ragweed

Mulches

Mulches are either organic or inorganic material placed on the soil around vegetable plants. Mulches perform a number of useful functions. They protect against soil erosion by breaking the force of heavy rains; they help prevent soil compaction; they discourage the growth of weeds; and they reduce certain disease problems. Mulches are insulators, making it possible to keep the soil warmer during cool weather and cooler during warm weather. Organic mulches also improve the soil texture. Sometimes mulches can improve the appearance of a vegetable garden by giving it a neater, more finished look.

Your plants will need less water if you use a mulch, increasing the time that plants can go between watering. When the soil dries out, plants slow their growth—or stop growing altogether. Swift, steady growth is important for the best-tasting fruits and vegetables. Mulches keep the soil evenly moist.

Mulches do not eliminate weeds. They can, however, help control them if the area has been cleared of weeds to begin with. If the mulch is thick enough, weeds that are already growing won't be able to push through and darkness will frustrate the germination of others. Persistent weeds can push their way through most mulch, but if they're cut off at the soil level a few times, they will die.

Whether you use an organic or an inorganic mulch, take care not to put it down before the soil has warmed up in the spring. If you put it down too soon, mulch will prevent the soil from warming and slow down root development.

Organic mulches are organic materials that, when laid on the soil, decompose to feed soil microorganisms and improve the quality of the soil. If the mulch you've put down is decomposing quickly, add nitrogen to make up for nitrogen consumed by bacteria.

The following are organic materials commonly used as mulches in vegetable gardens.

Compost—Partially decomposed compost looks a little rough, but it makes a great mulch and soil conditioner.

Lawn Clippings—Do not use clippings from a lawn that has been treated with a herbicide or weed killer; these substances can kill the vegetables you're trying to grow. Let untreated clippings dry before putting them around your garden; fresh grass mats down and smells bad while it's decomposing.

Leaf Mold—Leaves are cheap and usually easy to find, but they blow around and are hard to keep in place. They will stay in place better if they're ground up and partially decomposed. Nitrogen should be added to leaf mold. Do not use walnut leaves; they contain iodine, which is toxic to some vegetable plants.

Mulches are a multipurpose item for any garden.

Sawdust—Sawdust is often available for the asking, but it requires added nitrogen to prevent microorganisms from depleting the soil's nitrogen supply. If possible, allow sawdust to decompose for a year before using it as a mulch.

Straw—Straw is messy and hard to apply in small areas, but it is an excellent mulch. Be sure not to use hay, which contains many weed seeds.

Wood Chips or Shavings—Wood chips, like sawdust, decompose slowly and should be allowed to partially decompose for a year before being used as mulch. Additional nitrogen will be needed to supply bacteria during decomposition.

Inorganic mulch, or landscape fabric, is used in small gardens for plants that are grown in a group or a hill, such as cucumbers, squash, or pumpkins. It can also be used for individual plants such as peppers, tomatoes, and eggplants. Fabric should not be used for crops that need a cool growing season—cabbage or cauliflower, for instance—unless it's covered with a thick layer of light-reflecting material, such as sawdust.

There are several advantages to growing with a landscape fabric mulch. Fabric reduces the loss of soil moisture, raises the soil temperature, and speeds up crop maturity. Weeds are discouraged, because the fabric cuts off their light supply. This means you won't have to cultivate as much, reducing the risk of root damage. The fabric also helps keep the plants cleaner. When you're making a new garden in a formerly grassy area—if you've dug up a lawn, for instance—fabric can keep the grass from coming back.

There are some disadvantages to keep in mind as well. You will have to water more frequently, especially well-drained, sandy soils. On the other hand, plants can wilt and rot if the soil moisture is kept at too high a level and there isn't enough air in the soil. Remember too that the fabric is inorganic, and at the end of the season you'll have to remove it from the garden. If the fabric is of high grade, you may be able to reuse it the following season.

Using Organic Mulch

To use an organic mulch, such as straw or compost, spread a layer of the material on the surface of the ground around the plants after the soil has warmed up in the spring. If you're mulching around rows of direct-sown seedlings, wait until the plants are about four inches tall. Otherwise, the mulch will overwhelm the plants. Seedlings will poke through a light layer of organic matter, but several inches of mulch will prevent them from emerging. Avoid using a fluffy material with large particles, like bark chips, because you will have to put down a layer that is too thick. If you're using a denser material, such as straw or grass clippings, a two-inch layer will be enough. Be careful not to suffocate the vegetables while trying to frustrate weeds.

Laying Down Landscape Fabric Mulch

You can buy landscape fabric from many garden centers, hardware stores, and mail-order suppliers. It should be at least three or four feet wide. Put down the fabric before the plants are set out. Try to pick a calm day; a strong wind will whip the fabric around and make laying it down difficult. Prepare the soil with amendments and grade it smoothly with a garden rake. Lay out the row for the mulch with a string. Then, with a hoe, make a three-inch-deep trench along one side of the row for the entire length of the row. Pull some of the soil into the center of the area that will be covered with fabric: You want water to run off the fabric and into the soil rather than pooling on top of the fabric. Lay one edge of the fabric in the trench and cover the edge with soil. Smooth the fabric over the bed and repeat the process on the other side. Be sure the fabric is anchored securely, or the wind will get under it and pull it up.

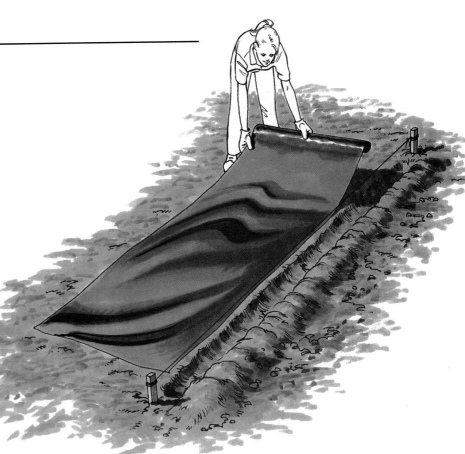

Planting in Landscape Fabric Mulch

When you're ready to plant, cut an "X" about three inches across for each transplant or seed. With a hand trowel, dig through the "X" and plant as usual. Thoroughly water the plants through the holes in the mulch. After a rain, check to see if there are any spots where water is standing. If there are, punch holes through the fabric so the water can run through.

51

Water for Your Garden

Watering, whether for rows of crops or in containers, is often necessary to supplement rainfall.

Some plants are composed of up to 95 percent water. Water is vital from the moment seeds are sown through sprouting to the end of the growing season. Plants need water for cell division, cell enlargement, and even for holding themselves up. If the cells don't have enough water in them, the result is a wilted plant. Water is essential, along with light and carbon dioxide, for producing the sugars that provide the plant with energy for growth. It also dissolves fertilizers and carries nutrients to the different parts of the plant.

Ideally, water for plants comes from rain or other precipitation and from underground sources. In reality, you'll often have to do extra watering by hand or through an irrigation system. How often you should water depends on how often it rains, how long your soil retains moisture, and how fast water evaporates in your climate. Soil type is another important factor. Clay soils hold water very well—sometimes too well. Sandy soils are like a sieve, letting the water run right through. Both kinds of soil can be improved with the addition of organic matter. Organic matter gives clay soils lightness and air; it gives sandy soils something to hold the water.

Other factors may also affect how often you need to water your garden.

- More water evaporates when the temperature is high than when it's low. Plants can rot if they get too much water in cool weather.
- More water evaporates when the relative humidity is low.
- Plants need more water when the days are bright.
- Wind and air movement will increase the loss of water to the atmosphere.
- Water needs vary with the type and maturity of the plant. Some vegetables are tolerant of low soil moisture.
- Sometimes water is not what a wilting plant needs. When plants are growing fast, the leaves sometimes get ahead of the roots' ability to provide them with water. If the day is hot and the plants wilt in the afternoon, don't worry about them; they will regain their balance overnight. But if plants are wilting early in the morning, water them immediately.

So much depends on climate and the ability of different soil types to hold moisture that it's difficult to give specific directions for watering your garden. Generally, however, vegetable plants need about an inch of water a week. The best time to water your garden is in the morning. If you water at night when the day is cooling off, the water is likely to stay on the foliage, increasing the danger of disease. Some people believe that you shouldn't water in the morning because water spots on leaves will cause leaf-burn when the sun gets hot; this isn't the case.

When watering your vegetable garden, there is one rule you should follow: Always soak the soil thoroughly. A light sprinkling can often do more harm than no water at all: It stimulates the roots to come to the surface, where they are more susceptible to high temperatures and dry soil.

Leaky-pipe Irrigation

Overhead watering is most commonly used, but it wastes water because of excessive evaporation and it encourages diseases to settle on the wet foliage. Controlled watering eliminates waste and supplies water to garden plants where they need it—at the base of the plants. Leaky-pipe, or soaker hose, is made of recycled rubber and is as flexible as an ordinary garden hose. Equipped with a female coupling on one end to attach to a water spigot, and a male coupling on the other end to cap off or attach another length of pipe, the soaker hose allows water to slowly permeate the soil. Arrange the soaker hose at the base of the plants in the row; water is then distributed evenly over the roots of the plants.

Trickle Irrigation

Also known as drip irrigation, trickle irrigation saves water. This is a good way to water vegetables that are spaced far apart as well as container gardens on a deck or terrace. Mini-tubes are inserted into holes in the main line at intervals to suit the gardener's needs. Weighted tips at the end of each mini-tube are placed at the base of each plant. Water is dispersed at low pressure wherever the tubes are placed. Kits for trickle systems are available at garden centers and through garden suppliers.

Measuring Precipitation

It's a good idea to keep a rain gauge in the garden to help determine whether plants are receiving enough water. Place a rain gauge or several straight-sided coffee cans in the garden away from plants that may hang over the container. Keep a record of the amount of rain that has fallen and supplement nature with irrigation. Typical garden soil will need about an inch of rain a week. If overhead irrigation is used, time a few waterings to determine how long it takes to supply the garden with one inch of water. By using several measuring cans, you can determine if the garden is being irrigated evenly. To encourage deep rooting, it's better to apply one heavy watering to the garden than several light waterings.

Preparing for Winter

After the final, bountiful harvest in the fall, it's time to prepare the garden for the winter.

The better a cleanup job you do in the fall, the easier it will be to start the new growing season in the spring. You may be tempted to skip some of these last-minute chores, but they're worth doing because they can make a big difference to the success of next year's garden. While these tasks can be put off until the start of the growing season, you can expect to be busy in the garden in the spring. You'll find it useful to have some of the work out of the way ahead of time.

As you finish harvesting crops and rows of garden space become available, it's a good idea to plant a cover crop, or green manure, as part of your preparation for the following year. This is a crop that you don't intend to harvest. It's simply to provide protection for the soil underneath. When you prepare for your spring planting, you dig the whole crop into the soil. A cover crop will keep your precious topsoil from blowing or washing away, and tilling it into the soil in the spring will provide valuable organic matter to enrich the soil. The cover crop will also shade the soil, preventing many cool-season weeds from germinating. It's not necessary to plant the whole cover crop at one time to cover the entire garden; you can plant in each area of the garden as space becomes available. Cover crops are not exclusively used over the winter. If you have a space in the garden that will be vacant for several weeks between plantings, a summer cover of buckwheat makes an ideal green manure. The buckwheat germinates quickly and covers the soil, preventing summer weeds from germinating. It's hollow-stemmed and easy to turn into the soil when you plant your next vegetable.

As an alternative to planting a cover crop, you can prepare the soil ahead of time. Tilling your soil in the fall can save you a great deal of time and help you get an earlier start in the spring because the soil is often too wet in early spring to use a spade or a rototiller. If you do till your soil in the fall, make sure to cover it with mulch to keep it from blowing away and to prevent massive winter weed germination. Consider soil preparation for the area of your garden where you plan to grow next season's cool-season vegetables.

If you're growing perennial vegetables, fall is the time to prepare them for winter survival. Remove old stems and foliage that have been killed back by frost to prevent the spread of disease organisms and insects that winter on old debris. In cold climates, perennial vegetables should be protected with a blanket of mulch to prevent root damage from extreme cold temperatures. In mild climates, a coating of mulch will protect plants from the alternating freeze-and-thaw and prevent plants from heaving from the soil.

COVER CROPS		
Variety	**Season to Grow**	**Amount of Seed/ 1000 Sq. Ft.**
Rye	Winter	1 to 2 lbs.
Crimson Clover	Winter	1 lb.
Soybeans	Summer	3 to 5 lbs.
Hairy Vetch	Winter	¾ to 1½ lbs.
Winter Wheat	Winter	1 to 2 lbs.
Buckwheat	Summer	2 to 3 lbs.
Rape	Winter	2 to 5 oz.
Cowpeas	Summer	3 to 4 lbs.

1 Preparing Perennial Crops

Perennial vegetable varieties grown in cold climates should be prepared and protected against winter temperatures. When frost has killed back the past season's leaves, plants such as asparagus and rhubarb should be cut down to a stubble.

Clear the garden of weeds and other debris and apply **2**
a mulch over the whole plant after the soil first
freezes. If you mulch when the soil is still warm, you'll
encourage root rot problems. Remember to remove
this mulch as soon as the soil starts to thaw in the
spring. The best mulches to use are organic materials,
such as straw, hay, leaves, and compost, that will let
the plants breathe. Crops you may need to mulch for
winter protection include artichokes (in some areas),
asparagus, chayotes, and rhubarb.

Planting a Cover Crop

When you close a section of the garden for the
winter, use a green manure, or cover crop. Clear the
area of weeds and debris and cultivate the soil. Till
and grade the soil as you would for spring planting
but leave the surface coarse. Choose a cover crop
and scatter the seeds over the area you want to
plant. If it's a large area, a hand spreader will do
the job well. With a garden rake, gently rake the
surface to work the seed into the top inch of soil.
Turn the rake over and tamp the soil to insure
contact between the seed and the soil. A light
covering of straw will help keep the soil moist and
speed germination. Water the area well to settle the
soil. When spring planting time arrives, turn the
cover crop into the soil with a spade or rototiller.

To remain healthy, these vegetables need protection from a wide range of pests and diseases. Both chemical and nonchemical means are available to the everyday gardener.

CHAPTER 5

GARDEN HEALTH

One of the most challenging—and sometimes frustrating—aspects of being a gardener is the natural forces you have to combat. Even in the unlikely event that you have perfect soil and a marvelous climate, you're still not home free; all sorts of pests are in competition with you for your crop.

In your vegetable garden, you're most likely to encounter insects and the like. Most gardeners have to contend with insect problems at some time during the growing season, but the problems are not always obvious. Just when it looks as though all your hard work is paying off and your plants are progressing toward a fine harvest, it can come as quite a surprise to find that pests are at work.

Your plants are subject to diseases, too. You know you're in trouble when the leaves turn yellow or the plants seem stunted and weak. Fortunately, you can take certain measures to forestall disease problems. Planting varieties that have been bred to be disease-resistant and rotating some crops when possible are just two of many options.

Controlling insect and disease pests can be quite a challenge, but it's not an insurmountable one. First identify the pest or disease. Once you've done this, you'll be able to make a wise choice as to the best means of control. We'll suggest the most effective means of control—both chemical and organic—for the pest and disease problems you're most likely to encounter.

Controlling Insect Pests

Chemical pesticides are effective and safe if used correctly.

For many people, anything in the garden that crawls or flies and is smaller than a chipmunk or a sparrow can be classified as an insect. In fact, many of the creatures that may damage your vegetable plants—mites, slugs, snails, nematodes, and sowbugs among them—are not insects at all. Another popular misconception is that insects and similar creatures are harmful or unnecessary and have no place in a garden. This just isn't true. While some insects are destructive, many are perfectly harmless. These insects are actually important to the healthy development of your garden crop. Some beneficial creatures perform a specific service by keeping down pests that do harm to your crop; others pollinate the plants. When you set out to control harmful pests, it's important to realize that indiscriminate controls may destroy useful creatures as well as the harmful ones.

The method you choose for controlling garden pests could be a cause for controversy. Many gardeners rely on chemical insecticides to eliminate the harmful insects competing for their crops. Some, however, object to the use of chemicals. These gardeners prefer to rely on organic, or nonchemical, means of control.

The surest way to control most insects and similar creatures that threaten your vegetable crop is by using an insecticide. A word here about terminology: The terms "pesticide" and "insecticide" are not interchangeable. A pesticide is any form of chemical control used in the garden. An insecticide is a pesticide used specifically to control insects. A herbicide is a pesticide used to control weeds. If you mistakenly use a herbicide to control insects, you'll lose your entire crop for the season because it will kill your vegetable plants.

Insecticides are chemical products that are sprayed or dusted on affected crops. The spray type is bought in concentrated form, diluted with water, and diffused with a hand sprayer or a spray attachment fitted to the end of your garden hose. Dust-on insecticides are powders that you pump onto the plants. Spraying is preferable because it gives more thorough coverage. It's also easier to treat the undersides as well as the tops of leaves and plants with a spray. Another technique is to apply insecticides directly to the soil to kill insects under the surface. This is known as applying a "soil drench."

Used correctly and responsibly, insecticides are not harmful to humans or other animals. However, they are toxic if used incorrectly. It is important to study the label of each pesticide and follow the directions exactly.

Because research is constantly being done to determine the safety of insecticides and improve their effectiveness, it's difficult to give long-term recommendations about their use. Certain basic rules, however, always apply. Read and reread the label and follow all precautions meticulously. Most important, never make the solution stronger than the label says because you think it will work better that way.

If you decide to use an insecticide to control insects in your garden, here are some important points to remember.
• Read the whole label and follow directions exactly.
• Wear rubber gloves, long sleeves and pants, and goggles while handling pesticides.
• Take care not to breathe the spray or dust.
• When the job is completed, wash your clothes separately from the family laundry and wash all exposed parts of your body with soap and water.
• Use equipment that you keep specifically for use with insecticides. Don't use equipment that has been used for herbicides.
• Use insecticides only when the air is still. Wind will carry the chemical away, creating a possible hazard somewhere else. The insecticide must dry on the plants to be effective; rain will wash it off.
• Treat only the affected portions of the plant. Use a light but thorough dose. Don't drench plants unnecessarily.
• Store unused, undiluted material in its original container in a locked area out of the reach of children.
• Dispose of the empty container carefully, according to the label's instructions.
• Wash all treated vegetables carefully before eating them.

Nonchemical Pest Control

Not all insects are harmful to garden plants. This lady bug can actually benefit your vegetables.

For various reasons, some people prefer to use nonchemical means for controlling diseases, insects, and other pests. Allergic reactions to chemicals, a desire to grow purely organic vegetables, or protection for young children are all reasons to use nonchemical controls for pests. If used correctly, nonchemical pest controls can be very effective in keeping your garden healthy.

VFNT Seeds—The easiest way to avoid disease problems is to choose varieties of vegetables that are resistant to disease. Over the years, many disease-resistant vegetable varieties have been developed. You'll notice that seed packages and catalog descriptions of some vegetable varieties include V, F, N, and T in the name. These abbreviations indicate disease resistance that has been bred into the variety. V and F stand for verticillium and fusarium wilts, which are fungi that cause tomato plants to turn yellow, wilt, and die. N indicates nematode tolerance. Nematodes are tiny parasitic worms that cause knots on stems and roots of vegetables. Tobacco mosaic virus, indicated by a T, affects foliage by yellowing and curling; it also causes severe root damage.

Water Early—If you irrigate your garden with a sprinkler from overhead, it's best to water early in the day so plants can dry off before night falls. Foliage that stays wet for long periods of time is susceptible to leaf diseases, fungi that grow on leaves, tender stems, and flower buds. This tends to be a problem when plants stay wet throughout the night: Fungi spread quickly during the cool, moist evening hours. The fungi will cause the plant to be weakened, flowers to fall off, and fruit to begin to spot and become soft.

Crop Rotation—Do not grow the same plant family in the same spot year after year. Repetition of the same crop gives diseases a chance to build up strength. Design your plan so that each family of vegetables—cabbage family, cucumber family, and tomato/pepper family—can be moved to another block of your garden on a three-year rotation.

Paper Collar

You may notice one morning that a couple of healthy young plants have keeled over and died. This is a pretty sure indication that cutworms are present. Feeding at night and hiding during the day, cutworms are most destructive early in the season, cutting off transplants at ground level. To prevent the cutworm from finding your cabbages, peppers, and tomatoes, wrap each stem with a paper or thin cardboard collar as you transplant it into the garden. The collar should reach at least one inch below and one inch above the soil level. In time, the collar will disintegrate; by then the danger of cutworm damage will have passed.

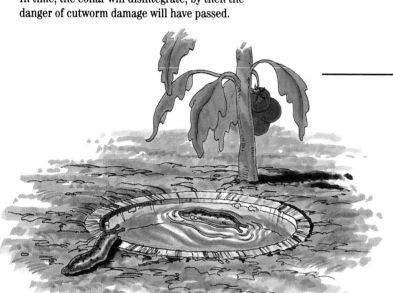

Beer: A Handy Bait

Snails and slugs pose a problem for many garden plants, especially during seasons with plenty of rain and rich, succulent growth. Lettuce and potatoes are especially susceptible to slug damage: Irregular holes will be found in the leaves. Snails and slugs feed mostly at night, hiding from the hot sun.

One way to control these pests is to remove the places where they hide; but if you're using mulch in the garden and supplying plants with the moisture they need, you're still likely to find snails and slugs. Although commercial baits are available, shallow pans of beer placed throughout the garden will attract and drown the pests.

Beneficial Insects

Not all insects in the garden are pests. Some are actually beneficial, providing a means to control insect pests. Insects such as ladybugs, lacewing flies, and praying mantises feed on bugs that are destructive to your crops. You should protect them when you find them in your garden. Harmless to your garden plants, these useful insects gorge on aphids, beetles, caterpillars, grasshoppers, and other bothersome insects.

Pests & Other Problems

A luscious garden is the gardener's reward for keeping pests in check.

The following lists are designed to help you identify the most common vegetable-garden insect and related problems. If you have difficulty identifying your garden's symptoms, take a sample to a garden center or county Cooperative Extension office to have it identified by an expert.

Once you know what your problem is, you can get a recommendation for controlling the pest. If the infestation is light, you may be able to pick the insects off by hand. For a heavy infestation, you'll probably need to turn to chemical insecticides. Disease problems are usually a little more difficult to control. The best method is prevention by choosing resistant varieties and keeping the garden area clear of weeds and infected debris.

INSECTS AND ANIMALS

SYMPTOM	CAUSE	CURE	PLANTS
Cluster of small, soft-bodied insects on buds and growth tips (gray, black, pink, green, red, or yellow in color); sticky secretions may be evident. Leaves are curled.	*Aphids*	Spray with contact poison labeled for aphids on vegetables.	Every garden vegetable
Irregularly shaped holes in the leaves; hard-shelled beetles of many colors and sizes	*Beetles of various kinds*	Pick off by hand or spray with a stomach poison insecticide.	Every vegetable crop can be infested by one or more variety of beetles.

Note: Consult your Cooperative Extension office for approved pesticides for vegetable plants.

INSECTS AND ANIMALS

SYMPTOM	CAUSE	CURE	PLANTS
Growth tips wilted or entire plant wilted; small hole in plant stem at point where wilting begins	*Borers*	Cut out borer, or destroy entire plant if affected at base of plant. Spray base of plant with suitable stomach poison insecticide in late spring and early summer.	Cucumber, Melon, Pumpkin, Squash
Irregular holes in foliage; green caterpillars under and on top of leaves	*Cabbage Worms*	Inspect plants and pick by hand. Spray with Bacillus thuringiensis—an organic insecticide—or a stomach poison insecticide.	Broccoli, Cabbage, Cauliflower, others
Corn kernels eaten within the husk; insides of tomatoes, peppers, and eggplants eaten; yellow-tan worms found inside	*Corn Earworm, Tomato Fruitworm*	Apply insecticide recommended for earworms. Remove infested plant debris at the end of the season.	Corn, Eggplant, Pepper, Tomato
Entire plant wilted or cut off at the base of the plant	*Cutworms*	Use paper collars, one inch above and one inch below ground level, around stems of transplants.	Cabbage, Pepper, Tomato
Slight wilting of the plant; plants growing poorly for no apparent reason; possible root damage	*Grubs*	Control adult beetles with a stomach poison. Apply soil drench of suitable insecticide.	Most vegetables
Foliage turns yellow and begins to curl; small green-patterned, winged insects on undersides of leaves	*Leaf Hoppers*	Spray off light infestations with garden hose. Apply a stomach poison labeled for use on vegetables.	Bean, Carrot, Chayote, Cucumber, Endive, Lettuce, Melon, Potato

INSECTS AND ANIMALS

SYMPTOM	CAUSE	CURE	PLANTS
Whitish trails visible on top sides of leaves; microscopic larvae of tiny flying insects	*Leaf Miners*	Remove infected leaves by hand. Keep garden weed-free. Remove and destroy infested plants in the fall.	Beet, Cabbage, Chard, Eggplant, Lettuce, Pepper, Squash, Tomato
Wilting of the plant; root inspection indicates yellowish, ¼- to 1¼-inch wormlike creatures.	*Root Maggots*	Discourage the fly from laying eggs near the seedlings by putting shields of plastic or paper 4 inches square around the seedlings. For heavy infestations, drench soil with insecticide labeled for control of root maggots.	Cabbage, Carrot, Radish, Spinach, Squash, Turnip
A slime trail from plants that have irregular holes in leaves and lower stems	*Snails and Slugs*	Remove debris where they hide during the day. Shallow pans of beer will attract and drown pests. Commercial baits are available.	Cabbage, Carrot, Lettuce, Tomato, Turnip
Yellowing leaves with speckled look; fine spider webs on backs of leaves and at point where leaves attach to stem; tiny reddish mites on webs and undersides of leaves	*Spider Mites*	Spray plants with miticide labeled for use on vegetables.	Bean, Cucumber, Eggplant, Tomato
Distorted leaf tips, white irregular marks on leaves	*Thrips*	Hose off infected areas (insects are nearly invisible to the naked eye). Spray with a contact poison labeled for vegetable garden use.	Bean, Cabbage, Carrot, Celery, Cucumber, Melon, Onion, Pea, Squash, Tomato, Turnip

INSECTS AND ANIMALS

SYMPTOM	CAUSE	CURE	PLANTS
Leaves and fruit of tomatoes and related plants eaten; four-inch green and white caterpillarlike worm found on plants.	*Tomato Hornworm*	Remove worms by hand as they are discovered. Spray with Bacillus thuringiensis or stomach poison insecticide.	Eggplant, Pepper, Tomato
Tiny white insects fly from plant when disturbed. Large infestations weaken plant by feeding on undersides of foliage.	*White Flies*	Light infestations can be sprayed off with garden hose. Spray contact poison labeled for white fly on vegetables.	Eggplant, Pepper, Sweet Potato, Tomato
Poorly grown, yellow, wilted plants; hard, one-inch, golden worms feed on seeds, roots, and lower stems.	*Wireworms*	Drench soil with recommended insecticide. Control adults (click beetles) later in the season.	Carrot, Lettuce, Potato, Tomato, others

DISEASES

SYMPTOM	CAUSE	CURE	PLANTS
Dead areas on leaves and fruits; areas are depressed with slightly raised edge around them. Occurs mostly during wet weather.	*Anthracnose*	Spray with sulfur fungicide labeled for vegetables.	Bean, Cucumber, Melon, Pepper, Potato, Pumpkin, Squash, Tomato, Watermelon
Water-soaked spots that spread and fuse into irregularly shaped blotches; fruit begins to rot.	*Blights*	Rotate crops; destroy infected garden debris.	Bean, Eggplant, Pepper, Squash, Tomato
Sunken, black patches on blossom end of fruit	*Calcium Deficiency, Nitrogen Excess*	Retain even soil moisture during dry periods. Mulch susceptible varieties.	Pepper, Squash, Tomato

DISEASES

SYMPTOM	CAUSE	CURE	PLANTS
White, powdery dust appears on leaves. Lower leaves and stem turn grayish.	*Mildews*	Increase air circulation and keep foliage dry. Spray with fungicide labeled for vegetable crops.	Bean, Corn, Cucumber, Melon, Onion, Pea, Pumpkin
Reddish or rusty spots on the leaves; leaves look wilted.	*Rust*	Water early enough for foliage to dry before nightfall. Destroy infected garden debris in fall. Spray with fungicide labeled for vegetables.	Asparagus, Bean, Beet, Chard
Masses of black spores on foliage and growing tips	*Smuts*	Use resistant varieties; rotate crops; destroy infected garden debris.	Corn, Onion
Stunted plants, yellowing of leaves or yellow and green mottled leaves	*Viruses*	Plant resistant varieties; remove infected plants and destroy. Do not smoke when handling plants.	Every garden vegetable variety
Leaves wilt and turn yellow, even when soil is moist.	*Wilt*	Use resistant varieties; rotate crops; remove and destroy affected plants before disease spreads.	Cabbage, Celery, Cucumber, Pea, Sweet Potato, Tomato

An herb garden can be part
of your vegetable garden,
or you can design a
separate, more formal
arangement. Herbs are a
perfect complement to
garden-fresh vegetables.

HERBS IN YOUR GARDEN

Herbs are probably the most popular and intriguing group of plants in existence. Undoubtedly, the explanation for this is that over the centuries herbs have been used in so many different ways. They flavor our foods, perfume our homes and bodies, decorate our gardens, and cure our ills. One way or another, herbs touch each of our lives.

Sooner or later, most of us decide to try our hand at growing a few favorite herbs. It usually starts with a pot of parsley on the kitchen windowsill or a short row of dill in the vegetable patch. Once started, many gardeners find themselves increasing the number of herbs they cultivate simply because so many of them flourish with little care. These rugged, hardy plants survive, and even thrive, in poor soil and wide temperature fluctuations that would prove too difficult for many other cultivated plant varieties. This same vigor makes them admirable choices for use in window boxes and other container situations where they're likely to be subjected to quite a bit of heat and dryness.

Because of their diversity, no group of plants is more difficult to define. How did we decide which plants to include? We simply chose those herbs we judged to be the most foolproof to grow and the most commonly useful to a beginning enthusiast. It should be noted that no attempt has been made to include the medicinal uses of herbs.

Growing Your Own Herbs

A few herb plants grown in a container can spice up a patio with their fragrance.

Herbs fit beautifully into any landscape. Ground-hugging thyme is a perfect choice for planting between the rocks in a flagstone walk. Tall clumps of angelica or rue provide attractive and dramatic accents in flower borders. Nasturtiums and chives add outstanding floral color to a garden, as well as making attractive cut flowers. The purple-leaf variety of basil is an eye-catching accent in any location.

The chart on page 71 will help you quickly identify those plants best suited to your site. It also notes whether plants are annuals, biennials, or perennials, and how large you can expect each herb to be at maturity. Especially attractive landscape varieties are also identified.

Although herbs are often planted in a formal layout separate from the rest of the garden, this is by no means a requirement for success in growing them. Herbs can be mixed into other plantings. The exceptions are those few herbs, such as mint, that will aggressively take over if not curbed. These are best planted in containers or separate beds, where strict control of their spread can be maintained. Most other herbs can be planted along with other row crops in your vegetable garden.

Herbs can be laid out in a very formal or an extremely informal design or anywhere in between. The choice is entirely up to your personal view regarding what will fit best with adjacent garden spaces.

When planning a vegetable garden that includes herbs, the same basic rules of good design apply as when designing any other garden. Tall plants should be located at the rear of side beds, plants of intermediate height in the middle of the bed, and low-growing plants at the front. This way they'll all obtain a maximum share of the available light. In central beds, the tallest plants can be located in the center of the bed, the shortest plants around the outer edge, and the intermediate heights between the two.

The best approach to deciding which herbs to grow is to make a list of herbs you're most likely to use. Write down their soil, light, and water needs; their height and spread; and any special notes such as unusual growth habit. Make a secondary list of plants you might enjoy having if there's any room left.

Sketch the garden area to scale (for example, one inch on the sketch equals one foot on the ground), decide on the size and shape of the planting beds, and determine which of the herbs on your list will be located where. Fill in any empty spots with appropriate species from your secondary list.

Harvesting—As a general rule of thumb, herbs have the highest level of flavor in their leaves just before they bloom. Harvesting is best done at this time. In the directory of vegetable and herb plants, you'll find notes regarding the best time to harvest each herb as well as the best methods of preservation.

Harvesting of herbs for fresh use can be done throughout the growing season. Thyme, sage, rosemary, and many other perennials need their active growing shoots snipped in 4- to 6-inch lengths. For annuals collect a few leaves.

When harvesting herbs to preserve for future use, wait until the plant is at its aromatic peak as noted in the directory. Pick it early in the morning when aromatics are at their highest level of the day. Discard any diseased or insect-infested portions. If there is dust present, wash the plant thoroughly and shake off as much of the excess water as possible before processing. If possible, wash the plant a day before harvesting.

Be especially careful when harvesting seeds. The timing must be precise enough to allow the seeds to ripen completely, but they must be caught before they disperse. One way to solve this problem is to keep watch on a daily basis and harvest as soon as the seeds begin to dry. Carefully snip off the heads over a large paper bag, allowing the seeds to fall directly into the bag. Keep

Formal Herb Garden Designs

Formal balanced geometric layouts usually revolve around some sort of special garden feature, such as a fountain, sundial, garden seat, statue, an unusual feature plant, or birdbath. All paths and attention lead to this feature, whether it's in the center of the garden or along one edge.

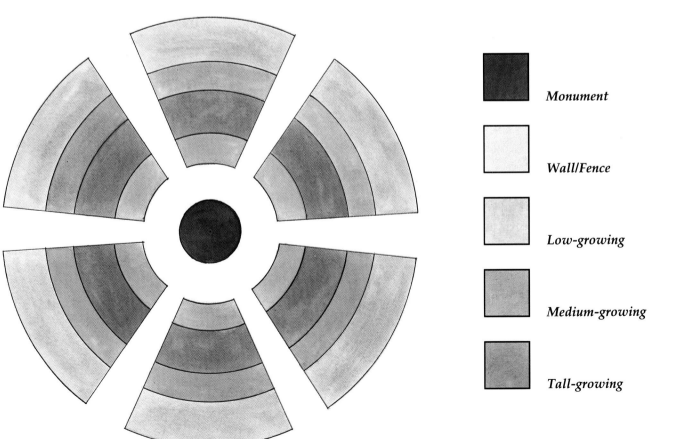

Monument

Wall/Fence

Low-growing

Medium-growing

Tall-growing

them in the bag to complete the drying process. Be careful not to compact the seed heads; air circulation in and around the seed heads is needed to cut down on the possibility of the growth of undesirable molds.

If you cannot keep such close track of the maturation process, another alternative is to enclose each seed head while still on the plant in a small paper bag once all flowering has ended and the green seeds become obvious. Then, when the heads dry, any seeds that fall out will be captured in the bag. Once you notice that seeds are being released, snip off the heads, bag and all, and dry them indoors.

The most common method of herb preservation is by hang drying. Another good way to preserve many herbs is by freezing them. This method is quick and easy, and the flavor is usually closer to fresh than dried. If you have the freezer space available, freezing is probably the most desirable choice for cooking herbs. Some herbs lose flavor when exposed to air, but they will retain it if stored in oil or liquor. Some herbs don't retain as much flavor when preserved by any means—they can only be used fresh. You can, however, extend their season by growing them indoors as pot plants during the winter months.

Informal Herb Garden Layouts

Here are two informal layouts. One backs a wall or fence and the other stands as an island in the middle of a lawn area.

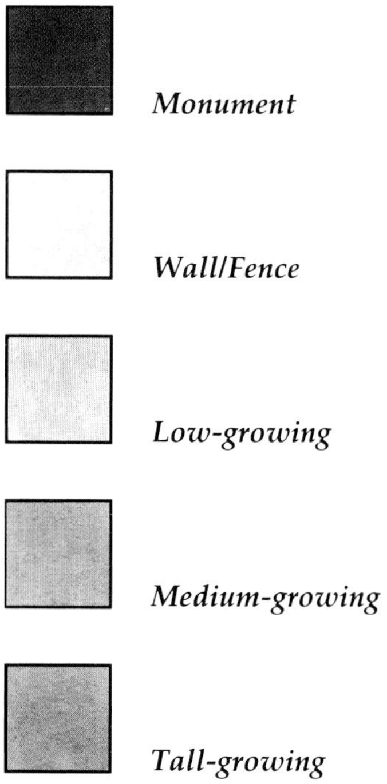

Monument

Wall/Fence

Low-growing

Medium-growing

Tall-growing

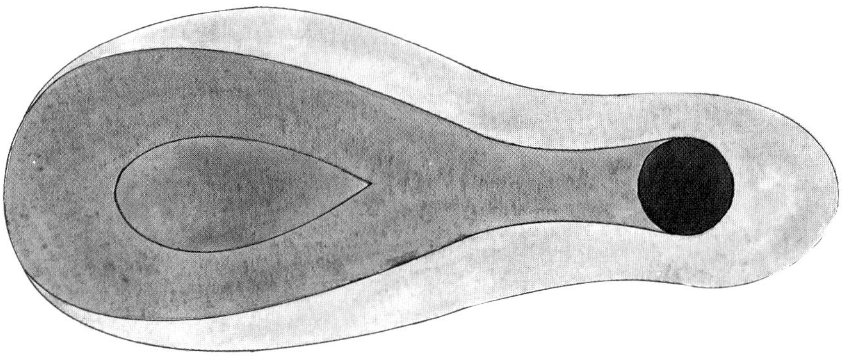

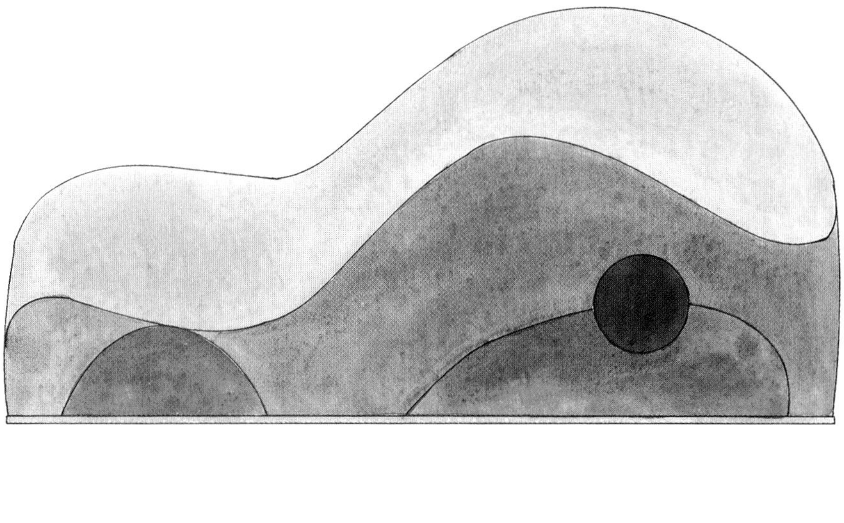

HERB CHART

Name	Plant	Landscape	Light	Soil	Height*	Spread*	Culture
Angelica	B	•	FS,PS	A,M	60–72	36	E
Anise	A		FS	A,D	18–24	4–8	E
Basil	A	•	FS	R,M	18	10	E
Chervil	A		PS	A,M	18	4–8	A–D
Chives	P	•	FS,PS	A–R,M	8–12	8	E
Coriander	A		FS	R	24–36	6	E
Costmary	P		FS,PS	R	30–36	24	E
Dill	A		FS	A–S,M	24–36	6	E
Fennel	P		FS	R	50–72	18–36	E
Garlic	P		FS	A–P	18	8	E
Geraniums, scented	P	•	FS	A–R	VARIES	VARIES	A
Horehound	P	•	FS	A–P	30	12	E
Marjoram	P,A		FS	R	8–12	12–18	E
Nasturtium	A	•	FS,PS	A–P,M	12–72	18	E
Oregano	P		FS	A–S	18	12	E
Parsley	B	•	FS,PS	R,M	12	8	E
Peppermint	P		FS,PS	R,M	24–30	12	E,R
Rosemary	P	•	FS	S	48–72	18–24	A
Rue	P	•	FS	P,S	24	18	A
Sage	P	•	FS	S	20	24	E
Savory, Summer	A		FS	R–A	18	8	E
Sorrel, French	P		FS,PS	R,M	18	10	E
Southernwood	P	•	FS	ANY	30	24	E
Spearmint	P		FS,PS	R,M	20	12	E,R
Sweet, Woodruff	P	•	S	R,M	6–8	6–8	D
Tansy	P		FS,PS	A–P	40	12–18	E,R
Tarragon, French	P	•	FS,PS	S–R	24	24	A
Thyme	P	•	FS,PS	P–A	1–10	12–18	E,R
Wormwood	P	•	FS	ANY	30–48	15–20	A

*inches
PLANT: A=Annual   B=Biennial   P=Perennial
LIGHT: FS=Full Sun   PS=Partial Shade   S=Shade
SOIL: P=Poor   A=Average   R=Rich   S=Sandy   M=Moist   D=Dry
CULTURE: E=Easy to Grow   A=Average   D=Difficult   R=Rampant Grower/Keep Restricted

Kale is just one of many vegetables you can grow in your backyard. With careful planning, you can reap a plentiful harvest from early spring to late autumn.

ENCYCLOPEDIA OF VEGETABLES & HERBS

The vegetable and herb garden is unlike any other garden on your property. It can be as attractive as a flower border—with many different types of plants: annuals and perennials, warm-season and cool-season plants—as well as productive. Try different types or new varieties of vegetables and herbs. You're not locked into what you planted last year.

Different parts of different plants are considered vegetables: We use carrot roots, asparagus stems, broccoli flower buds, spinach leaves, tomato fruits, and corn seeds all for food. Some varieties, such as turnips, are grown as a dual-purpose plant, where the leaves as well as the roots are edible. Herbs can serve many purposes: culinary, cosmetic, potpourri and sachet, and fresh or dried arrangement material.

There are so many varieties of vegetables and herbs we can't begin to describe them all. Instead, we've chosen a few of the tried and true varieties that will perform best in your garden. You'll find information about what the plant looks like and how to grow it. Use this guide as a handy reference while planning your garden to determine planting dates, soil preferences, and harvesting tips.

Globe Artichoke

Cynara Scolymus
Tender

Description: This thistlelike tender perennial grows 3 to 4 feet tall and 3 to 4 feet wide. The globe artichoke is grown for its flower buds, which are eaten before they begin to open. Since it is tender and reacts poorly to cold weather, it is not for all gardens.

How to grow: Artichokes have a definite preference for a long frost-free season with damp weather. They will be damaged by heavy frost or snow, and in areas where the temperature goes below freezing, they need special care and mulching. Artichokes are grown from offshoots, suckers, or seed. For best results, start with offshoots or suckers from a reputable nursery or garden center. Plants grown from seed vary tremendously in quality. Artichokes need a position in full sunlight and a rich, well-drained soil that will hold moisture. Too much nitrogen will keep the plant from flowering. Artichokes bear best the second year and should be started from new plants every three to four years. To enable the roots to survive the winter in cooler areas, cut the plant back to about 10 inches, cover it with a bushel basket, and then place mulch around the basket to a thickness of two feet to help maintain an even soil temperature.

Harvest: Timing from planting to harvest is 50 to 100 days for plants grown from suckers. The first buds will take at least a year to form when they are grown from seed. To harvest, cut off the bud with 1 to 1½ inches of stem before the bud begins to open.

Varieties: 'Green Globe' is the best variety; it has 4-inch-large round buds.

Jerusalem Artichoke

Helianthus tuberosus
Hardy

Description: Jerusalem artichoke is a large, upright, hardy perennial. It has small yellow flowers 2 to 3 inches across and rough, hairy leaves 4 to 8 inches long. This plant, which is not related to the globe artichoke, is a type of sunflower and will grow 5 to 10 feet tall. The edible tubers are low in starch and taste a bit like water chestnuts.

How to Grow: Jerusalem artichokes will grow anywhere and in almost any soil, as long as it's warm and well drained. Plant the tubers two to three weeks before the average date of last frost. Plant tubers 2 to 6 inches deep and 12 to 18 inches apart in ordinary soil. Don't fertilize Jerusalem artichokes; rich garden soil will encourage lush leafy growth with a low yield of tubers. Water only during extremely dry periods. The plants themselves can survive long dry periods, but the tubers will not develop without a regular supply of water. As the plants grow, cut off the flower buds as soon as they appear; this will encourage tuber production.

Harvest: The time from planting to harvest is 120 to 150 days. Harvest the tubers when the leaves die back; dig them up with a spading fork. Leave a few in the ground for next year. Plants spread quickly if not harvested.

Varieties: There are no named varieties available. Use tubers found in your grocery.

Asparagus

Asparagus officinalis
Hardy

Description: Asparagus is a long-lived hardy perennial with fleshy roots and fernlike, feathery foliage. The plant grows about 3 feet tall. The part that is eaten is the tender young stem. The popular houseplant asparagus fern is not a fern at all but a diminutive relative of edible asparagus.

How to grow: Asparagus grows well in most areas of the United States, except the Deep South. It thrives in a climate where the winters are cold enough to freeze the top few inches of soil and provide it with the necessary period of dormancy. Although asparagus can be started from seeds, the best-quality plants come from crowns that can be ordered from a nursery. Plant asparagus four to six weeks before the area's average date of last frost. Asparagus needs well-drained soil with a pH above 6. Full sun is best. To plant asparagus crowns, dig a trench or furrow 10 inches wide and 10 to 12 inches deep. Put in 2 to 4 inches of soil mixed with organic matter. Place the crowns on the soil with the roots well spread out. Cover with 2 more inches of soil. As the spears grow, gradually fill in the trench to the top. It's important to give asparagus sufficient water when the spears are forming.

Harvest: Asparagus should not be harvested until it is three years old; the crowns need time to develop fully. During the third season, cut off the spears at or slightly below soil level. Harvest asparagus when the spears are 8 to 10 inches tall; if the stalks have started to feather out, it's too late to eat them. Stop harvesting when the stalks begin coming up pencil-thin.

Varieties: 'Mary Washington' is widely available and resistant to asparagus rust. 'UC 157' was developed for Southern climates. It is resistant to fusarium root.

Green (Snap) Bean, Yellow (Wax) Bean

Phaseolus vulgaris
Tender

The most commonly grown beans are the green, or snap, bean and the yellow, or wax, bean, which is a variety of the green bean. Since 1894, when Burpee introduced the Stringless Green Pod, most beans have been stringless. Beans grow as bushes or vines. Bushes are generally easier to handle; they grow only 1 to 2 feet tall, and they mature earlier. Pole beans grow 6 to 8 feet tall and require a trellis for support. They grow more slowly but produce more beans per plant.

Description: Leaves are usually composed of three leaflets; flowers are pale yellow, lavender, or white. The size and color of the pods and seeds vary.

How to grow: Snap beans require a short growing season—about 60 days of moderate temperatures from seed to first crop. They grow anywhere in the United States and are an encouraging vegetable for the inexperienced gardener. Snap beans require warm soil to germinate and should be planted on the average date of last frost. You can plant bush beans every two weeks to extend the harvest, or you can start with bush beans and follow up with pole beans. Plant seeds an inch deep, directly in the garden. For bush beans, plant the seeds 2 inches apart in single rows or wide rows. Seeds of pole beans should be planted 4 to 6 inches apart in rows 30 to 36 inches apart. Or, plant them in inverted hills, five or six seeds to a hill, with 30 inches of space around each hill. For pole bean varieties, set the trellis at the time of planting to avoid disturbing the roots. Keep the soil evenly moist until the beans have pushed through the ground. When seedlings are growing well, thin the plants to 4 to 6 inches apart. Thin plants by cutting excess seedlings with scissors to avoid disturbing the roots of neighboring seedlings.

Harvest: The immature pod is the part that is eaten. When pods are large enough to eat, harvest by pulling the pods off the plant, taking care not to break the stem. Beans will flower twice and provide a second harvest. Smaller pods are more tender.

Bush varieties: 'Burpee's Tenderpod,' 50 days, has 5-inch-long green pods. 'Blue Lake,' 58 days, has green, 6½-inch pods with white seeds. 'Roma II,' 53 days, has green, flattened pods, 4½ inches long. 'Brittle Wax,' 52 days, has rounded, yellow pods, 7 inches long. 'Royal Burgundy,' 51 days, has 6-inch-long purple pods.

Pole varieties: 'Kentucky Wonder,' 65 days, is a proved standard variety with heavy yields of 9-inch green pods. 'Blue Lake,' 60 days, has pods that are 6 inches long with white seeds. 'Scarlet Runner Bean,' 65 days, is often grown ornamentally for its scarlet flowers; pods are green and up to 12 inches long.

Lima Bean

Phaseolus limensis
Very Tender

This large-seeded annual bean grows as either a bush or a vine. Bush lima beans are generally easier to handle than pole varieties. Bushes grow only 1 or 2 feet tall, and they mature earlier. Pole beans require a trellis for support. They grow more slowly but produce more beans per plant.

How to grow: To germinate properly, lima beans need warmer soil than snap beans. They also need higher temperatures and a longer growing season for a good crop. Lima bean seeds require soil temperatures of at least 65 degrees Fahrenheit for a minimum of five days to germinate. They should be planted two weeks after the average date of the last frost. Plant bush beans every two weeks to extend the harvest, or start with bush beans and follow up with pole varieties. Plant seeds directly in the garden, an inch deep. For bush beans, plant the seeds 2 inches apart in single rows or wide rows. Seeds of pole beans should be planted four to six inches apart in rows 30 to 36 inches apart. Or, plant them in inverted hills, five or six seeds to a hill, with 30 inches of space around each hill. For pole bean varieties, set the trellis at the time of planting to avoid disturbing the roots. The lima bean seed sometimes has trouble pushing through the soil, although this should not happen if the soil is well worked.

Harvest: With this type of bean, the maturing seed is eaten, not the entire pod. Pick pods before the seeds have become tough. Ripe pods usually pop open when you press them along the seams.

Bush varieties: 'Fordhook 242,' 75 days, is a large-seeded lima bean with high yields. 'Henderson Bush,' 65 days, has white beans, three or four to a flattened pod.

Pole varieties: 'Burpee's Best,' 92 days, has 'Fordhook' characteristics: thick, 4½-inch pods with high yield. 'Prizetaker,' 90 days, has 6-inch-long pods with three to five beans.

Beet

Beta vulgaris
Hardy

Description: The beet has a round or tapered swollen root—red, yellow, or white—from which sprouts a rosette of large leaves.

How to grow: Beets tolerate frost and do best in the cooler areas of the country, but they will go to seed without making roots if the plants get too cold when young. Plant them as a winter crop in the southern parts of the country. In a hot climate, pay special attention to watering and mulching to give seedlings a chance to establish themselves. The roots become woody in very hot weather. Plant beets two to three weeks before the average date of last frost. Beets thrive in well-worked, loose soil that is high in organic matter. They do not do well in a very acid soil, and they need a good supply of potassium. Beets are grown from seed clusters that are slightly smaller than a pea and contain several seeds in each. Plant the clusters an inch deep, directly in the garden, an inch apart in rows spaced 12 to 18 inches apart. The seedlings may emerge over a period of time, giving you a group of seedlings of different sizes. Since several seedlings will emerge from each seed cluster, they must be thinned to 2 to 3 inches apart when the seedlings develop true leaves.

Harvest: Both the leaves and the root can be eaten. Eat thinned seedlings like spinach; they do not transplant well. It takes about 60 days for a beet to reach 1½ inches in diameter, a popular size for cooking or pickling. They will quickly grow larger if they have plenty of water. Pull the beets up when they reach your desired size.

Varieties: 'Detroit Dark Red,' 60 days, is a deep red, finely-grained sweet standard beet. 'Golden,' 55 days, has gold-colored skin and flesh. 'Lutz Green Leaf,' 80 days, is often grown as a fall crop; its red flesh has lighter zones.

Broccoli

Brassica oleracea; Botrytis **Group**
Very Hardy

Description: Broccoli is a member of the cabbage, or cole, family. It grows 1½ to 2½ feet tall and looks a bit like cauliflower. Broccoli will grow in most areas of the United States at one season or another, but it is not a suitable crop for very hot climates.

How to grow: The head formation stage of development is essential for the production of the vegetable. Broccoli that's held in check by severe frost, lack of moisture, or too much heat will bolt (go directly to seed without forming a head). Broccoli is frost hardy and can tolerate low 20 degree Fahrenheit temperatures. It's a cool-season crop and does best with day temperatures less than 80 degrees Fahrenheit and night temperatures 20 degrees Fahrenheit lower. Broccoli likes fertile, well-drained soil with a pH within the 6.5 to 7.5 range. Broccoli is usually grown from transplants except where there's a long cool period, in which case you can sow seed directly in the garden in fall for winter harvest. Plant transplants that are four to six weeks old with four or five true leaves. If transplants are leggy with crooked stems, plant them deeply so they won't grow top-heavy. Plant the seedlings 18 to 24 inches apart.

Harvest: Time planting to harvest during cold weather. Transplants can be harvested in 40 to 80 days, depending on the variety. Harvesting can continue over a relatively long period. When it is well developed, cut off the central head with five to six inches of stem. Harvest before the head begins to loosen and separate. If small yellow flowers have started to show, it's past the good eating stage.

Varieties: 'Green Comet Hybrid,' 55 days, is disease resistant and heat resistant and produces 7-inch heads. 'Premium Crop,' 58 days, is an All America Selection.

Brussels Sprouts

Brassica oleracea; Gemmifera **Group**
Very Hardy

Description: Miniature cabbagelike heads, 1 or 2 inches in diameter and nestled in among large green leaves, sprout from a tall main stem. Brussels sprouts belong to the cabbage, or cole, family and are similar to cabbage in their growing habits and requirements. They're hardy—they are the most cold tolerant of the cole family vegetables—and easy to grow in the home garden.

How to grow: Brussels sprouts grow well in fertile soils and are frost-tolerant. They do best in a cool growing season with day temperatures less than 80 degrees Fahrenheit and night temperatures 20 degrees Fahrenheit lower. Weather that's too cold for too long or too warm will make the sprouts taste bitter. If they develop in hot weather, they may not form compact heads but instead will remain loose tufts of leaves. Brussels sprouts are usually grown from transplants. Where there's a long cool period, seeds can be sown directly in the garden in the fall for winter harvest. Plant transplants that are four to six weeks old. If the transplants are leggy or have crooked stems, plant them deeply so they won't grow top-heavy.

Harvest: You can harvest brussels sprouts 75 to 90 days after transplanting. The sprouts mature from the bottom of the stem upward, so start from the bottom and remove leaves and sprouts as the season progresses.

Varieties: 'Jade Cross Hybrid,' 95 days, is resistant to yellow virus. 'Long Island Improved' matures in 90 days.

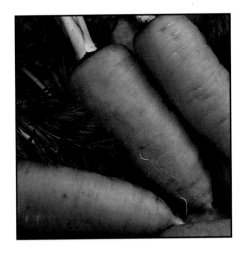

Cabbage

Brassica oleracea; Capitata **Group**
Very Hardy

Description: Cabbage, a hardy biennial that is grown as an annual, has an enlarged terminal bud made of crowded and expanded overlapping leaves shaped into a head. The leaves are smooth or crinkled in shades of green or purple. The head can be round, flat, or pointed. Cabbage is easy to grow in the home garden.

How to grow: Cabbage is a cool-weather crop that can tolerate frost but not heat. If the plants are cold for too long, or if the weather is too warm, the plants will bolt (go to seed without forming a head). If the head has already formed, it will split in hot weather. Splitting happens when the plant takes up water so fast the excess cannot escape through the tightly overlapped leaves, and the head bursts. Cabbage likes fertile, well-drained soil with a pH in the 6.5 to 7.5 range. Cabbages are usually grown from transplants. Where there's a long cool period, seed can be sown directly in the garden in the fall for winter harvest. Plant transplants that are four to six weeks old; plant two to three weeks before the average date of the last frost.

Harvest: Cabbages mature in 60 to 105 days from transplants. To harvest, cut off the head, leaving the outer leaves on the stem.

Varieties: 'Earliana,' 60 days from transplants, is a small, compact early variety. 'Early Jersey Wakefield,' 63 days, produces heads that are full-sized, pointed, and with a sweet flavor. 'Ruby Ball,' 68 days, produces purple heads that are four to six pounds; it is an All America Selection.

Cardoon

Cynara cardunculus
Tender

Description: Cardoon is a tender perennial grown as an annual for its young leaf-stalks, which are blanched and eaten like celery. A member of the artichoke family, cardoon has the same deeply cut leaves and heavy, bristled flower heads. Cardoon, which will grow anywhere in the United States, can grow to 4 feet tall and 2 feet wide, so it will need plenty of space in your garden.

How to grow: Plant cardoon from transplants in the garden on the date of the last frost in your area. If you're growing your own transplants from seed, start them indoors six to eight weeks before planting in the garden. New plants may also be started from suckers. Cardoon prefers full sun but can tolerate partial shade. It grows quickly in any well-drained, fertile soil. Cardoon stalks can get very tough, so the plant is blanched to improve flavor and make it more tender. Blanch when the plant is about three feet tall, four to six weeks before harvesting. Tie the leaves together in a bunch and wrap paper or burlap around the stems. Or, form a hill of soil around the stem.

Harvest: Harvest the plants four to six weeks after blanching. Cut them off at ground level and trim off the outer leaves.

Varieties: The two most common are 'Large Smooth' and 'Ivory White Smooth.'

Carrot

Daucus Carota sativis
Hardy

Description: Carrots are hardy biennials that are grown as annuals. They have a rosette of finely divided, fernlike leaves growing from a swollen, fleshy taproot. The root, which varies in size and shape, is generally a tapered cylinder that grows up to 10 inches long in different shades of orange.

How to grow: There are all types of carrots—long, short, fat, thin—they differ only in size and shape. Your soil type will influence the variety you choose. Shorter varieties will tolerate heavy soil. Carrots are cool-weather crops and tolerate cold. For a continuous crop, plant carrots every two to three weeks starting two to three weeks before the date of last frost. Sow the seeds directly in the garden. Wide-row planting of carrots gives a good yield from a small area. Carrot seedlings grow slowly when young, so it's important to control weeds during the first few weeks. In areas with high soil temperatures, mulch to regulate soil temperature.

Harvest: The time from planting to harvest is from 55 to 80 days, depending on variety. Pull carrots when the soil is moist: If you try to pull them from hard ground, you'll break the roots. In warmer areas, late season carrots can be kept in the garden throughout most of the winter and harvested as needed.

Varieties: 'Danvers Half Long,' 75 days, is uniform-size at 7½ inches; it is bright orange and sweet. 'Short 'n' Sweet,' 68 days, produces 4-inch roots and is good for heavy soil. 'Thumbelina,' 60 to 70 days, is an All America Selection; bred for heavy soils, it produces 2-inch round carrots. 'Juwarot,' 70 days, is dark orange and grows to 8 inches long.

Cauliflower

Brassica oleracea, Botrytis Group
Very Hardy

Cauliflower is a single-stalked, half-hardy, biennial member of the cole, or cabbage, family. It's grown as an annual, and the edible flower buds form a solid head that may be white, green, or purple. Cauliflower is more restricted by climatic conditions than other cole family members. It's less adaptable to extremes of temperature.

How to grow: Cauliflower needs two cool months to mature and is planted as a spring or fall crop in most areas. Plant for a winter crop if your winters are mild. For a spring crop, plant transplants four to six weeks before the average date of last frost. Start your own transplants from seed indoors about six weeks before garden planting. Plant leggy and crooked transplants deeply in the garden to prevent them from being top-heavy. Unless the buds are supposed to be green or purple, the color should be untinged creamy-white. To protect the head from discoloring, blanch the head when it gets to the size of an egg by gathering three or four leaves and tying them together to cover the head. Self-blanching cauliflower doesn't need to be covered, but it will not blanch in hot weather.

Harvest: Time from planting transplants to harvest is 55 to 100 days. The mature head should be compact and about 6 to 8 inches in diameter. Cut the whole head from the main stem.

Varieties: 'Snow Crown Hybrid,' 52 days, has pure white, 8-inch-diameter heads. 'Super Snowball' is ready to harvest in 55 days. 'Royal Purple,' produces 6- to 7-inch-diameter purple heads.

Celeriac

Apium graveolens rapaceum
Hardy

Description: Celeriac is a form of celery: a member of the same family and similar in growing habits and requirements. The edible root of celeriac is large and swollen and develops at soil level. A rosette of dark green leaves sprouts from the root.

How to grow: Celeriac does best in cool weather and especially enjoys cool nights. To grow celeriac, start in the spring in the North, in late summer in the South. In the North, start from transplants; sow seeds indoors two to three months before your planting date. Plant transplants on the average date of last frost. Celeriac prefers rich soil that is high in organic matter, well able to hold moisture but with good drainage. It needs constant moisture and does well in wet locations. The plant is a heavy feeder and needs plenty of fertilizer to keep it growing quickly. Celeriac cannot compete with weeds. Cultivate conscientiously, but be careful to not disturb the shallow roots. As the root develops, snip off the side roots and hill the soil over the swollen areas for a short time to blanch the tubers. The outer surface will be whitened, but the interior will remain a brownish color.

Harvest: Harvest celeriac when the swollen root is 3 to 4 inches wide. Celeriac increases in flavor after the first frost, but it should be harvested before the first hard freeze.

Varieties: Both 'Alabaster' and 'Prague' mature in 120 days.

Celery

Apium graveolens dulce
Hardy

Description: Celery is a hardy biennial that is grown as an annual. It has a tight rosette of stalks 8 to 18 inches long, topped with divided leaves. It's a versatile vegetable—you can eat the stalks, leaves, and seeds—but it needs a lot of attention. It's not an easy crop for the home gardener.

How to grow: Celery does best in cool weather and especially enjoys cool nights. Grow celery in spring in the North, planting transplants two to three weeks before the average date of last frost; in the South plant in the late summer. Celery prefers rich soil high in organic matter that is well able to hold moisture but with good drainage. It does well in wet locations. Celery is a heavy feeder and needs plenty of fertilizer for quick growth. If you're sowing seeds for transplants, start them two to four months before your estimated planting date: They germinate slowly. Transplant them to trenches 3 to 4 inches deep and two feet apart. Space the seedlings 8 to 10 inches apart. Celery will be bitter if it isn't blanched. Blanching is achieved by covering the plants to protect them from the sun. As the plants grow, pile soil up around them to blanch the stems. Having the plants fairly close together will also help blanching.

Harvest: The time from planting transplants to harvest is 100 to 130 days. Start harvesting before the first hard frost, when the head is about 2 to 3 inches in diameter at the base. Cut off the head at or slightly below soil level.

Varieties: 'Summer Pascal,' 115 days, is medium green in color and is slow-bolting. 'Utah 52-70,' 125 days, is the standard thick-stalked variety.

Swiss Chard

Beta vulgaris, Cicla **Group**
Hardy

Description: Chard is basically a beet without the bottom. It's a biennial that is grown as an annual for its big crinkly leaves. The stalks are red or white with large, dark green leaves.

How to grow: Chard prefers cool temperatures. High temperatures slow down leaf production, but chard tolerates heat better than spinach. In mild regions, you can plant chard from fall to early spring. In the North, plant from spring to midsummer. Plant chard from seed clusters—each cluster contains several seeds—about a week before the average date of last frost. Chard prefers well-worked soil with good drainage and a high organic content; it does not like acid soil. Plant the seeds directly in the garden 2 to 6 inches apart in single or wide rows. Thin seedlings to 12 inches apart when they're large enough to handle. The crop needs enough water to keep the leaves growing quickly, so keep the soil moist at all times.

Harvest: The time from planting to harvest is 55 to 65 days. Start harvesting chard when the outside leaves are three inches long. Don't let the leaves get much longer than 10 inches, or they'll taste earthy. Either take a few leaves off at a time or cut the entire plant down to three inches and let it grow back. If you harvest the leaves as they grow, the plant will go on producing all season.

Varieties: 'Rhubarb Chard,' 60 days, produces red stalks. 'Lucullus,' 50 days, is somewhat like spinach with white stalks and light green leaves. 'Fordhook Giant,' 60 days, produces green leaves and white stalks and is tolerant to heat.

Chicory

Cichorium intybus
Hardy

Description: Chicory is a hardy perennial with a long fleshy taproot and a flower stalk that rises from a rosette of ragged lobed leaves. The shoots are known as Belgian endive, which should not be confused with the salad endive, or escarole.

How to grow: Chicory tolerates cold and can be grown for its roots anywhere in the United States. Plant seeds an inch deep in the garden two to three weeks before the average date of last frost. Thin the plants to 12 to 18 inches apart. If chicory is planted in well-cultivated soil rich in organic matter, it should develop large roots. To produce blanched heads, dig the roots out before a hard freeze. Cut off the tops about two inches above the crown, or top, of the root; store the roots in a cool place. In winter, force the roots in a cool, dark room by planting them in moist sand. Keep the emerging shoots covered with seven or eight inches of sawdust and water the plant occasionally. In three to four weeks, when new shoots emerge, cut the heads from the root.

Harvest: Chicory is grown either for its root, which is roasted as a coffee substitute, or for its tender shoots, which are known as Belgian endive. If planting for the roots alone, they'll be ready to harvest in about 120 days.

Varieties: 'Magdeburg,' 100 days, is grown for its root, which is roasted as a coffee substitute. 'Witloof,' 110 days, is also known as Belgian endive; it is grown for its blanched heads, or chicons.

Chinese Cabbage

Brassica Rapa; Pekinensis **Group**
Very Hardy

Description: Chinese cabbage is a hardy biennial that is grown as an annual. It has broad, thick, tender leaves with heavy midribs; it can be either loosely or tightly headed. The plant grows 15 to 18 inches tall. The variety with a large compact heart is called celery cabbage, or Michihli.

How to grow: Chinese cabbage can be grown in cool weather only because it bolts (goes to seed) quickly in hot weather and long days. It's usually grown as a fall crop in the North and as a winter crop in the South. It can be started inside and transplanted outside in the spring. However, Chinese cabbage shocks easily, and transplanting sometimes shocks it into going to seed. Therefore, it's best to sow the seed directly in the garden and thin them to stand 8 to 12 inches apart. Water them frequently to help the young plants grow fast and become tender. They'll probably go to seed if growth slows down.

Harvest: The time from planting to harvest is 50 to 80 days, depending on the variety. Harvest when the heads are compact and firm and before seed stalks form. With a fall crop, harvest before hard-freezing weather. Cut off the whole plant at ground level.

Varieties: 'Pak Choi,' 47 days, produces non-heading, white, celerylike stalks with green leaves. 'Wong Bok,' 85 days, is the standard head-type Chinese cabbage. 'Michihli,' 75 days, has large heads with blanched inside leaves.

Collards

Brassica oleracea; Acephala **Group**
Very Hardy

Description: A hardy biennial that is grown as an annual, collards grow 2 to 4 feet tall and have tufted rosettes of leaves growing on sturdy stems. Collards are a kind of kale, a primitive member of the cabbage family that does not form a head.

How to grow: Collards are hardy and can tolerate low temperatures. They're also more tolerant of heat than some members of the cabbage family. In the South, get ahead of warm weather by planting collards from fall through March. In the North, you can get two crops by planting in early spring and again in July or August. Collards like fertile, well-drained soil with a pH between 6.5 and 7.5. Collards are usually grown from transplants planted four to six weeks before the average date of last frost. Set transplants deeply if the stems are leggy or crooked to prevent the plants from becoming top heavy. Where there is a long cool period, seeds can be sown directly in the garden in the fall for a winter harvest. Sow seeds an inch deep and thin seedlings to 12 inches apart.

Harvest: The time from planting to harvest is 75 to 85 days for transplants and 85 to 95 days for seeds. Collards become sweeter if harvested after a frost but harvest them before a hard freeze. In warmer areas, harvest the leaves from the bottom up before the leaves get tough.

Varieties: Both 'Georgia' and 'Vates' mature in 75 days.

Corn

Zea mays
Tender

Description: Corn, a tender annual that can grow 4 to 12 feet tall, is a member of the grass family. It produces one to three ears on a stalk. The kernels of sweet corn can be yellow, white, black, red, or a combination of colors. Corn is not the easiest crop to grow in a home vegetable garden, and it doesn't give a lot of return for the space it occupies.

How to grow: Corn can be grown in any region, but the time it will take to mature depends on the amount of heat it gets. Corn doesn't really hit its stride until the weather warms up. Depending on the varieties planted, two crops may be possible. Corn likes well-worked, fertile soil with good drainage, and it must have full sun. Sow the seeds directly in the garden on the average date of last frost. Plant the seeds 2 to 4 inches apart in short rows forming a block rather than a single, long row. Planting in clumps ensures pollination. For a continuous supply, plant early, mid-season, and late varieties at the same time. When the corn is about 6 inches tall, thin short varieties to two feet apart and tall varieties to three feet apart. Although corn can be grown closer together than this, the roots are then more crowded and more watering and feeding are needed. Corn is a heavy user of nitrogen. Fertilize in the spring, again when the corn is 8 inches tall, and again when the plants are 18 inches tall. Side-dress between the rows, using one-third of a pound of complete, well-balanced fertilizer on each side of a 10-foot-long row. Hill soil around the plant roots at this time to help support the stalks. Watering is very important. Keep the soil evenly moist. Corn often grows so fast in hot weather that the leaves wilt because the roots can't keep the leaves supplied with moisture. Although corn requires much water, avoid getting water on the tassels. The pollen from the tassels must fall onto the corn silk to produce kernels, and if pollination does not occur, all that will grow is the cob. Weed early and keep the weeds cut back. Remember that corn has shallow roots, and a vigorous attack on the weeds may destroy the crop.

Harvest: From planting to harvest takes 55 to 95 days, depending on the variety and, to some extent, the weather. Harvest your corn when the kernels are soft and plump and the juice is milky.

Varieties: A large number of varieties are available; just a few of the good varieties available are listed here. 'Early Sunglow,' 63 days, is an early yellow variety that is good for short seasons. 'Butter & Sugar,' 78 days, produces white and yellow kernels. 'Illini Xtra-Sweet,' 85 days, has yellow kernels and is good for freezing. 'Silver Queen,' 92 days, is a very popular white-kernel, sweet, large-ear variety.

Cucumber

Cucumis sativus
Very Tender

Description: Cucumbers are tender annual vines that can sprawl on the ground or be trained to climb. Both the large leaves and the stems are covered with short hairs; the flowers are yellow. Some plants have both male and female flowers on the same vine, and there may be ten male flowers to every female flower. Only the female flowers produce cucumbers. Some hybrid cucumbers have only female flowers but need some male flowers to produce. Seed companies will include seeds—usually indicated by a pink dye on the seed—that will produce male flowers with such hybrid varieties. These hybrids are usually more productive and set earlier than other varieties.

How to grow: Cucumber is a warm-weather vegetable and very sensitive to frost. It will grow anywhere in the United States, however, because it has a very short growing season—only 55 to 65 days from planting to harvest—and most areas can provide it with at least that much sunshine. Cucumbers respond to a rich, well-worked, well-drained soil that is high in organic matter. Sow seeds directly in the garden two to three weeks after the average date of last frost. To grow transplants indoors, sow seeds three to four weeks prior to planting in the garden. Plant cucumbers in inverted hills, leaving the three strongest plants per hill. Cucumbers need plenty of water to keep them growing fast; don't let the soil dry out. In hot weather the leaves may wilt during the day even when soil moisture is high because the plant is using water faster than its roots can supply it. This is normal; just be sure the plant is receiving regular and sufficient water. Mulch to avoid compaction caused by heavy watering.

Harvest: Harvest promptly; mature cucumbers left on the vine suppress the production of more flowers. Pick the cucumbers when they're immature—the size will depend on the variety. When the seeds start to mature, the vines will stop producing.

Varieties: There are many varieties available to the home gardener. The following are just a few of the good varieties. 'Early Pride Hybrid,' 55 days, grows straight, green fruit that is 8½ inches long. 'Cherokee,' 55 days, is smooth-skinned and good for pickling. 'Straight Eight,' 58 days, is an All America Selection. 'Bush Champion,' 55 days, has productive, compact vines producing 11-inch fruit; it's a good variety for containers. 'Sweet Success,' 58 days, is an All America Selection that is thin-skinned and seedless and produces 14-inch fruit. 'Tasty Green Hybrid,' 62 days, produces 10-inch fruit and is a burpless variety.

Dandelion

Taraxacum officinale
Hardy

The dandelion is best known—and feared—by gardeners as a remarkably persistent lawn weed, but its leaves are actually high in vitamin A and four times higher in vitamin C than lettuce. It's also versatile: Dandelion leaves are used raw in salads or boiled like spinach. The roots can be roasted and made into a coffeelike drink.

Description: The dandelion is a hardy perennial that is grown as an annual for its foliage and as a biennial for its roots. The jagged green leaves grow in a short rosette attached by a short stem to a long taproot. Bright yellow flowers 1 to 2 inches wide grow on smooth, hollow stalks.

How to grow: Dandelions are very hardy and can survive the hottest summers and the coldest winters. Plant the seeds in early spring, four to six weeks before the average date of last frost. Dandelions grow best in well-drained, fertile soil but do well in any soil anywhere. If you're growing dandelions for their foliage only, they'll tolerate soil in poorer physical condition. They prefer full sun but will do fine in partial shade. Plant seeds directly in the garden ¼ inch deep in single rows or wide rows. Thin seedlings to 8 inches apart when they have produced their first true leaves.

Harvest: Harvest dandelion greens at your pleasure throughout the growing season. Harvest the roots in the fall of the second year. Pull the whole root from the ground or lift the roots with a fork to avoid breaking them.

Varieties: The two most common varieties are 'Montmagny' and 'Improved Thick-leaved.'

Eggplant

Solanum Melongena
Very Tender

Description: Eggplant is grown as an annual and has large, hairy, grayish-green leaves. The star-shaped flowers are lavender with yellow centers. The long, slender or round, egg-shaped fruit can be creamy white, yellow, brown, or purple, depending on the variety. Eggplants will grow 2 to 6 feet tall, depending on the variety. Typical home garden varieties produce fruit that is rounded with shiny, dark purple skins. The Oriental varieties produce fruit that is slender and elongated with skin that is usually dull purple in color. Eggplant belongs to the tobacco family and is related to tomatoes, potatoes, and peppers.

How to grow: Eggplant is very sensitive to cold and needs a growing season with day temperatures between 80 and 90 degrees Fahrenheit and night temperatures between 70 and 80 degrees Fahrenheit. Although you can grow eggplant from seed, you'll wait 150 days for a harvest. It's easier to grow from transplants started inside about six to eight weeks before your outside planting date, which should be two to three weeks after the danger of frost. Eggplants must have full sun. They'll grow in almost any soil, but they do better in rich soil that is high in organic matter. Excellent drainage is essential. Set the plants 18 to 24 inches apart. Try to maintain an even soil moisture to ensure even growth. In hot climates the soil temperature may become too warm for the roots; in this case, mulch the plants about a month after you set them outside.

Harvest: The time from planting transplants to harvest is 70 to 85 days. Harvest the fruit young, before the flesh becomes pithy. The fruit should be firm and shiny with no brown streaks. The fruit is borne on a sturdy stem that does not break easily from the plant; cut it off with a sharp knife.

Varieties: 'Tycoon,' 54 days, is an Oriental type with slender, purple fruit. 'Bambino,' 60 days, produces small, rounded fruit on compact, 12-inch plants; it is an ideal variety for containers and small spaces. 'Victoria Hybrid,' 61 days, an Italian type with a deep purple skin color, produces fruit that is long and slender and good for slicing. 'Dusky Hybrid,' 62 days from transplants, is good for short seasons, producing slender, oval dark purple fruit. 'Black Beauty,' 80 days from transplants, has rounded, dark purple fruit.

Endive

Cichorium Endivia
Hardy

Description: Endive is a half-hardy biennial that is grown as an annual. It has a large rosette of toothed, curled, or wavy leaves that are used in salads as a substitute for lettuce. Endive is often known as escarole, and the two vegetables are varieties of the same plant. Escarole has broader leaves.

How to grow: Endive is a cool-season crop, although it's more tolerant of heat than lettuce. Grow it from seed planted in your garden four to six weeks before the average date of last frost. Long, hot summers will force the plant to bolt (go to seed). If your region has a short, hot growing season, start endive indoors from seed. Transplant it as soon as possible so the plants mature before the weather gets hot. Starting in midsummer, sow succession crops in well-worked soil with good drainage and water retention. If you're direct-seeding, sow seeds 1/4 inch deep in wide rows. Thin the plants to 9 to 12 inches apart; crowded plants may bolt early. Water regularly to keep the plants growing quickly; lack of water will slow growth and cause the leaves to become bitter. Endive tastes better if you blanch it by tying string around the leaves to hold them together. This deprives the plant of sunlight, discouraging the production of chlorophyll.

Harvest: The time from planting to harvest is 90 to 100 days from seed. To harvest, cut the plant off at soil level.

Varieties: 'Green Curled,' 90 days, has fringed leaves that are creamy white in the center. 'Sinco,' 80 days, is a large-headed escarole.

Garlic

Allium sativum
Very Hardy

Description: Garlic is a hardy perennial that looks similar to onion except that the bulb is segmented into cloves. The flower head looks like a tissue paper dunce cap and is filled with small flowers and bulblets.

How to grow: Garlic must have cool temperatures during its early growth period, but it's not affected by heat in the later stages. Plant garlic in the spring in the North; in the South you can get good results with fall planting. You grow garlic from cloves or bulblets, which are planted with the plump side down. The cloves need full sun and well-worked soil that drains well and is high in organic matter. Plant the cloves four to six weeks before the average date of last frost. Plant them 1 to 2 inches deep and 4 to 6 inches apart. Keep garlic slightly dry, especially when the bulbs are near maturity; this will improve flavor. Keep the area cultivated.

Harvest: Harvest the bulbs by digging the entire plant when the tops start to dry: that's the sign the bulbs are mature. Mature plants take 90 days from planting. Use the plumpest cloves for cooking and plant the others.

Varieties: Few varieties are available. Grow plants from cloves purchased from the grocery.

Horseradish

Armoracia rusticana
Very Hardy

Description: Horseradish looks like a giant, 2-foot radish. In fact, it's a hardy perennial member of the cabbage family. Growing up to 30 inches high, the plant has large, coarse leaves. The root of the horseradish has a very strong flavor.

How to grow: Horseradish is a cold-hardy plant that does well in the North and in cool, high-altitude areas in the South. Grow it from crowns or six-inch root cuttings. Plant crowns at soil level. Plant root cuttings with the narrow end downward and the cut end 2 to 3 inches below soil level. Space plants 1 foot apart. Horseradish tolerates partial shade and needs rich, well-drained soil. Turn over the soil to a depth of 10 to 12 inches, and remove stones and lumps that might cause the roots to split. Keep the soil evenly moist so that the roots will be tender and full of flavor; horseradish gets woody in dry soils.

Harvest: Plants grown from roots cannot be harvested until the second year. Horseradish makes its best growth in late summer and fall, so delay harvesting until October or later. Dig the roots as needed, but in areas where the ground freezes hard, dig them in the fall. Leave a little of the root in the ground so you'll have horseradish the following year.

Varieties: 'Maliner Kren' matures in 150 days from root cuttings.

Kale

Brassica oleracea; Acephala **Group**
Very Hardy

Description: Kale, a member of the cabbage family, is a hardy biennial that is grown as an annual. Scotch kale has gray-green leaves that are crumpled and curled. Siberian, or blue, kale is usually less curly.

How to grow: Kale is a cool-weather crop that grows best in fall. It will last through the winter as far north as Maryland and central Indiana. Frost even improves the flavor. Kale doesn't tolerate the heat as well as collards. If your area has cold winters, plant for summer to early fall harvest. In the South, plant for harvest in late fall or winter. Plant kale from transplants early in the spring, and again in the midsummer if your summers aren't too hot. Kale likes fertile, well-drained soil with a pH between 6.5 and 7.5. Plant transplants that are four to six weeks old. If the transplants are leggy or the stems are crooked, plant deeply so they don't become top-heavy. Plant transplants 8 to 12 inches apart. If you're planting seeds, set them ½ inch deep; thin them to 12 inches apart.

Harvest: The time from planting to harvest is 55 days from transplants, 70 to 80 days from seed. Leave kale in the garden until needed, but harvest before it gets old and tough. As the plant matures, take outside leaves, leaving the inner ones to grow. Or, cut off the entire plant.

Varieties: 'Dwarf Blue Curled Vates,' 55 days, produces short-stemmed plants with finely curled, bluish-green leaves. 'Dwarf Siberian Curled,' 65 days, has upright gray-green leaves.

Kohlrabi

Brassica oleracea; Gongylodes **Group**
Very Hardy

Description: Kohlrabi, a member of the cabbage family, is a hardy biennial that is grown as an annual. It has a swollen stem that makes it look like a turnip growing on a cabbage root. The swollen stem can be white, purple, or green, and is topped with a rosette of blue-green leaves.

How to grow: Although kohlrabi tolerates some heat, planting should be timed for harvesting during cool weather. Kohlrabi has a shorter growing season than cabbage and grows best in cool weather. If your area has cold winters, plant for summer to early fall harvest. In the South, plant for harvest in late fall or early winter. With spring plantings, start kohlrabi early so that most growth will occur before the weather gets too hot. Kohlrabi is usually grown from transplants started indoors, but you can sow seed directly in the garden. Plant the seeds ¼ to ½ inch deep; thin them to 5 to 6 inches when they're large enough to handle. Kohlrabi likes fertile, well-drained soil with a pH between 6.5 and 7.5. The soil should be high in organic matter. Kohlrabi should have even moisture so it doesn't become woody.

Harvest: When the swollen stem enlarges to 2 to 3 inches in diameter, harvest kohlrabi by cutting at ground level.

Varieties: 'Grand Duke,' 45 days, is an All America Selection. 'Early White Vienna,' 55 days, is a commonly grown, light green variety. 'Early Purple Vienna,' 60 days, is a light purple form.

Leek

Allium ampeloprasum; Porrum **Group**
Very Hardy

Description: The leek is a hardy biennial that is grown as an annual. It's a member of the onion family but has a stalk rather than a bulb. The plant's leaves are flat and straplike instead of hollow.

How to grow: Leeks are a cool-weather crop. They'll tolerate warm temperatures, but the results are better if the days are cool. Temperatures under 75 degrees Fahrenheit produce the best yields. Plant leeks from seed in the spring four to six weeks before the average date of last frost and from transplants in the fall for a late harvest. Plant transplants in spring if you want to speed up the crop to avoid a hot summer. Plant the seeds ⅛ inch deep and thin them to 6 to 9 inches apart. Plant transplants in 6-inch deep holes, in single rows or wide rows. Leeks like a place in full sun and thrive in rich, well-worked soil with good drainage. To grow large, white, succulent leeks, blanch the lower part of the stem by hilling the soil up around the stalk as it develops. Give leeks plenty of water to keep them growing strongly. Around midsummer, start removing the top half of the leaves. This will encourage greater growth of the leek stalk.

Harvest: The time from planting to harvest is about 80 days from transplants and 120 days from seed. Pull the leeks as you need them, but harvest them all before frost.

Varieties: 'Broad London,' 130 days from seed, produces thick mild-flavored stems. 'Titan,' 100 days, is earlier and larger than 'Broad London' and has a broader base.

Lettuce

Lactuca sativa
Very Hardy

Description: Lettuce is a hardy, fast-growing annual with either loose or compact leaves. Leaf color ranges from light green through reddish-brown. When it bolts, or goes to seed, the flower stalks are 2 to 3 feet tall, with small, yellowish flowers on the stalk. The lettuce most commonly found in supermarkets (iceberg, or crisphead, lettuce) is the most difficult to grow in the home vegetable garden. Butterhead lettuces, which have loose heads and delicate crunchy leaves, are easier to grow. Cos, or romaine, lettuce forms a loose, long head and is between a butterhead and leaf lettuce in flavor. Leaf lettuce is easy to grow, grows fast, and provides bulk and color to salads.

How to grow: Lettuce is a cool-season crop, usually grown from seed planted in the garden four to six weeks before the average date of last frost. Long, hot summer days will make the plants bolt. If your area has a short, hot growing season, start head lettuce from seed indoors eight to ten weeks before the average date of last frost; transplant as soon as possible so the plants will mature before the weather gets really hot. Sow succession crops, beginning in midsummer. In climates with mild winters, grow spring, fall, and winter crops. If you are direct-seeding lettuce in the garden, sow seeds ¼ inch deep in wide rows. When the seedlings are large enough to handle, thin leaf lettuce to 8 inches apart and head lettuce to 12 inches apart. Thinning is important: Heading lettuce won't head, and all lettuce may bolt if the plants are crowded. Lettuce needs well-worked soil with good drainage and moisture retention. Always keep the soil evenly moist. Don't allow the shallow-rooted lettuce plants to dry out.

Harvest: As the lettuce grows, either pick the outer leaves and let the inner leaves develop or harvest the whole plant at once by cutting it off at ground level. Try to harvest when the weather is cool; in the heat of the day the leaves may be limp. Chilling will crisp the leaves again.

Butterhead varieties: 'Bibb,' 75 days, has a delicate-flavored, dark green, open head. 'Buttercrunch,' 75 days, is an All America Selection with compact heads and a buttery texture; it can tolerate some heat.

Cos (Romaine) varieties: 'Little Gem,' 65 days, gives early, compact, and productive plants. 'Paris Island,' 70 days, is the standard romaine type; it has 10-inch heads and resists bolting.

Crisphead varieties: 'Great Lakes,' 90 days, produces a large, full head that will tolerate some heat. 'Iceberg,' 85 days, is compact with a light green color.

Loosehead (Leaf) varieties: 'Green Ice,' 45 days, has crisp, sweet, heavily ruffled green leaves. 'Red Salad Bowl,' 50 days, produces finely divided, dark burgundy leaves. 'Oak Leaf,' 50 days, is a heat-tolerant, deeply lobed, dark green leaf variety.

Muskmelon, Cantaloupe

Cucumis Melo; Reticulatus Group
Very Tender

Description: The muskmelon is a long trailing annual vine that belongs to the cucumber family. The netted melon, or muskmelon, is usually called a cantaloupe, but it should not be confused with the real cantaloupe, which is not often grown in home gardens. Honeydew melons have a smoother surface than muskmelons and lack their distinctive odor; they ripen later and require a longer growing season. The following growing information for muskmelons also applies to honeydews.

How to grow: Muskmelon is a warm-weather plant that will not tolerate even the slightest frost. It also has a long growing season, which means you must select a variety suited to your region's climate. In cool areas, grow muskmelons from transplants; use individual, plantable containers so the root system is not disturbed when you transplant. Set the plant in the garden when the ground is warm: two to three weeks after the danger of frost. Muskmelons must have full sun and need a well-drained soil that is high in organic matter. Grow muskmelons in inverted hills spaced 4 to 6 feet apart. If you're planting from seed, plant six to eight seeds per hill and then thin to the strongest two or three seedlings. If you're using transplants, put two or three in each hill. Muskmelons need a lot of water while the vines are growing, but stop watering when the fruit ripens.

Harvest: The time from planting to harvest is 60 to 110 days, depending on the variety. Leave the melons on the vine until they're ripe; mature melons will easily slip off the stem.

Varieties: 'Ambrosia Hybrid,' 86 days, produces thick, firm fruit about 6½ inches in size. 'Sweet 'n' Early Hybrid,' 75 days, is an early variety that is good for short seasons. 'Burpee Hybrid,' 82 days, produces deep orange, firm fruit.

Mustard

Brassica juncea
Tender

Description: Mustard is an annual with a rosette of large light to dark green crinkled leaves that grow up to 3 feet in length.

How to grow: Mustard is a cool-season crop. It's hardy, but the seeds will not germinate well if you sow them too early; plant the seeds in your garden on the average date of last frost. Mustard is grown like lettuce. It is more heat tolerant than lettuce, but long hot summer days will force the plant to bolt (go to seed). Mustard tolerates partial shade. The plant needs well-worked soil that is high in organic matter and with good drainage and moisture retention. Plant the seeds ½ inch deep. Plant a few seeds at intervals rather than as an entire row at one time. When the seedlings are large enough to handle, thin them to 6 to 12 inches apart. As soon as the plants begin to seed, pull them up or they will produce a great number of seeds and sow themselves all over the garden. Plant mustard again when the weather begins to cool off.

Harvest: The leaves and leaf stalks are eaten. The seeds can be ground and used as a condiment. Pick off individual leaves as they grow, or cut the entire plant at ground level. Harvest when the leaves are young and tender; in summer, the texture may become tough and the flavor strong. Harvest the entire crop when some of the plants start to go to seed.

Varieties: 'Southern Giant Curled,' 40 days, has wide, curled leaves on an upright plant. 'Fordhook Fancy,' produces deeply curled, dark green leaves with some heat tolerance.

Okra

Hibiscus esculentus
Very Tender

Description: Okra, a member of the cotton and hibiscus family, is an erect, tender annual with hairy stems and large maplelike leaves. It grows from 3 to 6 feet tall, and has large flowers that look like yellow hibiscus blossoms with red or purplish centers.

How to grow: Okra is very sensitive to cold; the yield decreases with temperatures less than 70 degrees Fahrenheit. However, okra has a short season, which permits it to be grown almost anywhere in the United States. The plant will grow in any warm, well-drained soil and needs a place in full sun. Plant okra from seed in your garden about four weeks after the average date of last frost. Plant the seeds ½ to 1 inch deep. When the seedlings are growing strongly, thin them to stand 12 to 18 inches apart. Keep the plants on the dry side. The stems rot easily in wet or cold conditions. Okra will grow for a year if not killed by frost and if old pods are not left on the plant.

Harvest: The time from planting to harvest is 50 to 65 days. When mature, the pods are 6 to 10 inches long and filled with buckshotlike seeds. When the plants begin to set their pods, harvest them at least every other day. Pods grow quickly, and unless the older ones are cut off, the plant will stop producing new ones. Keep picking the pods when they're quite small; the pods are less gluey when they're only about two inches long.

Varieties: 'Clemson Spineless,' 56 days, an All America Selection, is a compact plant with dark green, straight, spineless pods. 'Annie Oakley,' 52 days, is a compact variety with a short season.

Onion

Allium cepa
Very Hardy

Description: Onions are hardy biennial vegetables that are usually grown as annuals. They have hollow leaves, and the base of the stem enlarges to form a bulb. The bulbs vary in color from white to yellow or red. The flower stalk is also hollow, taller than the leaves, and topped with a cluster of white or lavender flowers.

How to grow: Most onions are sensitive to the length of the day. Bulb-type varieties are classified as either long-day or short-day onions. Long-day onions will produce bulbs when grown in the summer months in the North. Short-day onions produce bulbs in the mild winter climate of the South. American onions and Spanish onions need long days to produce their bulbs; Bermuda onions prefer short days. Onions are also sensitive to temperature. Generally, they require cool weather to produce their tops and warm weather to produce their bulbs. They're frost-hardy, and you can plant four weeks before the average date of last frost. In the South, onions can be planted in the fall or winter, depending on the variety.

Onions are available in three forms: sets, transplants, and seeds. Sets are small bulbs that are dormant. The smaller the sets are, the better. Sets are easiest to plant, but they come in the smallest number of varieties. Transplants are usually more reliable about producing bulbs and are available in more varieties than sets. Seeds are the least expensive and offer the greatest number of varieties, but they take the longest to develop and are most prone to disease and environmental problems.

Onions need a well-prepared bed with all the lumps removed to a depth of at least 6 inches. The soil should be fertile and rich in organic matter. Bulbing onions need full sun, but green onions can be grown in partial shade. Plant transplants or sets 1 or 2 inches deep and 2 to 3 inches apart. If you're planting onions from seed, plant the seeds ¼ inch deep and thin to 1 to 2 inches apart. If you have limited space, you can grow onions between other vegetables, such as cabbages or tomatoes. The soil should not be allowed to dry out until the plants have started to mature, which is marked by the leaves starting to turn yellow and brown and droop over. At this point, let the soil get as dry as possible.

Harvest: All varieties can be eaten as green onions, though some varieties are grown especially for their bulbs. Harvest leaves whenever you need. Harvest green onions when the bulb is not much larger than the leaves. Harvest dry onion bulbs after the leaves have dried. Lift the bulbs completely out of the soil. Dry the bulbs thoroughly before storing.

Green onion (Scallion, Bunching) varieties: 'Evergreen Long White Bunching,' 120 days from seed to maturity, produce long silvery-white stalks in bunches and will not form bulbs. 'Beltsville Bunching,' 120 days, is heat-tolerant and has a mild flavor.

Bulbing onion varieties: 'Southport Red Globe,' 110 days, long-day, has sweet, purple-red flesh. 'Yellow Sweet Spanish,' 110 days, long-day, has large, white flesh. 'Bermuda,' 185 days, short-day, is large and produces white flesh with a mild flavor. 'Yellow Granax,' 120 days, short-day, is large with white flesh.

Parsnip

Pastinaca sativa
Hardy

Description: Parsnips are biennials that are grown as annuals. They belong to the same family as celery, carrots, and parsley. A rosette of celerylike leaves grows from the top of the whitish, fleshy root.

How to grow: Parsnips need a long, cool growing season. They will tolerate cold at the start and the end of the growing season, and they can withstand freezing temperatures. Parsnips prefer full sun but will tolerate partial shade. Plant parsnip seeds two to three weeks before the average date of last frost. Turn the soil completely to a depth of 10 to 12 inches and remove all lumps and rocks. The initial soil preparation is essential for a healthy crop: Soil lumps, rocks, or other obstructions in the soil will cause the roots to split, fork, or become deformed. Since it may also cause forking, don't use manure in the soil bed for root crops unless it is well rotted. Plant seeds ½ inch deep and thin them to 2 to 4 inches apart; parsnips must have adequate space for root development. Thin seedlings with scissors so you don't disturb the tender roots of the remaining plants. Parsnips need plenty of water until they approach maturity. At this point, cut back on watering so the roots don't split.

Harvest: Leave parsnips in the soil as long as possible or until you need them. The roots are not harmed by the ground's freezing, but dig them up before the ground becomes unworkable.

Varieties: 'Hollow Crown,' 105 days, is long and produces mild flavored, white flesh. 'Harris Model,' 110 days, has white flesh with a smooth texture.

California Black-eye Pea

Vigna unguiculata
Very Tender

Description: Black-eyed peas are tender annuals. Depending on the variety, they can be either bushy or climbing plants. The seeds on the dwarf varieties are usually white with a dark spot (the "black eye") where they're attached to the pod; sometimes the spots are brown or purple.

How to grow: Black-eyed peas can tolerate high temperatures but are very sensitive to cold: The slightest frost will harm them. They grow well in the South. Some Northern areas may not have a long enough growing season to accommodate them from seeds; unfortunately, they don't grow well from transplants. If your area has a long enough warm season, plant black-eyed peas from seed four weeks after the average date of last frost. Black-eyed peas will tolerate poor soil. In fact, like other legumes, they're often grown to improve the soil. Well-drained, well-worked soil that's high in organic matter increases their productivity. Sow seeds directly in the garden ½ inch deep and about 2 inches apart. Thin them to 3 to 4 inches apart when they're easy enough to handle.

Harvest: The time from planting to harvest is 70 to 110 days. Pick the pods at whatever stage of maturity you desire—either young and tender or fully matured to use dried.

Varieties: 'California Black-eye,' 75 days, produces 8-inch pods. 'Mississippi Silver,' 65 days, has green pods that are streaked with pink.

Green Pea

Pisum sativum
Very Hardy

Description: Peas are hardy, weak-stemmed climbing annual vines. They have leaflike stipules, leaves with one to three pairs of leaflets, and tendrils for climbing. The flowers are white, streaked, or colored. The fruit is a pod containing 4 to 10 seeds, either smooth or wrinkled depending on the variety.

How to grow: Unlike black-eyed peas, green peas are a cool-season crop that must mature before the weather gets hot. The ideal growing weather is moist with temperatures between 60 and 65 degrees Fahrenheit. Plant peas as soon as the soil can be worked in spring: about six weeks before the average date of last frost. Peas need good drainage in soil that is high in organic material. They produce earlier in sandy soil, but yield a heavier, later crop if grown in clayey soil. Plant peas directly in the garden 2 inches deep and 1 to 2 inches apart. Don't let the soil dry out; peas need ample moisture. Provide a three-foot-high trellis to support the vines.

Harvest: The time from planting to harvest is 55 to 80 days. Pick shelling peas when the pods are full and green, before the peas start to harden. Edible pod peas are grown the same way as sweet peas, but harvest the immature pods before the peas have developed to full size. Pods should be plump, but the individual peas should not be showing through the pod.

Varieties: 'Little Marvel,' 63 days, has compact growth and produces dark green pods. 'Wando,' 68 days, is tolerant of heat. 'Maestro,' 61 days, is prolific, producing 9 to 12 peas per dark green pod. 'Oregon Sugar Pod II,' 68 days, produces a 4½-inch edible snow pea. 'Sugar Snap,' 70 days, an All America Selection, is a 3-inch edible snap pea.

Peanut

Arachis hypogaea
Very Tender

Description: The peanut is a tender annual belonging to the pea family. It grows 6 inches to 2½ feet tall, depending on type. The bunch type grows upright; the runner type spreads out over the ground. Small clusters of yellow, sweet pealike flowers grow on stems called pegs. The pegs grow down and push into the soil, and the nuts develop 1 to 3 inches under ground from the pegs. Peanuts are not grown commercially north of Washington, D.C., but they can be grown farther north for fun.

How to grow: Peanuts need a frost-free growing season four to five months long. If your growing season is short, start peanuts inside two weeks before the average date of last frost then transplant them outside two to three weeks after the average date of last frost. Peanuts like a well-worked sandy soil that is high in organic matter. The pegs have difficulty penetrating soil that has a high clay content. Plant seeds from shelled raw peanuts 1 to 3 inches deep. Space both seeds and transplants 6 to 8 inches apart. Keep soil moisture even until the plants start to flower, then water less. Blind (empty) pods are the result of too much rain or humidity at flowering time. Use a heavy mulch to help the pegs become established.

Harvest: The time from planting to harvest is 120 to 150 days. Start harvesting when frost begins; pull up the whole plant and let the pods dry on the vine.

Varieties: Few varieties are available. You can plant raw peanuts from the grocery. 'Jumbo Virginia,' matures in 120 days.

Pepper, Hot and Sweet

Capsicum annuum
Tender

Peppers come in sweet or hot varieties. Bell peppers are the most familiar; most bell peppers are sweet, but some hot varieties exist. Hot peppers are intensely flavored, and there are more than a hundred varieties.

Description: Peppers are erect perennials that are grown as annuals. One or several flowers grow in the angle between the leaf and stem. America peppers are members of the tobacco family, which includes tomatoes, potatoes, and eggplant. Peppers range in size from the large, sweet bullnose, or mango, pepper to the tiny, fiery bird, or devil, pepper. Peppers grow in many shapes: round, long, flat, and twisted. The large, sweet ones are used raw, cooked, or pickled; the hot ones are used as an unmistakable flavoring relish. Choose peppers carefully when you make a selection to be sure the variety you're growing suits your palate.

How to grow: Peppers prefer a soil temperature above 65 degrees Fahrenheit. They don't produce well when the day temperature gets above 90 degrees Fahrenheit. Hot peppers tolerate hot weather better than sweet peppers. The ideal climate is a daytime temperature around 75 degrees Fahrenheit and a nighttime temperature around 62 degrees Fahrenheit. The easiest way to grow peppers is from transplants. Set transplants in the garden 18 to 24 inches apart two to three weeks after the average date of last frost. You can also grow peppers from seed, starting indoors 7 to 10 weeks before the average date of last frost. If you have a long growing season, you can seed peppers directly in the garden. Peppers do best in a soil that is high in organic matter and that holds water but drains well. Do not overfertilize peppers; too much nitrogen will cause the plants to grow large but produce few peppers. Peppers are shallow-rooted, so cultivate them gently. Use a mulch to keep the soil temperature and moisture even and to suppress weeds.

Harvest: Peppers are usually harvested when green. If you want sweet red peppers, leave the sweet green peppers on the vine until they ripen and turn red. Cut the peppers off the vine; if you pull them off, half the plant may come up with the fruit. Hot peppers can irritate the skin, so wear gloves when you pick them.

Sweet varieties: 'Better Belle,' 65 days, produces peppers that are large, thick-walled, and green. 'Bell Boy,' 70 days, are a large deep green turning to red. 'Golden Bell,' 68 days, is a light green that turns golden yellow. 'Pimento,' 78 days, is heart-shaped and sweet.

Hot varieties: 'Hungarian Yellow Wax,' 65 days, matures to red in color and is medium-hot. 'Red Chili,' 80 days, produces peppers that are 2½ inches long and very hot.

Irish Potato

Solanum tuberosum
Hardy

There are more than 100 varieties of potatoes in the United States. They fall into four basic categories: long whites, round whites, russets, and round reds.

Description: Potatoes are weak-stemmed plants with hairy, dark green compound leaves that look a little like tomato leaves. The plants produce underground stem tubers when mature. It is a member of the tobacco family, related to the tomato, eggplant, and pepper.

How to grow: Potatoes need a frost-free growing season of 90 to 120 days. They're a cool-weather crop, and they grow best in areas with cool summers. Hot weather cuts down on the production of tubers. Grow potatoes in summer in the North, and in fall, winter, and spring in the South. Plant early varieties just before the average date of last frost. Potatoes are grown from whole potatoes or pieces of potatoes, which are called seed pieces. Each piece must have at least one eye. Always plant certified disease-free seed pieces. Don't use supermarket potatoes, which have been chemically treated to prevent sprouting. Potatoes need well-drained, fertile soil that is high in organic matter. The pH level should be between 5.0 and 5.5. Plant potato pieces in full sun, 4 inches deep, and 12 to 18 inches apart. Keep the soil evenly moist and free of weeds.

Harvest: Dig up new potatoes after the plant blooms or when the leaves begin to turn yellow. For mature tubers, use a spading fork to dig up the potatoes two weeks after the vine dies.

Varieties: 'Red Pontiac,' 100 days, are red with thin skin and white flesh. 'Explorer,' 100 days, produces small, white flesh and can be grown from seed. 'White Cobbler,' 90 days, is a baking variety with a short growing season. 'Kennebec,' 105 days, is large and white; it stores well.

Sweet Potato

Ipomoea Batatas
Very Tender

There are two kinds of sweet potato—"dry" and "moist"—which describes the texture of the variety. The moist varieties are often called yams, but the yam is actually a different species that is found in tropical countries.

Description: The sweet potato is a tender vining or semierect perennial plant that is grown as an annual. It has small white, pink, or red-purple flowers. The swollen, fleshy roots range in color from creamy-yellow to deep red-orange.

How to grow: Sweet potatoes are extremely sensitive to frost and need warm, moist weather. They have a long growing season (about 150 days); in areas with a shorter season, the plants tend to produce small potatoes. Plant sweet potatoes four weeks after the average date of last frost or when the soil is thoroughly warm. Sweet potatoes are planted from rooted sprouts, or slips, taken from a mature root. To grow your own slips, place sweet potatoes in a coldframe and cover with two inches of sand or light soil. Keep the bed warm. Add more soil when shoots appear. The shoots will develop roots that can be planted in the garden. You can also buy slips from a reputable garden center or supplier. A light, well-worked soil that is not overly rich produces the best roots. Plant slips 12 inches apart in mounded ridges. Plants do best with even moisture throughout the season until three weeks before harvesting.

Harvest: Dig up the roots before the first frost. The roots are damaged by freezing and cold soils.

Varieties: 'Centennial,' 95 days, has a short growing season and produces orange flesh. 'Bush Porto Rico,' 125 days, has compact growth and produces red-orange flesh.

Pumpkin

Cucurbita species
Very Tender

Description: Pumpkins are tender annuals with large leaves on branching vines that can grow 20 feet long. The male and female flowers grow on the same vine, and the fruit can weigh as much as 100 pounds.

How to grow: Pumpkins need a long growing season. They will grow almost anywhere in the United States, but in cooler areas you'll get better results with a smaller variety. Pumpkins are sensitive to cold soil and frost. Plant them from seed two to three weeks after the average date of last frost, when the soil has warmed up. Bush varieties can be grown if space is limited. Pumpkins prefer well-drained soil that is high in organic matter. Too much fertilizer encourages the growth of vines rather than the production of fruit. Plant seeds directly in the garden in inverted hills six feet apart. Plant several seeds per hill and thin to one plant in each hill. Thin seedlings at soil level to avoid disturbing the roots of the chosen survivor. Pumpkins need plenty of water to keep the fruit growing steadily.

Harvest: The time from planting to harvest is 95 to 120 days. Leave the pumpkins on the vine as long as possible before frost. They become soft after freezing. Cut off the pumpkin with one or two inches of stem.

Varieties: 'Bushkin,' 95 days, produces bright orange, 10-pound fruit; it is good for limited space. 'Jack Be Little,' 95 days, produces 3-inch fruit. 'Jack-O-Lantern,' 110 days, has 10-inch, bright orange fruit. 'Big Max,' 120 days, has reddish pink skin and can weigh up to 100 pounds.

Radish

Raphanus sativus
Hardy

Description: Radishes are hardy biennials that are grown as annuals. They produce rosettes of lobed leaves and white, red, or black roots, depending on the variety.
How to grow: Radishes are cool-season crops that can tolerate temperatures below freezing. They can grow anywhere in the United States. They mature in such a short time that you can get two to three crops in spring alone. Start planting radishes from seed in the garden two to three weeks before the average date of last frost. Radishes germinate quickly and are often used with seeds of slower-growing plants to mark rows. Radishes like well-worked, well-drained soil. Sow seeds directly in the garden ½ inch deep. Thin spring varieties 1 to 3 inches apart; give winter varieties a little more space. Radishes sometimes bolt (go to seed) in the summer, but this is often a question more of day length than of temperature. Cover the plants in midsummer so they get only an 8-hour day; a 12-hour day produces flowers and seeds but no radishes.
Harvest: The time from planting to harvest is 20 to 30 days for spring radishes, 50 to 60 days for winter radishes. Pull up the whole plant when the radishes are the right size.
Varieties: 'Cherry Belle,' 22 days, is an All America Selection producing round, red, ¾-inch roots. 'White Icicle,' 28 days, gives white, icicle-shaped roots that are 5 inches long. 'French Breakfast,' 23 days, is oblong and red with white on the bottom. 'Summer Cross Hybrid,' 45 days, is an Oriental-type, all-season variety that gives white flesh.

Rhubarb

Rheum rhabarbarum
Hardy Perennial

Description: A hardy perennial, rhubarb grows 2 to 4 feet tall, with large, attractive leaves on strong stalks. The leaf stalks are red or green and grow up from a stout rhizome. The flowers are small and grow on top of a dense flower spike.
How to grow: Rhubarb is very hardy and prefers cool weather. In areas where the weather is warm or hot, the leaf stalks become thin and spindly. Although rhubarb can be grown from seed, the plants will not grow 'true,' meaning they won't be the same variety as the parent plant. For a close or exact copy of the parent plant, grow from the divisions separated from the parent stems. Buy divisions or divide your own plants in early spring. Rhubarb likes rich, well-worked soil that is high in organic matter and drains well. Plant the divisions 3 feet apart with the growing tips slightly below the soil surface. Keep the soil evenly moist. Keep weeds away and mulch around the plant, especially in winter. To get earlier and longer leaf stalks, surround the plants with boxes in early spring but do not cover the plant from light. When flower stalks appear, remove them to keep the leaf stalks growing strongly. Divide the plant every three to four years.
Harvest: You'll have to wait two to three years from the time of planting to the first real harvest. To harvest, twist the leaf stalk at the soil line; do not take more than a third of the leaves in any given year. Eat only the stalk, not the leaf.
Varieties: 'MacDonald,' is brilliant red with tender skin. 'Valentine,' has deep red stalks. 'Victoria,' produces green stalks tinged with pink.

Rutabaga

Brassica napus; Napobrassica **Group**
Very Hardy

This plant was created by crossing a cabbage with a turnip.
Description: Rutabaga is a hardy biennial that is grown as an annual. A rosette of smooth, grayish green leaves grows from a swollen stem. The root can be yellow, purple, or white.
How to grow: Rutabagas are very hardy and grow best in cool weather. In hot weather they produce many leaves but only small, stringy roots. Plant rutabagas in late summer in the North, and in the late fall in the South or where the weather gets very hot. For spring plantings sow seed directly in the garden 4 to 6 weeks before the average date of last frost. Rutabagas do best in well-drained soil that is high in organic matter. The plants need well-worked soil with all rocks and soil lumps removed. Plant the seeds ½ inch deep and thin them to 8 inches apart. Thinning is important: Like all root crops, rutabagas must have room to develop. Water often enough to keep the plants growing steadily; if growth slows, the roots will be tough.
Harvest: The time from planting to harvest is 90 to 100 days. To harvest, dig up the whole root when the rutabaga is 3 to 5 inches in diameter. In cold areas, mulch heavily to extend the harvesting period.
Varieties: 'American Purple Top,' 90 days, gives fine-grained, yellow flesh.

Salsify, Oyster Plant

Tragopogon porrifolius
Hardy

Description: Salsify is a hardy biennial that is grown as an annual. It's related to dandelion and chicory, and its flowers look like lavender chicory blossoms. The edible part is the long taproot. Some people claim that salsify has a slight oyster flavor, hence the name "oyster plant."

How to grow: Salsify is hardy and tolerates cold. Like its prolific cousin the dandelion, it's easy to grow anywhere in the United States. Prepare rich soil by removing all stones and lumps. Plant salsify from seed two or three weeks before the average date of last frost. Plant the seeds ½ inch deep. When seedlings are large enough to handle, thin them to stand 2 to 4 inches apart. Don't overfertilize; it will cause the roots to fork and split. Keep the plants evenly moist to prevent the roots from getting stringy.

Harvest: The time from planting to harvest is about 120 days. Salsify roots can tolerate freezing, so leave them in the ground until you want them. The longer they're out of the ground, the less they taste like oysters. To harvest, dig up the whole root.

Varieties: 'Sandwich Island Mammoth,' 120 days, is the most widely available variety.

Shallot

Allium Cepa
Very Hardy

Description: The shallot is a very hardy biennial onion that is grown as an annual. Shallot plants grow 8 inches tall in a clump with narrow green leaves; they look very much like small onions. The roots are very shallow and fibrous, and mature bulbs are about ½ inch in diameter. The small bulbs have a more delicate flavor than regular onions.

How to grow: Shallots are easy to grow. You can grow them anywhere in the United States from cloves planted early in spring. Shallots have shallow roots, and they need little soil preparation. The plants seldom form seed, so they're usually grown from cloves, which should be planted four to six weeks before the average date of last frost. Plant the cloves 6 to 8 inches apart and set them so the tops of the cloves are even with the soil but no deeper. Carefully cultivate when they're small; the shallow root systems don't like to compete with weeds.

Harvest: Cut the green leaves throughout the growing season, but be careful not to cut away any new growth coming from the central stem. Dig up bulbs when the tops wither and fall over.

Varieties: No named varieties are available. Shallots take 90 days to mature from a clove.

Sorrel

Rumex Acetosa
Very Hardy

Description: Garden sorrel grows about 3 feet tall and produces sour-tasting leaves that are good when used fresh in salads. French sorrel grows only 6 to 12 inches tall; its fiddle-shaped leaves make good salad greens. The weed variety is bitter and is not good for eating.

How to grow: Sorrels are very hardy and can be grown in almost every area of the United States. Sorrels require a sunny location with well-drained fertile soil. Plant sorrels from seed two to three weeks before the average date of last frost. Plant the seeds ½ inch deep. When the plants are 6 to 8 weeks old, thin them to 12 to 18 inches apart. Sorrel plants should be kept moist; water them more often than the rest of the garden.

Harvest: Pick the fresh leaves of sorrel throughout the growing season. Pick off flowers before they mature to keep the plant producing new leaves long into the fall.

Varieties: Garden sorrel and French sorrel are sold under their common names. From seed to maturity is about 100 days.

Spinach

Spinacia oleracea
Very Hardy

Description: Spinach is a hardy annual with a rosette of dark green leaves. The leaves may be crinkled (savoy leaf) or flat. Spinach is related to beets and chard.

How to grow: Spinach is very hardy and can tolerate cold; in fact, it thrives in cold weather. Heat and long days make spinach bolt (go to seed) quickly. Spinach grows well in the winter in the South, and in early spring and late summer in the North. Plant spinach about four weeks before the average date of last frost. Spinach tolerates partial shade and requires well-drained soil that's rich in organic matter. Spinach does not like acid soil. The plant is grown from seed clusters that each produce several seedlings. Spinach must be thinned when the seedlings appear. Plant spinach seed clusters ½ inch deep and 2 to 4 inches apart. When the seedlings are large enough to handle, thin them to leave the strongest seedling from each cluster. Spinach does best when the soil is kept uniformly moist. Try not to splash muddy water on the leaves, which will make the spinach difficult to clean after harvesting. Mulch to retain moisture and avoid getting soil on the leaves.

Harvest: The time from planting to harvest is 40 to 45 days. To harvest, either pick the outside leaves periodically or pull up the entire plant.

Varieties: 'Melody Hybrid,' 42 days, is an All America Selection that gives semierect plants with dark green leaves. 'Bloomsdale Long-Standing,' 48 days, produces thick-textured, crinkled, dark green leaves.

New Zealand Spinach

Tetragonia tetragonioides
Hardy

Description: New Zealand spinach is an annual with weak, spreading stems 2 to 4 feet long that are covered with dark green leaves 2 to 4 inches long. New Zealand spinach is not really a spinach at all, but when it's cooked, the two are virtually indistinguishable. The leaves are smaller and fuzzier than those of regular spinach.

How to grow: New Zealand spinach likes long warm days. It grows best at 60 to 75 degrees Fahrenheit. It won't start growing until the soil warms up. The plant has a short season (55 to 65 days), so it can be grown successfully in most areas of the United States. Plant seed directly in the garden on the average date of last frost. When seedlings are large enough to handle, thin the plants to stand 12 to 18 inches apart. New Zealand spinach does not like competition from weeds; cut weeds at ground level to avoid damaging the shallow roots of the crop.

Harvest: The time from planting to harvest is about 60 days. Harvest tender leaves as you need them by cutting them from the tips of the branches. Plants will continue to produce new foliage as leaves are harvested.

Varieties: New Zealand spinach is sold under its common name.

Summer Squash

Cucurbita Pepo
Very Tender

Description: Summer squashes are weak-stemmed, tender annuals. They have large, cucumberlike leaves, and separate male and female flowers appear on the same plant. A summer squash usually grows as a bush, rather than as a vine. The fruits have thin, tender skin and are generally eaten in the immature stage before the skin hardens. Of the many kinds of summer squashes, the most popular are crookneck, straightneck, scallop, and zucchini.

How to grow: Squashes are warm-season crops and are very sensitive to cold and frost. They like night temperatures of at least 60 degrees Fahrenheit. Direct seeding is best for squashes, but if a variety requires a longer growing season than your area has, use transplants from a reputable nursery or garden center or grow your own transplants. To grow transplants, start four to five weeks before the outside planting date. Use individual plantable containers to lessen the risk of shock when the seedlings are transplanted. Squash varieties like well-worked soil with good drainage. They're heavy feeders, so the soil must be well-fertilized. Two to three weeks after the average date of last frost, when the soil is warm, plant squash in inverted hills. The hills should be 3 to 4 feet apart; plant four or five seeds in each hill. When the seedlings are about a week old, thin them to leave the two to three strongest plants. Keep the soil evenly moist: Squashes need a lot of water in hot weather. The vines may wilt on hot days because the plant is using water faster than the roots can supply it. If the vines are getting a regular supply of water, don't worry about the wilting; the plants will liven up as the day cools. If the vines are wilting first thing in the morning, water them immediately.

Winter Squash

Cucurbita maxima
Very Tender

Harvest: The time from planting to harvest, as well as the expected yield, depends on the variety. Harvest summer squashes when they're young: They taste delicious when they're small. If you leave them on the plant too long, they will suppress flowering and reduce your crop. Harvest zucchini and crookneck varieties when they're 6 to 8 inches long. Harvest round types when they're 4 to 8 inches in diameter. Break or cut the fruit from the plant.

Crookneck varieties: 'Early Golden Summer,' 53 days, gives fruit with bright yellow, warted skin. 'Pic-N-Pic,' 50 days, has golden-yellow, smooth skin.

Scallop varieties: 'Peter Pan Hybrid,' 50 days, is an All America Selection that provides meaty, light-green fruit. 'Early White Bush Scallop,' 60 days, produces fruit that has pale green skin and creamy-white flesh.

Straightneck varieties: 'Butterstick,' 50 days, produces bright yellow fruit and has a long harvest period. 'Goldbar,' 53 days, has compact growth and provides fruit with smooth, golden-yellow skin.

Zucchini varieties: 'Burpee Hybrid,' 50 days, has medium-green skin and compact plants. 'Golden Zucchini,' 54 days, gives glossy, bright golden skin.

Description: Winter squashes are weak-stemmed tender annual vines. They have large cucumberlike leaves, and separate male and female flowers grow on the same plant. Most winter squashes grow as vines, but some newer varieties have been bred to have a more compact, bushy habit of growth. Vining types of winter squash can be caged or trained to climb up a fence or trellis to save space. If you're growing a variety that will need support, set the support in place at the time of planting. If you do it later, you risk damaging the plant's roots. Winter squash varieties have hard skins when they're harvested and eaten. Popular types of winter squashes include acorn, banana, buttercup, butternut, cushaw, hubbard, and Turk's turban. Spaghetti squash is technically a small pumpkin and is cared for in the same way as pumpkins.

How to grow: Contrary to what its name suggests, winter squashes are warm-season crops and are very sensitive to cold and frost. Don't plant the seeds until the soil has warmed up in the spring, about two to three weeks after the average date of last frost. Direct-seeding is best. If you're planting a variety that requires a longer growing season than your area has, use transplants from a reputable nursery or garden center, or grow your own transplants. Start four to five weeks before the outdoor planting date, and use individual plantable containers to lessen the risk of shock when the seedlings are transplanted. Squashes like well-worked soil with good drainage. They're heavy feeders so the soil must be well-fertilized. Two to three weeks after the average date of last frost, when the soil is warm, plant squash in inverted hills. Place the hills 3 to 4 feet apart, and plant four or five seeds in each hill. When the seedlings are about a week old, thin them to leave the two to three strongest plants. Keep the soil evenly moist; squashes need a lot of water in hot weather.

Harvest: Leave winter squashes on the vine until the skin is so hard it cannot be dented with your thumbnail. Harvest before the first frost. Break or cut it off the vine. Cure squashes in a dark, humid place for 10 days at 80 to 85 degrees Fahrenheit; then store them at 50 to 60 degrees Fahrenheit in a moderately dry, dark place for five to six months.

Acorn variety: 'Early Acorn,' 75 days, produces fruit with smooth texture and orange flesh on a compact plant. 'Table King,' 75 days, has large fruit and a small seed cavity; it is an All America Selection.

Butternut variety: 'Butter Boy Hybrid,' 80 days, has a sweet, nutty flavor and reddish orange flesh. 'Waltham,' 85 days, is an All America Selection and has orange flesh.

Hubbard variety: 'Blue Hubbard,' 120 days, provides large fruit with blue-gray skin and orange flesh. 'Hubbard Improved Green,' 120 days, has dark green skin and orange flesh.

Spaghetti variety: 'Vegetable Spaghetti,' 100 days, has yellow skin and flesh; it should be stored like winter squash.

Turban variety: 'Buttercup,' 105 days, has dark green skin and orange flesh with a very small seed cavity. 'Turk's Turban,' 105 days, has bright red or orange skin with white and green stripes.

Tomatillo

Physalis ixocarpa
Tender

Description: Tomatillo, a member of the tobacco family, is a tender annual grown for its pulpy fruit, which resembles a small, green tomato. Tomatillo, or ground cherry, grows to 4 feet tall. It has deeply lobed leaves, yellow flowers, and a papery husk that contains a 2½-inch green fruit. The fruit is widely used in making jams and salsa.

How to grow: Tomatillo requires warm soil and a long, warm growing season. It needs full sun and prefers a well-drained soil that is rich in organic matter. Plant tomatillo from transplants on the average date of last frost. Start transplants indoors from seed six to eight weeks before the planting date. When transplants are large enough to be planted in the garden, set plants 18 to 24 inches apart. Established plants are drought tolerant.

Harvest: The time from planting to harvest is about 100 days. When the husk begins to turn brown, pick the fruit.

Varieties: Tomatillo is sold under its common name.

Tomato

Lycopersicon lycopersicum
Tender

Description: Tomatoes are tender perennials that are grown as annuals. They have weak stems and lobed and toothed leaves that have a distinctive odor. The yellow flowers grow in clusters. Most tomatoes have vining growth habits and need a fair amount of space. Some tomatoes are described as bush varieties that will save space, but they'll still sprawl if you let them. You may still have to stake or cage the bush types. Depending on the variety, tomatoes vary by the size and shape of the fruit (cherry, plum, pear, etc.), by their color (red, pink, yellow, orange), and by their use (slicing, canning, juicing).

Tomatoes are divided into two main groups according to growth habits: determinate and indeterminate. On the determinate tomato (bush tomato), the plant stops growing when the end buds set fruit, usually at about 3 feet tall. Determinate tomatoes seldom need staking, but a single stake or short cage will help keep them confined. Determinate varieties produce a crop of tomatoes that will all ripen at one time. This type of tomato is used for canning and processing. On the indeterminate tomato (vine tomato), the end buds do not set fruit; the plant continues to grow until it's killed by frost. Indeterminate tomatoes will get quite large, so these varieties should be staked or caged. Staked and caged tomatoes provide cleaner fruit and less loss from rot or problems that occur in warm, humid areas. In addition, they require less room for each plant.

How to grow: Tomatoes grow best when the daytime temperature is between 65 and 85 degrees Fahrenheit. They stop growing above 95 degrees Fahrenheit. If nighttime temperatures are above 85 degrees Fahrenheit, the fruit will not turn red. Tomatoes need full sun and warm, well-drained soil. Start tomatoes either by seed planted in the garden on the average date of last frost or from transplants set in the garden about a week after the average date of last frost. If you use transplants, either purchase them from a reputable nursery or garden center or start your own indoors six to eight weeks before the planting date. Plant transplants 18 to 36 inches apart, depending on whether you will stake or cage the plants or let them sprawl. Set the plants out on a cloudy day or in the late afternoon. If the sun is very hot, protect the plants with a temporary shade of newspapers. Disturb the roots of transplants as little as possible. If the stems are leggy or crooked, set the plants deeply or in a trench. Side roots will develop along the stem, and the top will turn in the right direction. Tomatoes need plenty of water; water before the soil dries out.

Harvest: The time from planting to harvest is 50 to 180 days from transplants, depending on the variety. The color when ripe depends on the variety. Ripe tomatoes should feel firm, neither squashy nor too hard.

Indeterminate varieties: 'Avalanch F,' 77 days, produces medium-size red fruit. 'Beefmaster VFN,' is large and red and resists cracking. 'Better Boy VFN,' 72 days, has large, round, red fruit. 'Better Girl VFN,' 62 days, gives fruit that is early, round, red, and meaty. 'Champion VFNT,' 62 days, produces an early, large beefsteak-type fruit. 'Early Girl V' matures in 54 days. 'Whopper VFNT,' 70 days, provides very large, meaty, red fruit. 'Pink Girl VFT,' 76 days, gives a medium-size fruit with pink skin. 'Golden Boy,' 80 days, has medium-size, round fruit that is bright yellow.

Determinate varieties: 'Celebrity VFNT,' 70 days, produces medium-size, red, round fruit. 'Floramerica VF,' 70 days, is an All America Selection that provides meaty, red, all-purpose fruit. 'The Juice VF,' 65 days, has red, juicy fruit and is good for juice making.

Turnip

Brassica Rapa, Rapifera **Group**
Hardy

Description: The turnip, a hardy biennial that is grown as an annual, sports a rosette of hairy, bright green leaves growing from a swelling at the base of the stem. The turnip is more commonly grown for use as a root vegetable, but it can also be grown for the leaves, which are used as greens.

How to grow: Turnips are a cool-weather crop. They are grown in the fall, winter, and spring in the South, and in the spring and fall in the North. Turnips need soil that's high in organic matter and well-drained but able to hold moisture. Too much nitrogen in the soil encourages the plant to produce leaves and a seed stalk rather than a good-size root. Turnips don't transplant well, so grow them from seed sown directly in the garden. Sow seeds 1 to 2 inches apart in single or wide rows. When the seedlings are large enough to handle, thin to 3 or 4 inches apart; if you're growing turnips for greens, thin to 2 to 3 inches apart. Water before the soil dries out; water is important to keep turnips growing as fast as possible. If growth is slow, the roots become strong-flavored and woody and the plant will often send up a seed stalk.

Harvest: Harvest turnips when they are 2 to 4 inches in diameter—before they get pithy and bitter. Pull them easily when the soil is moist. Pick greens when they are young and tender; use thinned seedlings for greens.

Varieties: 'Purple Top White Globe' matures in 58 days. 'Tokyo Cross Hybrid,' 35 days, is an All America Selection that produces 2- to 6-inch pure white roots.

Watercress

Nasturtium officinale
Hardy

Description: Watercress is a trailing perennial of European origin with dark green peppery leaves. Plants usually grow in water. If you're fortunate enough to have a stream running through your garden, you can grow watercress on the bank. You can also grow it indoors in pots set in a tray of water. Watercress adds a kick to salads and makes a popular garnish. It's full of vitamin C and minerals.

How to grow: Although watercress is easily grown from seed, it is usually propagated in temperate climates from stem-pieces, which root easily in wet soil. Sow seeds of watercress directly in wet garden soils two to three weeks before the average date of last frost. Cuttings can be taken from the watercress you buy at the grocery. Watercress prefers sun in the North, dappled shade in the South. Sow the seeds thickly ¼ inch deep. Mulch lightly if high water is likely to wash seeds from their bed. As watercress becomes established, the plants will spread and float on the edges of streams, rooting into the soil below.

Harvest: Pick plants when needed for a pungent, peppery flavor.

Varieties: 'Dutch' matures in 53 days.

Watermelon

Citrullus lanatus
Very Tender

Description: The watermelon is a spreading, tender annual vine related to the cucumber. It produces round, oval, or oblong fruits that can weigh anywhere from 5 to 100 pounds. The fruit can have pink, red, yellow, or grayish white flesh. Male and female flowers appear on the same vine. Although smaller varieties are available, watermelons still need a lot of room. They also take a lot of nutrients from the soil.

How to grow: Watermelons require warm soil and warm days. Night temperatures below 50 degrees Fahrenheit will cause the flavor of the fruit to deteriorate. They must have full sun and prefer well-drained soil that holds moisture well. Grow watermelons in inverted hills either by seed or transplants. You can either purchase transplants or start your own indoors three to four weeks before the planting date. Sow seeds or set out transplants two to three weeks after the average date of last frost, when the soil has warmed up. Space the hills 6 feet apart and plant four to five seeds in each hill. When the seedlings have grown large enough, thin to leave the strongest one or two seedlings in each hill. With transplants, set one or two transplants per hill. Watermelons are 95 percent water, so make sure they have enough water to keep them growing well. Don't let the soil dry out and use a mulch to keep the moisture even.

Harvest: A watermelon is ready to harvest when the vine's tendrils begin to turn brown and die off. A ripe watermelon will sound dull and hollow when you tap it with your knuckles.

Varieties: 'Golden Crown Hybrid,' 80 days, is an All America Selection that produces juicy, golden-yellow flesh. 'Sugar Baby,' 75 days, gives round, 12-pound fruits with red flesh and thin rinds. 'Bush Sugar Baby,' 80 days, provides sweet, 12-pound fruit on a compact bush. 'Redball Seedless,' 80 days, gives fruit with red flesh that has a few white seeds.

HERBS

Angelica

Biennial
Angelica archangelica

Height: 60 to 72 inches
Spread: 36 inches
Description: This large, boldly attractive biennial has very lush growth, making it a striking focal point in the garden. It is similar in appearance to celery and parsnip plants. The flowers are white umbels followed by decorative yellow-green seedpods. Its flavor is licoricelike.
Ease of care: Easy
How to grow: Angelica likes a cool, moist location and average to well-drained soil. It will grow in sun or partial shade. Sow seeds in place or transplant them when still very small as they don't like to be moved. One plant is enough to supply the needs of an average family.
Propagation: By seed. Seeds must be no more than a few weeks old to be viable. Sow in late fall or early spring while the ground is still cool. Leave seeds on top of the soil; do not cover them.
Uses: Fresh leaves—soups, stews; Dried leaves—salads, soups, stews, potpourris; Fresh foliage—floral arrangements; Seeds—teas, baked goods; Stems—candy, pork, baked goods; Dried roots—teas, breads; Root oil—baths, lotions.
Preservation: Harvest stems during second spring, leaves throughout summer season, roots in fall, and seeds when ripe. Stems can be candied or frozen. Hang-dry or freeze leaves, depending on planned use.

Anise

Annual
Pimpinella anisum

Height: 18 to 24 inches
Spread: 4 to 8 inches
Description: Feathery leaves and a lacy flower umbel are held on a tall and not very strong stem. These annuals look similar to dill and, like that plant, do best when grown closely together either in rows or clumps so that the multiple stems provide support for one another. The flavor is licoricelike.
Ease of care: Easy, but it will take at least 4 frost-free months to grow seeds to maturity. Therefore, in northern areas only the leaves can be obtained from home-grown plants.
How to grow: Plant in full sun and average, light dry soil. Either seed in place where they'll grow or transplant them when they are very small.
Propagation: By seed in early spring.
Uses: Fresh or frozen leaves—salads, cottage cheese, teas, jellies; Seeds—perfumes, soaps, breads, cookies, fish stocks, teas, soups, stews
Preservation: Harvest leaves during late summer for freezing. Harvest seeds when fully ripe, watching carefully to cut plants at ground level when first seeds ripen. Hang-dry the seed heads inside paper bags in a warm, dry place. Store them in tightly sealed containers.

Basil

Annual
Ocimum basilicum

Height: 18 inches
Spread: 10 inches
Description: Basil has a very neat, dense growing habit with attractive, glossy, bright-green, triangular leaves. All varieties of this annual make effective additions to any garden. They can also be clipped into a neat hedging, if desired. Flowers are not an important feature.
Ease of care: Easy
How to grow: Full sun and rich, moist soil are preferred. Sow seeds when soil is warm, or get a head start by starting them indoors and transplanting seedlings to the garden after danger of frost is past.
Propagation: By seed outdoors in late spring or indoors 8 weeks before the last frost.
Uses: Fresh, dried, and frozen leaves—vinegars, sauces, stews, salads, fish, shellfish, chicken, veal, lamb, tomatoes, potatoes; Dried leaves—potpourris, saches; Fresh branches—floral arrangements; Cosmetic uses—hair rinses, toilet waters, soaps
Preservation: The ideal harvest time, when flavor is at its peak, is when flower buds are about to blossom. Prunings can be used whenever they are taken. Hang-dry and store in airtight containers; better flavor is retained if frozen or stored in oil or vinegar.
Related varieties: Compact dwarf variety, 'Spicy Globe,' makes an outstanding edging or an attractive container plant. 'Purple Ruffles' and 'Dark Opal' are two dramatic, purple-leaved varieties. 'Green Ruffles' has a great lime-green color. Lemon basil has a distinct lemon flavor.

Chervil

Annual

Anthriscus cerefolium

Height: 18 inches
Spread: 4 to 8 inches
Description: Lacy, fernlike, dark green leaves have a coarser texture than carrot foliage, but finer than parsley. Chervil has a very delicate flavor of a licorice/parsley blend. Of the two forms available, the curly variety is more decorative in the garden than the flat variety.
Ease of care: Average to difficult.
How to grow: Chervil likes coolness and does well in partial shade. It likes a moist, well-drained, average or better soil. Do not try to move plants. For a fresh supply throughout the season, plant at 3-week intervals.
Propagation: By seed in the fall or very early spring.
Uses: Fresh or frozen leaves—eggs, salads, soups, fish, stews, veal, add during the last few minutes of cooking; Dried flowers—floral arrangements; Dried leaves—potpourris
Preservation: Pick chervil just before blooming. For culinary use, freeze leaves or store them in a small amount of oil. For potpourri, dry rapidly in an oven and store immediately.

Chives

Perennial

Allium schoenoprasum

Height: 8 to 12 inches
Spread: 8 inches
Description: Chives have very tight clumps of long, skinny, grasslike onion leaves. They produce an abundance of small, rosy purple, globe-shaped flowers in early summer. They can be used as edging plants, grown alone, or with other plants in containers. Chives have a mild onion flavor.
Ease of care: Easy
How to grow: This herb prefers an average to rich, moist soil, but will manage in almost any soil if kept moist. It grows in full sun to partial shade. It can also be grown as a pot plant indoors any time of the year for a source of fresh supply.
Propagation: By seed or division taken at any time during the growing season.
Uses: Fresh, dried, or frozen leaves—cream cheese spreads, cottage cheese, potatoes, salads, eggs, soups, poultry, fish, shellfish, veal; Fresh flowers—vinegars, salads, garnishes; Dried flowers—floral arrangements, wreaths.
Preservation: Harvest only part of the plant at a time for continuous production through the season. Mince leaves and then freeze them for full flavor; dried leaves are less flavor-filled. Hang-dry the flowers for decorative uses. Pick them before any seeds begin to appear.

Coriander, Cilantro, Chinese Parsley

Annual

Coriandrum sativum

Height: 24 to 36 inches
Spread: 6 inches
Description: The bright green, lacy leaves look very similar to flat-leaved Italian parsley on the lower part of the plant, but become more finely fernlike further up. This large annual has a leaf and root flavor that is a cross between sage and citrus; the seeds, however, are simply citruslike.
Ease of care: Easy
How to grow: Plant in rich, well-drained soil in sun. Coriander plants are best located where they are protected from the wind, since they blow over easily.
Propagation: By seed once the soil is warm in spring.
Uses: Fresh or frozen leaves—potatoes, clams, oysters; Seeds—marinades, cheeses, pickles, mushrooms, stews, curries, chicken, quick breads, potpourris; Fresh roots—salads, relishes
Preservation: Harvest only fresh, young leaves and freeze them promptly. Harvest seeds when they have turned brown, but are not yet released. Cut a whole plant and hang-dry inside paper bags to catch seeds.

Costmary

Perennial
Chrysanthemum balsamita

Height: 30 to 36 inches
Spread: 24 inches
Description: Basal clusters of elongated oval leaves look similar to horseradish growth. This perennial sends up tall flower stems that produce clusters of unremarkable blooms. When the leaves are young and fresh, they're mint scented; the scent changes to balsam when the leaves are dried.
Ease of care: Easy
How to grow: Grow in fertile, well-drained soil, in full sun to partial shade. Divide every few years as the clump becomes too large.
Propagation: By division as needed.
Uses: Fresh leaves—tuna fish, shrimp, eggs, lemonade; Dried leaves—sachets, potpourris, baths, lotions
Preservation: Pick leaves when they are young and tender for immediate fresh use or a few at a time to dry. Costmary retains its scent for a long period when dried.

Dill

Annual
Anethum graveolens

Height: 24 to 36 inches
Spread: 6 inches
Description: Dill has extremely fine-cut, fernlike leaves on tall stems. It is a blue-green annual with attractive yellow flower umbels and yellow-green seed heads.
Ease of care: Easy
How to grow: Dill likes acid, light, moist, and sandy soil in full sun. Since it does not transplant well, sow it in place and thin. Grow it in clumps or rows so stems can give support to one another.
Propagation: By seed in late fall or early spring. Plant at 3-week intervals during spring and early summer for a fresh supply all season.
Uses: Fresh leaves—potatoes, tomatoes, vinegars, pickles, fish, shrimp, stews, cheeses, lamb, pork, poultry; Fresh and dried seed heads—floral arrangements; Seeds—pickles, cheeses
Preservation: Clip fresh leaves as needed. Flavor is best retained for winter use if frozen; pick the leaves just as flowers begin to open. For seeds, harvest entire plants when seed heads are brown but not yet releasing seeds. Hang-dry in paper bags to catch seeds.

Fennel

Perennial
Foeniculum vulgare

Height: 50 to 72 inches
Spread: 18 to 36 inches
Description: Fennel has very fine-cut leaves that look very similar to dill. This half-hardy perennial has a sweetish, licoricelike flavor. The flowers and seed heads are attractive and make appealing additions to floral arrangements.
Ease of care: Easy
How to grow: Fennel likes alkaline soil; add lime if soil is very acidic. Grow in full sun in well-drained, rich soil. Locate them where plants are sheltered from heavy winds since they blow over easily.
Propagation: By seed in cold climates, where it will grow as an annual. Sow in late fall or early spring.
Uses: Fresh leaves—sauces, salads, eggs, fish, add during the last few moments of cooking; Dried leaves—cosmetic oils, soaps, facials; Seeds—desserts, cakes, breads, potatoes, spreads
Preservation: Snip individual leaves to use fresh or to freeze. Harvest whole plants just before blooming and hang-dry. To harvest seeds, cut down entire plants when seeds turn brown but before they release. Hang-dry in paper bags to catch the seeds.
Related varieties: Sweet fennel, *Foeniculum vulgare dulce,* is a closely related annual, the base stems of which are eaten as a vegetable in the same manner as celery.

Garlic Chives, Chinese Chives, Chinese Leeks

Perennial
Allium tuberosum

Height: 18 inches
Spread: 8 inches
Description: Garlic chives have compact, grasslike clumps of large, flattened, blue-green leaves that look like a larger version of chives. This perennial has attractive, white, globe-shaped blossoms that last a long time in floral arrangements. It has a definite garlic flavor.
Ease of care: Easy
How to grow: Plant seeds in full sun in average to poor soil.
Propagation: By seed in spring; by division anytime during the growing season.
Uses: Fresh leaves—salads, soups, spreads, vinegars; Dried leaves—soups, cheeses, sauces; Fresh and dried flowers—floral arrangements
Preservation: Harvest only part of the plant at a time for continuous production throughout the season. Mince leaves and then freeze them for full flavor; drying causes some flavor loss. Hang-dry flowers for decorative uses.

Geraniums, Scented

Half-Hardy Perennial
Pelargonium **species**

Height: Varies with variety
Spread: Varies with variety
Description: These aromatic-leaved perennials come in a variety of scents, including rose, orange, pepper, lemon, lime, mint, and apple. The leaf shapes are also varied, ranging from round to deeply cut, and their color ranges from yellow-green to reddish-purple according to the variety involved. Most make attractive potted plants and many have beautiful flowers.
Ease of care: Average
How to grow: All prefer full sun and well-drained, rich to average soil. Geraniums over-winter as pot plants in cold climates.
Propagation: By cuttings before flowering.
Uses: Fresh leaves—cakes, cookies, jellies; Dried leaves—potpourris, sachets, baths, facials, teas; Fresh flowers—salads
Preservation: Pick single leaves just as plants begin to develop flower buds and dry them on screens.
Related varieties: Lemon geranium is *P. mellissinum,* lime is *P. nervosum,* apple is *P. odoratissimum,* and peppermint is *P. tomentosum.* These are probably the most common of the many special scented geranium varieties available; choose those you prefer from the selection offered by your local plant supplier.

Horehound

Perennial
Marrubium vulgare

Height: 30 inches
Spread: 12 inches
Description: Horehound has attractive, round, gray, mintlike foliage. The overall look of this perennial is that of a woolly gray bush. It makes an attractive addition to any garden. Flower arrangers will find it an outstanding decorative foliage for fresh or dried use.
Ease of care: Easy
How to grow: Grow in full sun in average to poor, well-drained soil.
Propagation: By seed or division in late spring
Uses: Fresh or dried leaves—candy flavorings, teas; Dried branches—floral arrangements
Preservation: Remove the leaves from the stems at the time of flowering and dry them on screens. Store in airtight containers. Hang-dry whole branches.

Marjoram

Perennial, often grown as Annual
Origanum majorana or
Majorana hortensis

Height: 8 to 12 inches
Spread: 12 to 18 inches
Description: Marjoram is a bushy, spreading, half-hardy perennial that is grown as an annual in climates where it freezes. It has small, oval, gray-green, velvety leaves. This plant is attractive when grown as a pot plant and brought indoors to overwinter.
Ease of care: Easy
How to grow: Marjoram likes rich, well-drained alkaline soil and full sun. Where winters are severe, treat it as an annual or as a pot plant. Locate it in a sheltered spot for best overwinter survival outdoors.
Propagation: By seed early indoors, transplanting seedlings outdoors after danger of frost has passed; by cuttings in spring.
Uses: Fresh or dried leaves—stuffings, soups, stews, meat loaf, pork, poultry, fish, eggs, potatoes, cheeses. Can be used in place of oregano; Dried leaves—baths, potpourris, sachets; Dried flowers—floral arrangements, wreaths
Preservation: Snip fresh when needed. For drying, harvest just before flowering and hang-dry.

Nasturtium

Annual
Tropaeolum majus

Height: 12 inches for bush, 72 inches for vines
Spread: 18 inches for bush
Description: Distinctive, blue-green circular leaves are held up on fleshy stems. These annuals come in a variety of types ranging from compact bushes to long-spreading vines. They make an eye-catching addition to any garden. In addition, they have large attractive blooms that range in color from palest yellows, pinks, and apricots to deep, rich yellows, oranges, and burgundy. The vining types are great in hanging planters, window boxes, or for use on trellises and fences. Aphids love nasturtiums, so be on the lookout for them.
Ease of care: Easy
How to grow: Plant in full sun to partial shade in average to poor, moist soil.
Propagation: By seed in late spring. They're large and can be planted individually where the plants are going to grow.
Uses: Fresh leaves and flowers—salads; Fresh flowers—floral arrangements; Unripe seeds and flower buds—pickled for salads
Preservation: Pickle unripe seeds in vinegar and use them in salads.

Oregano

Perennial
Origanum vulgare

Height: 18 inches
Spread: 12 inches
Description: Oregano is a bushy, spreading perennial with abundant oval leaves and purple blooms. Be careful to get the correct species. To be sure of avoiding disappointment, buy a plant that you've tested by crushing a few leaves and smelling or tasting them beforehand. It should have the distinct aroma of oregano.
Ease of care: Easy
How to grow: Grow in full sun, in average to sandy and preferably alkaline soil (add lime generously if soil is acidic).
Propagation: Buy your first plant, then use division, layering, or cuttings to obtain additional ones.
Uses: Fresh or dried leaves—tomatoes, cheeses, eggs, beef, pork, poultry, shellfish, potatoes, sauces; Flowers—floral arrangements; Dried branches—baths
Preservation: Clip fresh as needed. Harvest at the time of bloom and hang-dry or freeze.

Parsley

Biennial grown as Annual
Petroselinum crispum

Height: 12 inches
Spread: 8 inches
Description: Attractive, rich, green, dense leaves form a rosette base. A biennial usually grown as an annual, parsley comes in two cut-leaf forms: ruffled and Italian. The latter has flat leaves and is stronger-flavored than the curly variety. The curly form makes a nice edging plant; both are also easily grown as indoor pot plants.
Ease of care: Easy
How to grow: Plant in place in full sun or partial shade in a moist, rich soil. Presoak seeds between several hours and overnight in warm water to help speed up germination.
Propagation: By seed once the soil is warm.
Uses: Fresh, dried, or frozen leaves—garnishes, potatoes, soups, sauces, pasta, poultry, jellies, baths, shampoos, lotions
Preservation: Snip as needed fresh. Hang-dry the flat variety; freeze the curly variety.

Peppermint

Perennial
Mentha piperita

Height: 24 to 30 inches
Spread: 12 inches
Description: Peppermint has dark green, spear-shaped leaves that come to a point. It has a neat, dense growth habit with tall stems arising from an underground network of spreading stems. Since it can become invasive, plant it in an isolated location or where it can be kept contained. Another alternative is to grow it as a pot plant.
Ease of care: Easy
How to grow: Likes full sun or partial shade and rich, moist soil.
Propagation: By cuttings taken in mid-summer; by division at any time during the growing season.
Uses: Fresh or frozen leaves—garnishes, vinegars, jellies, punches, candy, lamb; Dried leaves—teas.
Preservation: Pick peppermint shoots in early to mid-summer. Hang-dry or freeze.
Related varieties: Pineapple mint, apple mint, and lemon mint each have flavors as indicated by their names. (Also refer to the profile on Spearmint.)

Rosemary

Perennial
Rosmarinus officinalis

Height: 48 to 72 inches
Spread: 18 to 24 inches
Description: Rosemary is an attractive, evergreen perennial with a spreading habit of growth. Its gray-green, needle-shaped foliage can be pruned to form a low hedge. Grow rosemary as a pot plant in colder climates, protecting it from winter winds. It makes an attractive addition to any garden. There is a prostrate form that makes a wonderful ground cover where hardy.
Ease of care: Average
How to grow: Likes a sandy, alkaline soil and full sun.
Propagation: By cuttings or by seed in spring, or by layering.
Uses: Fresh or frozen leaves—fish, lamb, potatoes, soups, tomatoes, pork, poultry, cheeses, eggs, breads, fruit salads, jellies; Dried leaves—facials, hair rinses, sachets, potpourris, lotions, toilet waters; Fresh and dried branches—baths
Preservation: Pick rosemary fresh as desired. Hang-dry or freeze the active young 3- to 4-inch growth tips.

Rue

Perennial
Ruta graveolens

Height: 24 inches
Spread: 18 inches
Description: This perennial has blue-green, teardrop-shaped foliage in clusters. Rue is an attractive and unusual plant to use as a focal point in a garden design.
Ease of care: Average
How to grow: Full sun in poor, sandy, alkaline soil. It can also be easily grown as a pot plant.
Propagation: By seed in spring or started ahead of time indoors and transplanted into the garden after the danger of frost has passed; by cuttings in mid-summer.
Uses: Fresh leaves—floral arrangements, tussy mussies; Dried seed heads—floral arrangements
Preservation: Pick just before flowers open and hang-dry. Collect seeds when flower heads ripen.
Related varieties: The variety 'Jackman's Blue' is compact and very blue-leaved. It can also be trimmed to form a lovely low hedge.

Sage

Perennial
Salvia officinalis

Height: 20 inches
Spread: 24 inches
Description: Sage is a perennial with gray-green, pebblelike, textured leaves in a long, oval shape. It has an attractive, compact, spreading growth habit. This plant is also available in variegated and purple-leaved varieties. Sage is a good edging plant and is attractive in any garden.
Ease of care: Easy
How to grow: Grow it in full sun in a well-drained sandy, alkaline soil. Protect it from the wind.
Propagation: By seed, cuttings, or division by layering in the spring.
Uses: Fresh, frozen, or dried leaves—salads, breads, soups, stews, pork, beef, fish, lamb, poultry, stuffings, tomatoes, vegetables, cheeses, teas; Dried branches—baths, lotions, herbal wreaths
Preservation: Use fresh sage as needed. Pick active growth shoots or separate leaves to hang-dry, screen dry, or freeze.
Related varieties: Sage is available in gold and green variegated (*S. officinalis* 'Aurea') and purple-leaved (*S. officinalis* 'Purpurea') varieties.

Savory, Summer

Annual
Satureja hortensis

Height: 18 inches
Spread: 8 inches
Description: This attractive annual has flattened, gray-green, needle-shaped leaves. The leaves are soft rather than stiff and have a slightly peppery flavor. The overall look of the plant is light and airy.
Ease of care: Easy
How to grow: Plant seeds in place in full sun in a light, rich to average soil. They do not transplant well. Summer savory grows well as a container plant with seeds planted directly in a pot.
Propagation: By seed when the soil is warm.
Uses: Fresh, dried, or frozen leaves—tomatoes, pastas, soups, stews, roasts, beans, salads, cheeses, fish, vinegars, vegetables
Preservation: When it begins to flower, dry it on screens or paper.

Sorrel, French

Perennial

Rumex acetosa or *R. scutatus*

Height: 18 inches
Spread: 10 inches
Description: Succulent, bright green, spear-shaped leaves in a low rosette send up tall flower stalks that should be removed so that leaf supply will continue. The leaves of this hardy perennial have a pleasant acidity that brightens any salad. Sorrel can also be grown as an indoor pot plant.
Ease of care: Easy
How to grow: Provide full sun or partial shade in a moist, rich acid soil. Shady conditions produce a milder taste.
Propagation: By seed or division in spring.
Uses: Fresh or frozen leaves—soups, lamb, beef, sauces
Preservation: Remove single leaves and use them fresh or freeze them for winter use.

Southernwood

Perennial

Artemisia abrotanum

Height: 30 inches
Spread: 24 inches
Description: Woolly, silver-gray, cut leaves and a dense, branching growth habit make these perennials a very decorative addition to any garden.
Ease of care: Easy
How to grow: Full sun in any kind of soil. Prune southernwood back each spring to encourage new growth and a nice shape.
Propagation: By semi-hardwood cuttings in late summer.
Uses: Fresh branches—floral arrangements, tussy mussies; Dried branches—baths, floral arrangements, wreaths
Preservation: Pick branches just before flowering and hang-dry.

Spearmint

Perennial

Mentha spicata or *M. viridis*

Height: 20 inches
Spread: 12 inches
Description: Green, pointed leaves are somewhat hairy compared to peppermint, but the best way to tell them apart is to crush the leaves and taste or smell them. Spearmint has a neat, dense growth with tall stems arising from a network of spreading underground stems. It can become invasive, so plant it in an isolated location or where it can be kept contained. A good solution is to grow it as a pot plant.
Ease of care: Easy
How to grow: Full sun or partial shade in rich, moist soil.
Propagation: By cuttings in mid-summer; by division at any time during the growing season.
Uses: Fresh or frozen leaves—candy, garnishes, jellies, punches, lamb; Dried leaves—teas
Preservation: Pick spearmint shoots in early to mid-summer. Hang-dry or freeze.
Related varieties: Pineapple mint, apple mint, and lemon mint each have distinctive flavors as indicated by their name. (Also refer to the profile on Peppermint.)

Sweet Woodruff

Perennial
Galium odoratum or *Asperula odorata*

Height: 6 to 8 inches
Spread: 6 to 8 inches
Description: Single, small, and knife-shaped leaves circle in tiers around the stemlike flattened wheel spokes. This perennial has a rich green color and spreads by means of underground stems to make a lovely ground cover when it has its preferred growing conditions of shade and rich, moist soil.
Ease of care: Difficult unless conditions are exactly to its liking.
How to grow: Grow in rich, moist soil in fairly deep, woodland shade.
Propagation: By seed in fall that will sprout in the spring; by division after flowering.
Uses: Fresh leaves—wine punches; Dried leaves—potpourris, sachets, wreaths
Preservation: Pick fresh sweet woodruff as needed. Cut entire stems when they are in bloom and hang-dry.

Tansy

Perennial
Tanacetum vulgare

Height: 40 inches
Spread: 12 to 18 inches
Description: This hardy perennial has lush, dark green, cut leaves and tall flower stems that produce tight clusters of intense yellow, button-shaped blooms. These are vigorous growers that spread rapidly and can take over; keep them constantly under control or place them where they can be allowed to run wild. The foliage has a peppery odor and flavor.
Ease of care: Easy
How to grow: Grow in full sun or partial shade in average to poor soil.
Propagation: By seed in spring; by division in spring or fall; or by layering.
Uses: Fresh or dried flowers—floral arrangements
Preservation: Harvest leaves singly and dry them on screens or harvest entire stems with flowers and hang-dry.

Tarragon

Perennial
Artemisia dracunculus

Height: 24 inches
Spread: 24 inches
Description: This bushy, medium green perennial has long, narrow, pointed leaves and inconspicuous flowers that rarely appear. Be sure to get the French rather than the Russian variety that looks very much the same with somewhat narrower and lighter green leaves. The latter has none of the sweetly aromatic flavor wanted for culinary use. Test it by crushing, smelling, and tasting a few leaves.
Ease of care: Average
How to grow: Likes full sun to partial shade in a sandy to rich alkaline soil that is well drained. It can also be grown successfully as a pot plant. Cut it back in the fall or early spring. Protect it with a mulch during the winter in cold climates.
Propagation: Buy first plant, then by cuttings in summer and fall; by division in early spring; or by layering.
Uses: Fresh, dried, or frozen leaves—fish, vinegars, tomatoes, salads, eggs, chicken, pickles, add during the last few minutes of cooking
Preservation: Pick separate leaves or 3- to 4-inch growth tips at any time for fresh use. Pick just before blooming to freeze or dry. Be careful because the delicate flavor is easily lost if dried too long. Store immediately in an airtight container. The flavor can also be captured in vinegar or oil.
Related varieties: Since it does not produce seeds, if tarragon seeds are offered, they will be those of Russian rather than French tarragon. Buy plants only.

Thyme

Perennial
Thymus vulgaris

Height: 1 to 10 inches depending on variety
Spread: 12 to 18 inches
Description: These tiny-leaved, wide-spreading perennials make a good and inexpensive ground cover. They can be clipped and mowed regularly, if desired. Their profuse blooms are especially attractive to bees; clip off flower heads just before blooming. The lowest-growing varieties are excellent to plant in flagstone walks.
Ease of care: Easy
How to grow: Thyme does well in full sun to partial shade in poor to average, well-drained soil. Trim it back each spring to encourage abundant new growth. It can also be grown as a pot plant.
Propagation: By seed or division in spring or fall; by cuttings in early summer; or by layering.
Uses: Fresh, frozen, or dried leaves—marinades, stuffings, soups, vinegars, poultry, shellfish, fish, cheeses; Dried leaves—sachets, potpourris, floral arrangements, baths, facials, wreaths; Dried flowers—sachets, lotions, baths
Preservation: Harvest anytime for fresh use. Pick before and during flowering to hang-dry.
Related varieties: There are many different thyme species and varieties with self-descriptive names: woolly thyme, silver thyme, lemon thyme, and golden thyme. The variations in their foliage colors, growth habits, and flower colors make them all good candidates for use in garden designs.

Wormwood

Perennial
Artemisia absinthium

Height: 30 to 48 inches
Spread: 15 to 20 inches
Description: A handsome, very fine cut-leaf, silver-green foliage and a spreading growth habit makes this an attractive perennial.
Ease of care: Average
How to grow: Plant in full sun in almost any kind of soil as long as it's alkaline. Add lime if soil is naturally acid.
Propagation: By seed or cuttings in summer; by division in spring or fall.
Uses: Fresh leaves—floral arrangements; Dried leaves—sachets, floral arrangements, wreaths
Preservation: Harvest when in flower and hang-dry.

GARDEN BOUNTY

A vegetable and herb garden can be both beautiful and productive. The recipes that follow will give you dozens of delicious ways to enjoy fresh, healthy vegetables and herbs from artichokes and watermelon to basil and savory.

Pepper-Stuffed Artichokes

4 large artichokes, outer leaves removed
¼ cup lemon juice
2 teaspoons olive oil
½ cup chopped onion
2 cloves garlic, minced
½ cup diced red bell pepper
½ cup diced yellow bell pepper
½ cup fresh whole wheat bread crumbs
2 tablespoons chopped fresh parsley
2 teaspoons dried oregano leaves
⅛ teaspoon black pepper
1 can (14½ ounces) no-salt-added peeled tomatoes, undrained
2 tablespoons freshly grated Parmesan cheese

1. Trim 1 inch off top and stem of each artichoke. Dip artichokes in lemon juice.

2. Bring 5 cups water to a boil in large saucepan over high heat. Reduce heat to low. Add artichokes; simmer 30 minutes. Drain and cool slightly. Cut in half lengthwise. Scoop out and discard center of artichoke.

3. Preheat oven to 350°F. Heat oil in small nonstick skillet over medium heat. Add onion and garlic; cook and stir 3 to 4 minutes or until onion is tender. Remove from heat; stir in bell peppers, bread crumbs, parsley, oregano and black pepper. Stuff artichokes with bell pepper mixture.

4. Spray 9-inch square baking pan with nonstick cooking spray. Arrange stuffed artichokes in prepared pan. Set aside.

5. Place tomatoes in food processor or blender; process until smooth. Pour over artichokes. Sprinkle with cheese. Cover; bake 30 minutes or until lightly browned.
Makes 4 servings

Nutrients per Serving

Calories	162
Total Fat	4 g
Cholesterol	2 mg
Sodium	217 mg

🌿 *Pepper-Stuffed Artichokes*

Cold Asparagus with Lemon-Mustard Dressing

12 fresh asparagus spears
2 tablespoons fat-free mayonnaise
1 tablespoon sweet brown mustard
1 tablespoon fresh lemon juice
1 teaspoon grated lemon peel, divided

1. Bring ½ cup water to a boil in medium saucepan over high heat. Add asparagus; cook until crisp-tender. Immediately drain and run under cold water. Cover; refrigerate until chilled.

2. Combine mayonnaise, mustard and lemon juice in small bowl; blend well. Stir in ½ teaspoon lemon peel; set aside.

3. Divide asparagus between 2 plates. Spoon 2 tablespoons dressing over top of each serving; sprinkle each with ¼ teaspoon lemon peel. Garnish with carrot strips and edible flowers, such as pansies, violets or nasturtiums, if desired.
Makes 2 appetizer servings

Nutrients per Serving

Calories	39
Total Fat	1 g
Cholesterol	0 mg
Sodium	294 mg

🌿 *(left) Cob Corn in Barbecue Butter (recipe on page 120)*

🌿 *Shanghai Chicken with Asparagus and Ham*

Shanghai Chicken with Asparagus and Ham

- 2 cups diagonally cut 1-inch asparagus pieces
- 2 teaspoons vegetable oil
- ¾ cup coarsely chopped onion
- 2 cloves garlic, minced
- 1 pound boneless skinless chicken breasts, cut into 1-inch pieces
- 2 tablespoons teriyaki sauce
- ¼ cup diced deli ham
- 2 cups hot cooked rice

1. Place asparagus in large saucepan; cover with water. Bring to a boil over high heat. Cook 3 minutes. Plunge asparagus into cold water. Drain well.

2. Heat oil in large nonstick skillet over medium heat. Add onion and garlic; cook and stir 2 minutes. Add chicken; cook and stir 2 minutes. Add asparagus; cook and stir 2 minutes or until chicken is no longer pink in center.

3. Add teriyaki sauce; mix well. Add ham; cook until heated through. Serve over rice. Garnish with carrot strips and fresh herbs, if desired. *Makes 4 servings*

Nutrients per Serving

Calories	289	
Total Fat	5	g
Cholesterol	46	mg
Sodium	265	mg

Country Green Beans with Ham

- 2 teaspoons olive oil
- ¼ cup minced onion
- 1 clove garlic, minced
- 1 pound fresh green beans, rinsed and drained
- 1 cup chopped fresh tomatoes
- 6 slices (2 ounces) thinly sliced low-fat smoked turkey-ham
- 1 tablespoon chopped fresh marjoram
- 2 teaspoons chopped fresh basil
- ⅛ teaspoon black pepper
- ¼ cup herbed croutons

1. Heat oil in medium saucepan over medium heat. Add onion and garlic; cook and stir about 3 minutes or until onion is tender. Reduce heat to low.

2. Add beans, tomatoes, turkey-ham, marjoram, basil and pepper. Cook about 10 minutes, stirring occasionally, until liquid from tomatoes is absorbed. Transfer mixture to serving dish. Top with croutons. *Makes 4 servings*

Nutrients per Serving

Calories	100	
Total Fat	3	g
Cholesterol	12	mg
Sodium	194	mg

Green Bean Bundles

- 8 ounces fresh haricot vert beans or other tiny, young green beans, rinsed and drained
- 1 yellow squash, about 1½ inches in diameter
- 1 tablespoon olive oil
- 1 clove garlic, minced
- ¼ teaspoon dried tarragon leaves
  Salt and black pepper

1. Divide beans evenly into 8 stacks. Cut squash into 8 (½-inch-thick) slices; hollow out with spoon to within ¼ inch of peel.

2. Thread stacks of beans through squash pieces as if each piece were a napkin ring.

3. Place steamer basket in large saucepan; add water to 1 inch depth. (Water should not touch bottom of basket.) Place bean bundles in steamer basket; cover. Bring to a boil over high heat; cook 5 minutes or until beans are crisp-tender. Add water, as necessary, to prevent pan from boiling dry.

4. Meanwhile, heat oil in small nonstick skillet over medium-high heat. Add garlic and tarragon; cook and stir until garlic is tender.

5. Transfer bean bundles to warm serving plate; pour garlic oil over top. Season to taste with salt and pepper. Garnish as desired. Serve immediately.
Makes 8 side-dish servings

Nutrients per Serving

Calories	27	
Total Fat	2	g
Cholesterol	0	mg
Sodium	4	mg

Frenched Beans with Celery

¾ pound fresh green beans, rinsed, drained and sliced lengthwise
2 ribs celery, thinly sliced
2 tablespoons butter, melted
2 tablespoons sunflower seeds, toasted

1. Bring ½ cup water to a boil in 2-quart saucepan over high heat. Add beans and celery. Cover; reduce heat to medium-low. Simmer 8 minutes or until beans are crisp-tender. Drain.

2. Add butter to bean mixture; toss to coat. Transfer to warm serving dish. Sprinkle with sunflower seeds. Garnish as desired. Serve immediately.

Makes 6 side-dish servings

Nutrients per Serving

Calories	66
Total Fat	5 g
Cholesterol	10 mg
Sodium	57 mg

Fresh Lima Beans in Onion Cream

1 pound fresh lima beans
⅔ cup milk
½ teaspoon instant minced onion
1 tablespoon butter or margarine
1 small onion, sliced into rings
⅓ cup sour cream
Salt and black pepper
2 teaspoons sliced pimientos

1. Open bean pods at seams by pinching pods between thumb and forefinger. Remove beans; discard shells.

2. Place beans in small heavy saucepan. Add milk and minced onion. Bring just to a boil over medium-high heat. Reduce heat to low. Simmer, uncovered, 20 to 25 minutes or until tender.

3. Meanwhile, melt butter in small skillet over medium-high heat. Add onion rings; cook and stir until golden. Stir in sour cream. Season to taste with salt and

pepper. Gently stir in pimientos. Stir onion ring mixture into lima bean mixture. Transfer to warm serving dish. Garnish as desired. Serve immediately.

Makes 4 side-dish servings

Nutrients per Serving

Calories	432
Total Fat	9 g
Cholesterol	19 mg
Sodium	107 mg

Apricot-Glazed Beets

1 large bunch fresh beets *or* 1 pound loose beets
1 cup apricot nectar
1 tablespoon cornstarch
2 tablespoons cider vinegar or red wine vinegar
8 dried apricot halves, cut into strips
¼ teaspoon salt
Additional apricot halves (optional)

1. Cut tops off beets, leaving 1 inch of stem. Do not trim root ends. Scrub beets under cold running water with soft vegetable brush, being careful not to break skins.

2. Place beets in medium saucepan; add enough water to cover. Cover. Bring to a boil over high heat; reduce heat to medium. Simmer about 20 minutes or until skins rub off easily and beets are barely firm when pierced with fork. Transfer to plate; cool. Rinse pan.

3. Combine apricot nectar with cornstarch in same saucepan. Stir in vinegar. Add apricot strips and salt. Cook over medium heat until mixture thickens.

4. Cut roots and stems from beets on plate.* Peel, halve and cut beets into ¼-inch-thick slices. Add beet slices to apricot mixture; toss gently to coat. Transfer to warm serving dish. Garnish as desired. Serve immediately with apricot halves, if desired.

Makes 4 side-dish servings

* *Do not cut beets on cutting board because the juice will stain the board.*

Nutrients per Serving

Calories	111
Total Fat	<1 g
Cholesterol	0 mg
Sodium	184 mg

Fresh Lima Beans in Onion Cream

Cream of Broccoli Soup

1 medium onion, chopped
1 carrot, chopped
1 rib celery, chopped
1 potato, peeled and chopped
1 clove garlic, minced
½ teaspoon dried basil leaves
3 cups chicken broth
1 bunch fresh broccoli, rinsed,
    drained and cut into ½-inch
    pieces
2 tablespoons butter
2 tablespoons all-purpose flour
1½ cups milk
1 cup half-and-half
½ teaspoon salt
¼ teaspoon black pepper
½ cup (2 ounces) shredded Cheddar
    cheese
6 to 8 teaspoons sour cream
    (optional)

1. Bring onion, carrot, celery, potato, garlic, basil and chicken broth to a boil in large saucepan over high heat. Reduce heat to low; simmer 10 minutes. Add broccoli to saucepan. Simmer 10 minutes or until vegetables are fork-tender. Cool at room temperature 20 to 30 minutes. *Do not drain.*

2. Transfer vegetables to food processor or blender; process until smooth.

3. Melt butter in Dutch oven over medium heat. Add flour, stirring until mixture is smooth. Cook 1 minute. Gradually whisk in milk and half-and-half. Stir in salt, pepper and cheese. Add puréed vegetables. Cook 3 to 5 minutes or until mixture thickens, stirring occasionally.

4. Ladle into individual soup bowls. Top each serving with small dollops of sour cream, if desired. Garnish as desired.

Makes 8 servings

Nutrients per Serving

Calories	155	
Total Fat	10	g
Cholesterol	33	mg
Sodium	614	mg

Broccoli Timbales

1 pound fresh broccoli, rinsed,
    drained and cut into 1-inch pieces
3 eggs
1 cup heavy cream
1 tablespoon lemon juice
¼ teaspoon salt
⅛ teaspoon black pepper
    Boiling water

1. Preheat oven to 375°F. Generously grease six (6-ounce) ramekins or custard cups. Place in 13×9-inch baking pan.

2. Bring ½ cup water to a boil in medium saucepan over high heat. Reduce heat to medium-low; add broccoli stem pieces. Cover; simmer about 10 minutes or until tender. Transfer stems, with slotted spoon, to food processor or blender. Add flowerets to same saucepan. Cover; simmer about 5 minutes or until bright green. Remove flowerets with slotted spoon to cutting board.

 *Broccoli Timbales*

3. Add eggs to stems in food processor; process until smooth. Add cream; pulse to blend. Add lemon juice, salt and pepper; pulse once.

4. Reserve 6 small flowerets for garnish, if desired. Chop remaining flowerets; add to food processor. Pulse several times to blend.

5. Divide mixture evenly between prepared ramekins. Add boiling water to pan so water comes halfway up sides of ramekins. Bake 25 to 30 minutes or until knife inserted in centers comes out clean. Let stand 5 minutes. Garnish with reserved flowerets, if desired.

Makes 6 side-dish servings

Nutrients per Serving

Calories	193	
Total Fat	17	g
Cholesterol	161	mg
Sodium	152	mg

Vegetable Rings on Broccoli Spears

1 small bunch broccoli, cut into
   florets
3 (¼-inch-thick) slices mild white
   onion
1 red bell pepper, sliced into rings
2 tablespoons butter or margarine
½ teaspoon wine vinegar
½ teaspoon dried rosemary

1. Place steamer basket in large
saucepan; add water to 1 inch depth.
(Water should not touch bottom of
basket.) Place broccoli in steamer.
Separate onion slices into rings; place
on broccoli. Cover. Bring to a boil over
high heat; steam about 8 minutes or until
broccoli is crisp-tender. Add water, as
necessary, to prevent pan from
boiling dry.

2. Uncover; place pepper rings over
onion. Cover; cook 2 to 3 minutes or until
crisp-tender. Remove from heat; transfer
vegetables, with slotted spoon, to warm
serving dish.

3. Melt butter in small saucepan over
medium heat; stir in vinegar and
rosemary. Drizzle evenly over vegetables.
Serve immediately.

Makes 4 side-dish servings

Nutrients per Serving

Calories	89	
Total Fat	6	g
Cholesterol	15	mg
Sodium	78	mg

🌱 *Vegetable Rings on Broccoli Spears*

Broccoli Boutonnieres and Buttons

1 large bunch fresh broccoli
2 teaspoons lemon juice
1 tablespoon cornstarch
1 teaspoon instant chicken bouillon
   granules
   White pepper

1. Cut broccoli into florets. Peel stems;
cut crosswise into ⅛-inch pieces to make
"buttons."

2. Place steamer basket in large
saucepan; add water to 1 inch depth.
(Water should not touch bottom of
basket.) Place "buttons" in steamer; top
with florets. Cover. Bring to a boil over
high heat; cook 4 to 6 minutes or until
crisp-tender. Add water, as necessary, to
prevent pan from boiling dry.

3. Meanwhile, combine lemon juice and
cornstarch in small saucepan. Stir in
bouillon granules and 1 cup water. Cook
over medium heat until mixture thickens
and begins to boil, stirring constantly.

4. Arrange "buttons" around edge of
warm serving platter. Place florets in
center. Drizzle with lemon juice mixture;
season with pepper to taste. Garnish as
desired. Serve immediately.

Makes 6 side-dish servings

Nutrients per Serving

Calories	13	
Total Fat	<1	g
Cholesterol	0	mg
Sodium	168	mg

Broth-Simmered Brussels Sprouts

Broth-Simmered Brussels Sprouts

1 pound fresh Brussels sprouts
½ cup condensed beef broth *or* ½ cup water *plus* 2 teaspoons instant beef bouillon granules
1 tablespoon butter or margarine, softened
¼ cup freshly grated Parmesan cheese Paprika

1. Cut stem from each Brussels sprout; pull off outer or bruised leaves. Cut an "X" deep into stem end of each sprout. Rinse under cold water; drain.

2. Pour broth into large saucepan. Place sprouts, stem ends down, in single layer in broth. Bring to a boil over high heat; reduce heat to medium-low. Cover; simmer about 5 minutes or just until crisp-tender.

3. Uncover; simmer until liquid is almost evaporated. Add butter and cheese to saucepan; toss to combine. Transfer to warm serving dish; sprinkle with paprika to taste. Garnish as desired. Serve immediately.

Makes 4 side-dish servings

Nutrients per Serving

Calories	105	
Total Fat	5	g
Cholesterol	13	mg
Sodium	376	mg

Lemon Brussels Sprouts

2 pounds fresh Brussels sprouts
½ teaspoon lemon juice
¼ teaspoon grated lemon peel
⅛ teaspoon black pepper
⅛ teaspoon ground thyme

1. Cut stem from each Brussels sprout; pull off outer or bruised leaves. Cut an "X" deep into stem end of each sprout. Rinse under cold water; drain.

2. Combine sprouts, ½ cup water, lemon juice and lemon peel in large saucepan. Bring to a boil over high heat. Reduce heat; simmer, covered 8 to 10 minutes or until sprouts are crisp-tender. Uncover; simmer until liquid is almost evaporated. Sprinkle with pepper and thyme.

Makes 2 servings

Nutrients per Serving

Calories	30	
Total Fat	<1	g
Cholesterol	0	mg
Sodium	16	mg

Cabbage Wedges with Tangy Hot Dressing

1 slice uncooked bacon, cut crosswise into ¼-inch strips
2 teaspoons cornstarch
⅔ cup unsweetened apple juice
¼ cup cider vinegar or red wine vinegar
1 tablespoon brown sugar
½ teaspoon caraway seeds
1 green onion, thinly sliced
½ head red or green cabbage, cut into 4 wedges

1. Cook bacon in large skillet over medium heat until crisp. Remove bacon to paper towel; set aside. Reserve drippings in skillet.

2. Meanwhile, dissolve cornstarch in apple juice in glass measuring cup. Stir in vinegar, brown sugar and caraway seeds; set aside. Add onion to hot drippings. Cook and stir until tender.

3. Place cabbage wedges, flat sides down, in drippings mixture in skillet. Pour cornstarch mixture over cabbage wedges. Cook over medium heat 4 minutes. Carefully turn cabbage wedges over with spatula. Cook 6 minutes or until cabbage is fork-tender and dressing is thickened.

4. Remove cabbage to cutting board with spatula; cut core away from each wedge. Transfer wedges to warm serving dish. Pour hot dressing over cabbage wedges. Sprinkle with reserved bacon pieces. Garnish as desired. Serve immediately.

Makes 4 side-dish servings

Nutrients per Serving

Calories	66	
Total Fat	1	g
Cholesterol	1	mg
Sodium	36	mg

Cabbage Wedges with Tangy Hot Dressing

Warm Blackened Tuna Salad

- 5 cups torn washed romaine lettuce
- 2 cups coarsely shredded red cabbage
- 2 medium yellow or green bell peppers, cut into strips
- 1½ cups sliced zucchini
- 1 teaspoon onion powder
- ½ teaspoon garlic powder
- ½ teaspoon black pepper
- ½ teaspoon ground red pepper
- ½ teaspoon dried thyme leaves
- 12 ounces fresh or thawed frozen tuna steaks, cut 1 inch thick
- ¾ cup onion slices
- 2 tablespoons balsamic vinegar
- 1½ teaspoons Dijon mustard
- 1 teaspoon vegetable oil
- ½ teaspoon chicken bouillon granules

1. Preheat broiler. Combine romaine, cabbage, bell peppers and zucchini in large bowl; set aside.

2. Combine onion powder, garlic powder, black pepper, ground red pepper and thyme in small bowl. Rub spice mixture on both sides of tuna. Place tuna on broiler pan. Broil 4 inches from heat 6 minutes. Turn and broil 5 to 8 minutes or until tuna begins to flake easily when tested with fork. Cut tuna into bite-sized pieces; set aside.

3. For dressing, bring ⅓ cup water to a boil in small saucepan over high heat. Add onion slices; reduce heat to medium-low. Simmer, covered, 4 to 5 minutes or until onion is tender. Add vinegar, mustard, oil and bouillon granules; cook and stir until heated through.

4. Place romaine mixture on 4 individual salad plates; arrange tuna over mixture. Drizzle with dressing. Serve warm.

Makes 4 servings

Nutrients per Serving

Calories	196	
Total Fat	6	g
Cholesterol	32	mg
Sodium	185	mg

Nutmeg & Honey Carrot Crescents

Nutmeg & Honey Carrot Crescents

- 1 pound fresh carrots, cut into ¼-inch crescents
- 2 tablespoons honey
- ¼ teaspoon grated nutmeg
- 2 tablespoons chopped walnuts

1. Place carrots and ⅓ cup water in large saucepan; cover. Bring to a boil over high heat; reduce heat to medium-low. Simmer 8 minutes or until fork-tender.

2. Transfer carrots to warm serving dish. Bring remaining liquid in saucepan to a boil until liquid is almost evaporated. Add honey and nutmeg; stir. Pour over carrots. Toss gently to coat. Sprinkle with walnuts. Garnish as desired. Serve immediately.

Makes 4 side-dish servings

Nutrients per Serving

Calories	107	
Total Fat	2	g
Cholesterol	0	mg
Sodium	74	mg

Savory Matchstick Carrots

- ½ pound carrots, cut into thin strips
- 1 small turnip,* peeled and cut into thin strips
- 3 tablespoons butter or margarine, cut into pieces
- 1½ teaspoons fresh thyme *or* ½ teaspoon dried thyme leaves
- ⅛ teaspoon salt
- ⅛ teaspoon black pepper

* Or, substitute 2 additional carrots for turnip.

1. Place carrot and turnip strips in medium saucepan. Add ½ cup water; cover. Bring to a boil over high heat; reduce heat to medium. Simmer 5 to 8 minutes or until crisp-tender. Drain; set aside.

2. Melt butter over medium heat in same saucepan. Stir in thyme, salt and pepper. Return carrots and turnips to saucepan; toss gently to coat. Transfer carrot mixture to warm serving dish. Garnish as desired. Serve immediately.

Makes 4 side-dish servings

Nutrients per Serving

Calories	107	
Total Fat	9	g
Cholesterol	23	mg
Sodium	210	mg

 Carrot Cake

Carrot Cake

¼ cup walnuts, chopped
1 cup whole wheat flour
1 cup all-purpose flour
2 teaspoons baking soda
2 teaspoons ground cinnamon
½ teaspoon salt
1 whole egg
3 egg whites
1½ cups granulated sugar
¾ cup buttermilk
½ cup unsweetened applesauce
¼ cup vegetable oil
3 teaspoons vanilla, divided
2 cups grated peeled carrots
1 can (8 ounces) crushed pineapple
　 in juice, drained
1½ cups powdered sugar
1 tablespoon skim milk

1. Preheat oven to 350°F. Spray 13×9×2-inch baking pan with nonstick cooking spray. Toast walnuts 8 to 10 minutes or until golden brown. Set aside. *Do not turn off oven.*

2. Sift both flours, baking soda, cinnamon and salt together in large bowl; set aside. Lightly beat whole egg and egg whites in another large bowl. Add granulated sugar, buttermilk, applesauce, oil and 2 teaspoons vanilla; mix well. Stir in flour mixture, carrots, pineapple and walnuts.

3. Pour batter into prepared pan. Bake 45 to 50 minutes or until toothpick inserted into center comes out clean. Cool completely in pan on wire rack.

4. Combine powdered sugar, milk, 1 tablespoon water and remaining 1 teaspoon vanilla in medium bowl. Stir until smooth. Spread glaze over cooled cake.　　*Makes 15 servings*

Nutrients per Serving

Calories	263
Total Fat	5 g
Cholesterol	15 mg
Sodium	274 mg

Indian-Style Vegetable Stir-Fry

1 teaspoon vegetable oil
1 teaspoon curry powder
1 teaspoon ground cumin
⅛ teaspoon red pepper flakes
1½ teaspoons finely chopped, seeded
　 jalapeño pepper*
2 cloves garlic, minced
¾ cup chopped red bell pepper
¾ cup thinly sliced carrots
3 cups cauliflower florets
½ teaspoon salt
2 teaspoons finely chopped cilantro
　 (optional)

* Chili peppers can sting and irritate the skin; wear rubber gloves when handling peppers and do not touch eyes. Wash hands after handling chili peppers.

1. Heat oil in large nonstick skillet over medium-high heat. Add curry powder, cumin and red pepper flakes; cook and stir about 30 seconds. Stir in jalapeño and garlic. Add bell pepper and carrots; mix well to coat. Add cauliflower florets; reduce heat to medium.

2. Stir in ¼ cup water; cook and stir until water evaporates. Add an additional ¼ cup water; cover and cook about 8 to 10 minutes or until vegetables are crisp-tender, stirring occasionally.

3. Add salt; mix well. Sprinkle with cilantro, if desired. Serve immediately.
　　Makes 6 servings

Nutrients per Serving

Calories	40
Total Fat	1 g
Cholesterol	0 mg
Sodium	198 mg

Broccoli & Cauliflower with Mustard Sauce

2 cups broccoli florets
2 cups cauliflower florets
⅓ to ½ cup skim milk
1 tablespoon all-purpose flour
1½ teaspoons mustard
¼ teaspoon salt (optional)
⅛ teaspoon garlic powder
⅛ teaspoon ground white pepper

Microwave Directions:

1. Combine broccoli and cauliflower in microwavable baking dish; cover. Microwave at HIGH (100%) 8 to 11 minutes or until tender, stirring once. Drain; set aside.

2. Combine milk, flour, mustard, salt, garlic powder and pepper in medium microwavable bowl. Microwave at HIGH 2 to 3 minutes or until thickened, stirring every minute. Pour over vegetables. Toss to coat.　　*Makes 4 servings*

Nutrients per Serving

Calories	40
Total Fat	<1 g
Cholesterol	<1 mg
Sodium	55 mg

Cioppino

1 teaspoon olive oil
1 large onion, chopped
1 cup sliced celery, with tops
1 clove garlic, minced
1 fish-flavored bouillon cube
1 tablespoon salt-free Italian herb
  seasoning
¼ pound cod or other boneless
  mild-flavored fish fillets, cut into
  ½-inch pieces
¼ pound raw small shrimp
¼ pound raw bay scallops
1 large tomato, chopped
¼ cup flaked crabmeat or imitation
  crabmeat
1 can (10 ounces) baby clams, rinsed
  and drained (optional)
2 tablespoons fresh lemon juice

1. Heat oil in large saucepan over medium heat. Add onion, celery and garlic. Cook and stir 5 minutes or until onion is tender. Add 4 cups water, bouillon cube and Italian seasoning. Cover; bring to a boil over high heat.

2. Add cod, shrimp, scallops and tomato to onion mixture. Reduce heat to medium-low; simmer 10 to 15 minutes or until seafood is opaque. Add crabmeat, clams, if desired, and lemon juice. Cook until heated thoroughly. Garnish with lemon wedges, if desired.

Makes 4 servings

Nutrients per Serving

Calories	122
Total Fat	2 g
Cholesterol	75 mg
Sodium	412 mg

 Cioppino

Peach and Ricotta Filled Celery

2½ cups (1½-inch) celery pieces
 2 tablespoons coarsely chopped dried
   peaches
 ½ cup part-skim ricotta cheese
1½ teaspoons sugar
 ½ teaspoon grated lemon peel

1. Cut thin lengthwise slice from bottom of each celery piece to prevent tipping; set celery aside.

2. Add peaches to food processor or blender; process until finely chopped.

3. Add cheese, sugar and lemon peel to peaches; process until smooth. Fill celery pieces with cheese mixture. Cover; refrigerate up to 3 hours before serving.

Makes about 25 appetizers

Nutrients per Serving

Calories	10
Total Fat	<1 g
Cholesterol	2 mg
Sodium	26 mg

Celery Slaw with Cucumber-Mint Dressing

3 cups thinly sliced celery
2 cups finely chopped red or green
  cabbage
1 medium cucumber, trimmed, peeled
  and grated
1 cup plain low-fat yogurt
3 tablespoons sugar
1 to 2 tablespoons finely chopped
  fresh mint

1. Combine celery and cabbage in large bowl. Place cucumber in strainer; press out all liquid with back of spoon. Combine cucumber, yogurt, sugar and mint in small bowl; stir until sugar dissolves.

 Peasant Risotto

2. Pour dressing over celery mixture, tossing to coat. Serve immediately or refrigerate, covered, up to 1 hour. Stir well before serving.

Makes 4 servings

Nutrients per Serving

Calories	101
Total Fat	1 g
Cholesterol	4 mg
Sodium	123 mg

Peasant Risotto

- 1 teaspoon olive oil
- 3 ounces chopped low-fat turkey-ham
- 2 cloves garlic, minced
- 1 cup arborio or white short-grain rice
- 1 can (15 ounces) Great Northern beans, rinsed and drained
- ¼ cup chopped green onions with tops
- ½ teaspoon dried sage leaves
- 2 cans (14 ounces each) fat-free reduced-sodium chicken broth, heated
- 1½ cups Swiss chard, rinsed, stems removed and shredded
- ¼ cup freshly grated Parmesan cheese

1. Heat oil in large saucepan over medium heat. Add turkey-ham and garlic. Cook and stir until garlic is browned. Add rice, beans, green onions and sage; blend well. Add broth; bring to a boil. Reduce heat to low. Cook about 25 minutes or until rice is creamy, stirring frequently.

2. Add Swiss chard and cheese; mix well. Cover; remove from heat. Let stand covered 2 minutes or until Swiss chard is wilted. Serve immediately.

Makes 4 servings

Nutrients per Serving

Calories	372
Total Fat	5 g
Cholesterol	21 mg
Sodium	411 mg

Orange and Green Salad

- 3 slices whole wheat bread, cut into ½-inch cubes
  Nonstick cooking spray
- 1 clove garlic, minced
- 3 tablespoons frozen orange juice concentrate, thawed
- 3 tablespoons balsamic vinegar
- 2 teaspoons honey
- 1 clove garlic, crushed
- ½ teaspoon grated orange peel
- ½ teaspoon olive oil
- 6 cups torn washed mixed salad greens, such as chicory, escarole, arugula, radicchio, romaine, spinach and watercress
- 2 navel oranges, peeled, seeded and cut into thin slices
- ½ cup thinly sliced red onion

1. Preheat oven to 250°F. For croutons, spread bread cubes in shallow baking pan. Coat lightly with nonstick cooking spray; sprinkle with minced garlic. Bake 10 minutes. Stir bread cubes; coat lightly with nonstick cooking spray. Bake 5 minutes or until croutons are browned and crisp. Let cool to room temperature.

2. For dressing, combine orange juice concentrate, vinegar, honey, crushed garlic, orange peel and oil in medium bowl until smooth. Cover; let stand 1 hour.

3. Combine salad greens, oranges and onion in large bowl. Just before serving, remove garlic clove from dressing. Pour dressing over salad; toss gently to coat. Sprinkle with croutons.

Makes 6 servings

Note: Dressing may be stored, covered, in refrigerator up to 4 days.

Nutrients per Serving

Calories	113
Total Fat	1 g
Cholesterol	0 mg
Sodium	115 mg

Moo Shu Vegetables

½ package dried Chinese black mushrooms (6 or 7 mushrooms)
2 tablespoons vegetable oil
2 cloves garlic, minced
2 cups shredded napa or green cabbage, preshredded cabbage or coleslaw mix
1 red bell pepper, cut into short, thin strips
1 cup fresh or canned bean sprouts, rinsed and drained
2 large green onions, cut into short, thin strips
1 tablespoon teriyaki sauce
⅓ cup plum sauce
8 flour tortillas (6 to 7 inches), heated

1. Place mushrooms in small bowl; cover with warm water. Soak 20 minutes to soften. Drain; squeeze out excess water. Discard stems; slice caps.

2. Heat oil in wok or large nonstick skillet over medium heat. Add garlic; cook 30 seconds. Add cabbage, mushrooms and bell pepper; cook and stir 3 minutes. Add bean sprouts and onions; cook and stir 2 minutes. Add teriyaki sauce; cook and stir 30 seconds or until mixture is hot.

3. Spread about 2 teaspoons plum sauce on each tortilla. Spoon heaping ¼ cupful of vegetable mixture over sauce. Fold bottom of tortilla up over filling, then fold sides over filling.

Makes 8 side-dish servings

Nutrients per Serving

Calories	147	
Total Fat	4	g
Cholesterol	0	mg
Sodium	207	mg

Braised Oriental Cabbage

1 small head bok choy
½ small head green cabbage, cut into 1-inch pieces and stems trimmed
½ cup fat-free reduced-sodium chicken broth
2 tablespoons low-sodium soy sauce
2 tablespoons rice wine vinegar
1 tablespoon packed brown sugar
¼ teaspoon red pepper flakes (optional)
1 tablespoon cornstarch

1. Cut stems from bok choy leaves; slice into ½-inch pieces. Cut tops of leaves into ½-inch slices; set aside.

2. Combine cabbage and bok choy stems in large nonstick skillet. Add broth, soy sauce, vinegar, sugar and pepper flakes, if desired. Bring to a boil over high heat; reduce heat to medium. Cover; simmer 5 minutes or until vegetables are crisp-tender.

3. Blend 1 tablespoon water into cornstarch in small bowl until smooth. Stir into skillet. Bring sauce to a boil; cook and stir 1 minute or until sauce thickens. Stir in reserved bok choy leaves; cook 1 minute.

Makes 6 side-dish servings

Nutrients per Serving

Calories	34	
Total Fat	<1	g
Cholesterol	0	mg
Sodium	170	mg

❧ *Braised Oriental Cabbage*

🍃 *Cajun-Style Corn with Crayfish*

Cajun-Style Corn with Crayfish

 6 ears corn, shucked and rinsed
 1 tablespoon vegetable oil
 1 medium onion, chopped
 ½ cup chopped green bell pepper
 ½ cup chopped red bell pepper
 1 teaspoon salt
 ⅛ teaspoon black pepper
 ⅛ teaspoon ground red pepper
 ¾ pound crayfish tail meat

1. Cut corn from cobs in two or three layers. Scrape cobs to remove remaining juice and pulp.

2. Heat oil in large skillet over medium heat. Add onion and bell peppers; cook 5 minutes, stirring occasionally. Add corn, 1 cup water, salt, black pepper and ground red pepper; bring to a boil. Reduce heat to low; simmer 10 to 15 minutes.

3. Add crayfish; return mixture to a simmer. Cook 3 to 5 minutes or just until crayfish turn opaque.

Makes 6 servings

Nutrients per Serving

Calories	262
Total Fat	5 g
Cholesterol	125 mg
Sodium	631 mg

Collard Green Medley

1½ pounds collard greens, rinsed and coarsely chopped
 1 teaspoon olive oil
 1 small onion, thinly sliced
 3 large cloves garlic, minced
 ½ medium red bell pepper, cut lengthwise into ¼-inch-thick slices
 1 tablespoon lemon juice
 2 teaspoons margarine
 ¼ teaspoon salt

1. Fill large saucepan ¾ full with water; bring to a boil over high heat. Add greens; cook and stir until slightly wilted. Reduce heat to medium; cook 10 minutes or until tender, stirring occasionally. Drain in colander; rinse under cold water. Drain well, pressing out excess water. Set aside.

2. Heat oil in large nonstick skillet over medium heat. Add onion and garlic; cook and stir 2 minutes. Add pepper; cook and stir 3 minutes. Add greens, lemon juice, margarine and salt; cook and stir about 2 minutes or until heated through.

Makes 4 servings

Nutrients per Serving

Calories	94
Total Fat	3 g
Cholesterol	0 mg
Sodium	188 mg

Cob Corn in Barbecue Butter

 4 ears corn, shucked and rinsed
 2 tablespoons butter or margarine, softened
 ½ teaspoon dry barbecue seasoning
 ¼ teaspoon salt

1. Pour 3 cups water into large saucepan. (Do *not* add salt, as it will make corn tough.) Bring to a boil over medium-high heat. Add corn; cover. Cook 4 to 7 minutes or until kernels are slightly crisp when pierced with fork.*

2. Remove corn with tongs to warm serving platter. Blend butter, barbecue seasoning and salt in small bowl until smooth. Serve immediately with corn.

Makes 4 side-dish servings

* *Length of cooking time depends on size and age of corn.*

Nutrients per Serving

Calories	142
Total Fat	8 g
Cholesterol	15 mg
Sodium	238 mg

Roasted Corn & Wild Rice Salad

½ cup uncooked wild rice
1½ cups corn (about 3 medium ears)
½ cup diced seeded tomato
½ cup finely chopped yellow or green bell pepper
⅓ cup minced fresh cilantro
2 tablespoons minced seeded jalapeño pepper* (optional)
2 tablespoons fresh lime juice
2 tablespoons honey mustard
1 tablespoon olive oil
½ teaspoon ground cumin

Chili peppers can sting and irritate the skin; wear rubber gloves when handling and do not touch eyes. Wash hands after handling chili peppers.

1. Bring 1½ cups water to a boil in small saucepan over high heat. Stir in rice; cover. Reduce heat to medium-low. Simmer 40 minutes or until rice is just tender, but still firm to the bite. Drain.

2. Preheat oven to 400°F. Coat baking sheet with nonstick cooking spray. Spread corn evenly on prepared baking sheet. Bake 20 to 25 minutes or until corn is lightly browned, stirring after 15 minutes.

3. Combine rice, corn, tomato, bell pepper, cilantro and jalapeño, if desired, in large bowl. Combine lime juice, honey mustard, oil and cumin in small bowl. Drizzle mustard mixture over rice mixture; toss to coat. Cover; refrigerate 2 hours. Serve on lettuce leaves, if desired.

Makes 6 servings

Nutrients per Serving

Calories	116
Total Fat	3 g
Cholesterol	0 mg
Sodium	70 mg

Roasted Corn & Wild Rice Salad

Chilled Poached Salmon with Cucumber Sauce

½ teaspoon chicken or fish bouillon granules
⅛ teaspoon black pepper
4 (6 ounce) fresh or frozen thawed pink salmon fillets
½ cup chopped seeded peeled cucumber
⅓ cup plain low-fat yogurt
2 tablespoons sliced green onion, including tops
2 tablespoons nonfat salad dressing or mayonnaise
1 tablespoon chopped fresh cilantro *or* 1 teaspoon dried cilantro leaves
1 teaspoon Dijon mustard
2 cups shredded lettuce (optional)

1. Combine 1 cup water, bouillon granules and pepper in large skillet. Bring to a boil over high heat. Carefully place salmon in skillet. Return to a boil. Reduce heat to medium-low. Cover; simmer 8 to 10 minutes or until salmon flakes easily when tested with fork. Remove salmon. Cover and refrigerate.

2. Meanwhile, combine cucumber, yogurt, onion, salad dressing, cilantro and mustard in small bowl. Cover and refrigerate.

3. Serve chilled salmon fillets on lettuce-lined plates, if desired. Spoon sauce over salmon.

Makes 4 servings

Nutrients per Serving

Calories	223
Total Fat	6 g
Cholesterol	89 mg
Sodium	322 mg

Singapore Rice Salad

Singapore Rice Salad

1 can (8 ounces) pineapple tidbits or chunks in pineapple juice, undrained
3 cups chilled cooked rice
1 cup diced cucumber
1 red bell pepper, diced
1 cup shredded carrots
½ cup sliced green onions, including tops
2 tablespoons fresh lime juice
2 tablespoons dry sherry
1 tablespoon rice wine vinegar
1 teaspoon minced fresh ginger root
2 tablespoons chopped fresh cilantro
1 tablespoon chopped unsalted peanuts

1. Drain pineapple, reserving 3 tablespoons juice. Combine rice, cucumber, bell pepper, carrots, onions and pineapple in large bowl.

2. Combine lime juice, sherry, vinegar, ginger and reserved pineapple juice in small bowl; mix well. Pour over rice mixture; toss to coat. Cover and refrigerate at least 2 hours or up to 12 hours. Sprinkle with cilantro and peanuts before serving. Garnish with cucumber slices, if desired.

Makes 6 side-dish servings

Nutrients per Serving

Calories	188
Total Fat	1 g
Cholesterol	0 mg
Sodium	367 mg

Cucumber Salad

½ cup plain nonfat yogurt
1 teaspoon dried mint leaves
½ teaspoon sugar
2 cucumbers, thinly sliced

Combine yogurt, mint and sugar in small bowl. Add cucumbers to yogurt mixture; toss to coat. Serve immediately.

Makes 4 servings

Nutrients per Serving

Calories	37
Total Fat	<1 g
Cholesterol	1 mg
Sodium	25 mg

*Favorite recipe from **The Sugar Association, Inc.***

Italian Tomato and Dandelion Greens Soup

2 cans (14½ ounces each) no-salt-added stewed tomatoes, undrained
1 cup frozen vegetable combination, such as zucchini, carrots, cauliflower, lima beans and Italian beans
1 cup low-sodium tomato juice
1 tablespoon onion powder
1 teaspoon sugar
1 teaspoon dried oregano leaves
½ teaspoon dried basil leaves
¼ teaspoon garlic powder
¼ teaspoon black pepper
2 cups packed torn stemmed washed dandelion greens
¼ cup grated Parmesan cheese

1. Combine tomatoes with liquid, frozen vegetables, tomato juice, 1 cup water, onion powder, sugar, oregano, basil, garlic powder and pepper in large saucepan. Bring to a boil over high heat. Reduce heat to low. Simmer, covered, 5 to 6 minutes or until vegetables are tender, stirring occasionally.

2. Stir in dandelion greens. Cook about 1 minute or until greens wilt. Top each serving evenly with cheese.

Makes 4 servings

Nutrients per Serving

Calories	135
Total Fat	3 g
Cholesterol	5 mg
Sodium	178 mg

Plum Ratatouille

1 tablespoon vegetable oil
2½ cups diced eggplant
2 cups sliced zucchini
1 onion, cut into wedges
2 cups diced tomatoes
2 cups fresh plum wedges
2 teaspoons minced garlic
1½ teaspoons dried basil leaves
1 teaspoon dried oregano leaves
¼ teaspoon black pepper
Fresh lemon juice

1. Heat oil in large nonstick skillet over medium heat. Add eggplant, zucchini and onion; cook and stir 15 minutes or until tender. Add tomatoes, plums, garlic, basil, oregano and pepper. Reduce heat to low; cover.

2. Cook, stirring occasionally, about 4 minutes or until plum tomatoes are tender. Drizzle with fresh lemon juice just before serving. *Makes 6 servings*

Nutrients per Serving

Calories	69
Total Fat	3 g
Cholesterol	0 mg
Sodium	4 mg

*Favorite recipe from **California Tree Fruit Agreement***

Roasted Eggplant Dip

- 2 eggplants (about 1 pound each)
- 3 tablespoons tahini*
- ¼ cup lemon juice
- 4 cloves garlic, minced
- 2 teaspoons hot pepper sauce
- ½ teaspoon salt
  Paprika
- 1 tablespoon chopped fresh parsley
  Pita bread wedges

Tahini can be found in the ethnic section of the supermarket or in Middle Eastern grocery stores.

1. Prick eggplants in several places with fork. To roast over charcoal, place eggplants on grill over hot coals; cook about 30 to 40 minutes or until skin is black and blistered and pulp is soft, turning often. To roast in oven, preheat oven to 450°F. Place eggplants on baking sheet; bake about 30 to 40 minutes or until skin is blistered and pulp is soft. Peel eggplants when cool enough to handle. Let cool to room temperature.

2. Place eggplant pulp in food processor with tahini, lemon juice, garlic, pepper sauce and salt; process until smooth. Refrigerate at least 1 hour before serving to allow flavors to blend. Sprinkle dip with paprika and parsley; serve with pita bread wedges. Garnish with red chili pepper slices, if desired.

Makes 8 (¼-cup) servings

Nutrients per Serving

Calories	49	
Total Fat	2	g
Cholesterol	0	mg
Sodium	144	mg

Italian Eggplant with Millet and Peppers Stuffing

- ¼ cup uncooked millet
- 2 small eggplants (about ¾ pound total)
- ¼ cup chopped red bell pepper, divided
- ¼ cup chopped green bell pepper, divided
- 1 teaspoon olive oil
- 1 clove garlic, minced
- ⅔ cup fat-free reduced-sodium chicken broth
- ½ teaspoon ground cumin
- ½ teaspoon dried oregano leaves
- ⅛ teaspoon red pepper flakes

1. Heat large heavy nonstick skillet over medium heat. Add millet; cook and stir 5 minutes or until golden. Transfer to small bowl; set aside.

2. Cut eggplants lengthwise into halves. Scoop out flesh, leaving shells about ¼ inch thick; reserve shells. Chop eggplant flesh. Combine 1 teaspoon red bell pepper and 1 teaspoon green bell pepper in small bowl; set aside.

3. Heat oil in same skillet over medium heat. Add eggplant flesh, remaining red and green bell peppers and garlic; cook and stir about 8 minutes or until eggplant is tender.

4. Stir in toasted millet, chicken broth, cumin, oregano and red pepper flakes. Bring to a boil over high heat. Reduce heat to medium-low. Cook, covered, 20 minutes or until all liquid has been absorbed and millet is tender. Remove from heat; let stand, covered, 10 minutes.

5. Preheat oven to 350°F. Pour 1 cup water into 8-inch square baking pan. Fill reserved eggplant shells with eggplant-millet mixture. Sprinkle shells with reserved chopped bell peppers, pressing lightly. Carefully place filled shells in pan. Bake 15 minutes or until heated through. Serve immediately.

Makes 4 servings

Nutrients per Serving

Calories	89	
Total Fat	2	g
Cholesterol	0	mg
Sodium	130	mg

Garlicky Chicken Packets

- 1 cup julienned carrots
- ½ cup sliced onion
- 2 whole boneless skinless chicken breasts
- ¼ cup chopped fresh basil *or* 1 tablespoon dried basil leaves
- 2 tablespoons reduced-calorie mayonnaise
- 6 cloves garlic, minced
- ⅛ teaspoon black pepper

1. Cut parchment paper or foil into four 12-inch squares. Fold squares in half, then cut into shape of half hearts. Open parchment to form whole hearts.

2. Preheat oven to 400°F. Place carrots and onion on 1 side of each parchment heart near fold. Remove all fat from chicken breasts; cut in half. Combine basil, mayonnaise, garlic and pepper in small cup; spread mixture over chicken. Place chicken, mayonnaise side up, over carrot mixture.

3. Fold parchment over chicken; seal by creasing and folding edges of parchment in small overlapping sections from top of heart until completed at point. Finish by twisting point and tucking under.

4. Place parchment packages on ungreased baking sheet. Bake 20 to 25 minutes or until juices run clear and chicken is no longer pink in center.

Makes 4 servings

Nutrients per Serving

Calories	192	
Total Fat	5	g
Cholesterol	75	mg
Sodium	82	mg

🌿 *Roasted Eggplant Dip*

Spicy Island Chicken

1 cup finely chopped white onion
⅓ cup white wine vinegar
6 green onions, including tops, finely chopped
6 cloves garlic, minced
1 habañero or serrano pepper, finely chopped*
4½ teaspoons fresh thyme *or* 2 teaspoons dried thyme leaves
4½ teaspoons olive oil
1 tablespoon ground allspice
2 teaspoons sugar
1 teaspoon salt
1 teaspoon ground cinnamon
1 teaspoon ground nutmeg
1 teaspoon black pepper
½ teaspoon ground red pepper
6 boneless skinless chicken breast halves

* Chili peppers can sting and irritate the skin; wear rubber gloves when handling and do not touch eyes. Wash hands after handling chili peppers.

1. Combine white onion, vinegar, green onions, garlic, habañero pepper, thyme, oil, allspice, sugar, salt, cinnamon, nutmeg, black pepper and ground red pepper in medium bowl; mix well.

2. Place chicken in resealable plastic food storage bag and add seasoning mixture; turn bag to coat. Marinate in refrigerator 4 hours or overnight.

3. Spray cold grid with nonstick cooking spray. Adjust grid to 4 to 6 inches above heat. Preheat grill to medium-high heat.

4. Remove chicken from marinade. Grill 5 to 7 minutes per side or until chicken is no longer pink in center, brushing occasionally with marinade. Discard remaining marinade.

Makes 6 servings

Nutrients per Serving

Calories	203
Total Fat	7 g
Cholesterol	73 mg
Sodium	421 mg

Roasted Garlic Hummus

2 heads garlic
1 can (15 ounces) chick-peas, rinsed and drained
¼ cup parsley, stems removed
2 tablespoons lemon juice
½ teaspoon curry powder
3 drops sesame oil
Dash hot pepper sauce

1. To roast garlic, preheat oven to 400°F. Place garlic in small baking pan; bake 30 to 40 minutes or until garlic cloves are soft. When garlic is cool enough to handle, squeeze cloves to release garlic; discard skins.

2. Place 2 tablespoons roasted garlic, chick-peas, parsley, lemon juice, 2 tablespoons water, curry powder, sesame oil and pepper sauce in food processor or blender; process until smooth, scraping down side of bowl once.

Makes 6 servings (1¼ cups)

Note: Serve with pita bread triangles or crackers.

Nutrients per Serving

Calories	84	
Total Fat	1	g
Cholesterol	0	mg
Sodium	302	mg

Barbecued Pork Sandwiches

2 pork tenderloins (about 1½ pounds total)
⅓ cup barbecue sauce
½ cup prepared horseradish
4 pita bread rounds, cut into halves
1 onion, thinly sliced
4 romaine lettuce leaves
1 red bell pepper, cut lengthwise into ¼-inch-thick slices
1 green bell pepper, cut lengthwise into ¼-inch-thick slices

1. Preheat oven to 400°F. Place pork tenderloins in medium roasting pan; brush with barbecue sauce.

2. Bake tenderloins 15 minutes; turn and bake 15 minutes or until internal temperature reaches 155°F. Cover with foil; let stand 15 minutes.

3. Slice pork across the grain. Spread horseradish on pita bread halves; stuff with pork, onion, lettuce and bell peppers. *Makes 4 servings*

Nutrients per Serving

Calories	440	
Total Fat	9	g
Cholesterol	12	mg
Sodium	628	mg

🍂 *Spicy Island Chicken*

Grilled Flank Steak with Horseradish Sauce

1 pound beef flank steak
2 tablespoons low-sodium soy sauce
1 tablespoon red wine vinegar
2 cloves garlic, minced
½ teaspoon black pepper
1 cup nonfat sour cream
1 tablespoon prepared horseradish
1 tablespoon Dijon mustard
¼ cup finely chopped fresh parsley
½ teaspoon salt
6 sourdough rolls, split
6 romaine lettuce leaves

1. Place flank steak in large resealable plastic food storage bag. Add soy sauce, vinegar, garlic and pepper. Close bag securely; turn to coat. Refrigerate at least 1 hour.

2. Prepare grill or preheat broiler. Drain steak; discard marinade. Grill or broil over medium-high heat 5 minutes. Turn steak; grill 6 minutes for medium-rare or until desired doneness. Cover with foil; let stand 15 minutes. Thinly slice steak across the grain.

3. Combine sour cream, horseradish, mustard, parsley and salt in small bowl until well blended. Spread rolls with horseradish sauce; layer with sliced steak and lettuce. Garnish with small pickles, if desired. *Makes 6 servings*

Nutrients per Serving

Calories	220
Total Fat	6 g
Cholesterol	35 mg
Sodium	542 mg

Grilled Flank Steak with Horseradish Sauce

Picante Pintos and Rice

2 cups dried pinto beans
1 can (14½ ounces) no-salt-added stewed tomatoes, undrained
1 cup coarsely chopped onion
¾ cup coarsely chopped green bell pepper
¼ cup sliced celery
4 cloves garlic, minced
½ small jalapeño pepper, seeded and chopped*
2 teaspoons dried oregano leaves
2 teaspoons chili powder
½ teaspoon ground red pepper
2 cups chopped kale
3 cups cooked rice

* Chili peppers can sting and irritate the skin; wear rubber gloves when handling and do not touch eyes. Wash hands after handling chili peppers.

1. Place beans in large saucepan; add water to 2 inch depth. Bring to a boil over high heat; boil 2 minutes. Remove pan from heat; let stand, covered, 1 hour. Drain beans; discard water. Return to saucepan.

2. Add 2 cups water, tomatoes, onion, bell pepper, celery, garlic, jalapeño, oregano, chili powder and ground red pepper to saucepan; bring to a boil over high heat. Reduce heat to low. Simmer, covered, about 1½ hours or until beans are tender, stirring occasionally.

3. Gently stir kale into bean mixture. Simmer, uncovered, 30 minutes. (Beans will be very tender and mixture will have consistency of thick sauce.) Serve over rice. *Makes 8 servings*

Nutrients per Serving

Calories	386
Total Fat	2 g
Cholesterol	0 mg
Sodium	83 mg

Smoky Kale Chiffonade

¾ pound fresh young kale or mustard
   greens, rinsed and stemmed
3 slices uncooked bacon
2 tablespoons crumbled blue cheese

1. To prepare chiffonade,* roll up 1 kale leaf jelly-roll style. Slice crosswise into ½-inch-thick slices with chef's knife; separate into strips. Repeat with remaining leaves. Set aside.

2. Cook bacon in medium skillet over medium heat until crisp. Remove bacon to paper towel. Add reserved kale to drippings in skillet. Cook and stir over medium-high heat 2 to 3 minutes or until wilted and tender (older leaves may take slightly longer.**)

3. Crumble bacon. Toss bacon and blue cheese with kale. Transfer to warm serving dish. Serve immediately.

Makes 4 side-dish servings

* *"Chiffonade" in French literally means "made of rags." In cooking, it means "cut into thin strips."*

** *If using mustard greens, cook and stir 4 to 6 minutes or until wilted and tender.*

Nutrients per Serving

Calories	73	
Total Fat	4	g
Cholesterol	7	mg
Sodium	150	mg

Kohlrabi with Red Peppers

3 tablespoons cider vinegar
2 teaspoons olive oil
1 tablespoon sugar
1 clove garlic, minced
½ teaspoon dried tarragon leaves
⅛ teaspoon black pepper
2 pounds kohlrabies, peeled and
   sliced
¾ cup sliced red bell pepper
½ cup sliced onion

Combine vinegar, 3 tablespoons water, oil, sugar, garlic, tarragon and black pepper in large skillet. Bring to a boil over high heat. Add kohlrabies, bell pepper and onion; reduce heat to low. Cover; simmer, about 20 minutes or until kohlrabies are crisp-tender, stirring occasionally.

Makes 4 servings

Nutrients per Serving

Calories	76	
Total Fat	2	g
Cholesterol	0	mg
Sodium	24	mg

Kohlrabi and Carrot Slaw

2 pounds kohlrabies, peeled and
   shredded
2 medium carrots, shredded
1 small red bell pepper, chopped
8 cherry tomatoes, cut into halves
2 green onions, thinly sliced
¼ cup fat-free mayonnaise
¼ cup plain nonfat yogurt
2 tablespoons cider vinegar
2 tablespoons finely chopped fresh
   parsley
1 teaspoon dried dill weed
¼ teaspoon ground cumin
¼ teaspoon salt
⅛ teaspoon black pepper

1. Combine kohlrabies, carrots, bell pepper, tomatoes and green onions in medium bowl.

2. Combine mayonnaise, yogurt, vinegar, parsley, dill, cumin, salt and black pepper in small bowl until smooth. Add to vegetable mixture; toss to coat evenly. Cover; refrigerate until ready to serve.

Makes 8 servings

Nutrients per Serving

Calories	37	
Total Fat	<1	g
Cholesterol	<1	mg
Sodium	154	mg

Leek Cheese Pie

⅔ cup thinly sliced leek
1 clove garlic, minced
1 cup all-purpose flour
2 teaspoons baking powder
4 egg whites, divided
¼ cup skim milk
1½ tablespoons vegetable oil
¼ cup reduced-calorie soft cream
   cheese
1 carton (12 ounces) dry curd cottage
   cheese
¾ cup shredded carrots
2 tablespoons fine dry bread crumbs
2 tablespoons chopped fresh basil *or*
   2 teaspoons dried basil leaves
¼ teaspoon black pepper

1. Preheat oven to 325°F. Spray 9-inch pie plate with nonstick cooking spray. Combine leek, ¼ cup water and garlic in small saucepan. Bring to a boil over high heat. Reduce heat to medium-low. Cover; simmer 3 to 4 minutes or until leek is tender. Drain.

2. Combine flour and baking powder in medium bowl. Stir in leek mixture, 2 egg whites, milk and oil until almost smooth. Spread half of batter into prepared pie plate. Bake 20 to 22 minutes or until crust starts to brown.

3. Meanwhile, combine remaining 2 egg whites and cream cheese in medium bowl. Stir in cottage cheese, carrots, bread crumbs, basil and pepper. Spread over crust in pie plate. Spoon remaining batter over cottage cheese mixture. Bake 40 to 45 minutes or until golden brown. Let stand 10 minutes before serving.

Makes 6 servings

Nutrients per Serving

Calories	215	
Total Fat	6	g
Cholesterol	7	mg
Sodium	236	mg

Mexican Hot Pot

1 tablespoon vegetable oil
1 onion, sliced
3 cloves garlic, minced
2 teaspoons red pepper flakes
2 teaspoons dried oregano leaves
1 teaspoon ground cumin
1 can (28 ounces) tomatoes, chopped and undrained
1 can (15 ounces) chick-peas, rinsed and drained
1 can (15 ounces) pinto beans, rinsed and drained
2 cups corn, fresh or frozen
6 cups shredded iceberg lettuce

1. Heat oil in stockpot or Dutch oven over medium-high heat. Add onion and garlic; cook and stir 5 minutes. Add red pepper flakes, oregano and cumin; mix well.

2. Stir in tomatoes, chick-peas, pinto beans, corn and 1 cup water; bring to a boil over high heat. Reduce heat to medium-low. Cover; simmer 15 minutes. Top individual servings with 1 cup shredded lettuce. Serve hot.

Makes 6 servings

Nutrients per Serving

Calories	252
Total Fat	5 g
Cholesterol	0 mg
Sodium	765 mg

🥢 *Mexican Hot Pot*

Salad Primavera

Citrus-Caper Dressing (recipe follows)
6 cups romaine lettuce, washed and torn into bite-sized pieces
1 package (9 ounces) frozen artichoke hearts, thawed, drained and cut into bite-sized pieces
1 cup chopped watercress
1 orange, peeled, separated into segments and cut into halves
½ cup chopped red bell pepper
¼ cup chopped green onions, including tops
2 tablespoons freshly grated Parmesan cheese

1. Prepare Citrus-Caper Dressing.

2. Combine lettuce, artichoke hearts, watercress, orange segments, bell pepper and green onions in large bowl. Add dressing to lettuce mixture. Mix well. Sprinkle with cheese before serving.

Makes 8 servings

Citrus-Caper Dressing

⅓ cup orange juice
¼ cup white wine vinegar
2 tablespoons chopped fresh parsley
2 teaspoons Dijon mustard
¼ teaspoon olive oil
1 tablespoon minced capers
1 teaspoon sugar
1 teaspoon minced fresh garlic
¼ teaspoon black pepper

Combine all ingredients in jar or bottle with tight-fitting lid; shake well. Refrigerate until ready to serve. Shake well before using.

Makes ½ cup dressing

Nutrients per Serving

Calories	55
Total Fat	1 g
Cholesterol	1 mg
Sodium	102 mg

Chicken, Tortellini and Roasted Vegetable Salad

3 cups whole medium mushrooms
2 cups cubed zucchini
2 cups cubed eggplant
¾ cup red onion wedges
  Sun-Dried Tomato and Basil
    Vinaigrette (recipe follows)
1½ packages (9 ounces each) reduced-
    fat cheese tortellini
6 cups bite-sized pieces leaf lettuce
    and arugula
1 pound boneless skinless chicken
    breasts, cooked and cut into
    1×½-inch pieces

1. Preheat oven to 425°F. Place mushrooms, zucchini, eggplant and onion in 15×10-inch jelly-roll pan. Spray vegetables with nonstick cooking spray; toss to coat evenly. Bake 20 to 25 minutes or until vegetables are browned. Cool to room temperature.

2. Meanwhile, prepare Sun-Dried Tomato and Basil Vinaigrette. Cook tortellini according to package directions; drain. Cool to room temperature.

3. Combine roasted vegetables, tortellini, lettuce and chicken in large bowl. Drizzle with vinaigrette; toss to coat evenly. Serve immediately.　　　*Makes 8 servings*

Sun-Dried Tomato and Basil Vinaigrette

4 sun-dried tomato halves, not packed
    in oil
  Hot water
½ cup fat-free reduced-sodium
    chicken broth
2 tablespoons finely chopped fresh
    basil *or* 2 teaspoons dried basil
    leaves
2 tablespoons olive oil
2 tablespoons lemon juice
1 clove garlic, minced
¼ teaspoon salt
¼ teaspoon black pepper

1. Place sun-dried tomatoes in small bowl. Pour hot water over tomatoes to cover. Let stand 10 to 15 minutes or until tomatoes are soft. Drain well; chop tomatoes.

2. Combine tomatoes and remaining ingredients in small jar with tight-fitting lid; shake well. Refrigerate until ready to use. Shake well before using.
　　　Makes about 1 cup dressing

Nutrients per Serving

Calories	210
Total Fat	7 g
Cholesterol	31 mg
Sodium	219 mg

Minted Melon Soup

1 tablespoon sugar
1½ cups fresh mint, including stems
2 fresh basil leaves
1½ cups diced cantaloupe
4 teaspoons fresh lemon juice, divided
1½ cups diced and seeded watermelon

1. Combine 1 cup water and sugar in small saucepan; mix well. Bring to a boil over medium heat. Add mint and basil; simmer 10 minutes or until liquid is reduced by two thirds. Remove from heat.

Cover; let stand at least 2 hours or until cool. Strain liquid; set aside.

2. Place cantaloupe in blender or food processor; process until smooth. Add 2 tablespoons mint syrup and 2 teaspoons lemon juice. Blend to mix well. Pour into air-tight container. Cover and refrigerate until cold. Repeat procedure with watermelon, 2 teaspoons mint syrup and remaining 2 teaspoons lemon juice. Discard any remaining mint syrup.

3. To serve, simultaneously pour ¼ cup of each melon soup, side by side, into serving bowl. Place 1 mint sprig in center for garnish, if desired. Repeat with remaining soup.
　　　Makes 4 appetizer servings

Nutrients per Serving

Calories	48
Total Fat	<1 g
Cholesterol	0 mg
Sodium	7 mg

✒ *Chicken, Tortellini and Roasted Vegetable Salad*

Crab and Pasta Salad in Cantaloupe

1½ cups uncooked rotini pasta
1 cup seedless green grapes
½ cup chopped celery
½ cup fresh pineapple chunks
1 small red onion, coarsely chopped
6 ounces canned, fresh or frozen crabmeat, drained
½ cup plain nonfat yogurt
¼ cup mayonnaise
2 tablespoons lemon juice
2 tablespoons honey
2 teaspoons grated lemon peel
1 teaspoon Dijon mustard
2 small cantaloupes

1. Cook rotini according to package directions; drain. Rinse under cold water; drain.

2. Combine grapes, celery, pineapple, onion and crabmeat in large bowl. Combine yogurt, mayonnaise, lemon juice, honey, lemon peel and mustard in small bowl. Add yogurt mixture and pasta to crabmeat mixture; toss to coat evenly. Cover; refrigerate.

3. Cut cantaloupes into halves. Remove and discard seeds. Remove some of cantaloupe with spoon, leaving a shell about ¾ inch thick. Fill cantaloupe shells with salad. *Makes 4 servings*

Nutrients per Serving

Calories	331	
Total Fat	6	g
Cholesterol	42	mg
Sodium	463	mg

🦐 *Crab and Pasta Salad in Cantaloupe*

Garlicky Mustard Greens

2 pounds mustard greens
1 teaspoon olive oil
1 cup chopped onion
2 cloves garlic, minced
¾ cup chopped red bell pepper
½ cup fat-free reduced-sodium chicken broth
1 tablespoon cider vinegar
1 teaspoon sugar

1. Wash greens well; remove stems and any wilted leaves. Stack several leaves; roll up jelly-roll style. Cut crosswise into 1-inch slices. Repeat with remaining greens.

2. Heat oil in Dutch oven or large saucepan over medium heat. Add onion and garlic; cook and stir 5 minutes or until onion is tender. Stir in greens, bell pepper and chicken broth. Reduce heat to low. Cover; cook 25 minutes or until greens are tender, stirring occasionally.

3. Stir vinegar and sugar in small cup until sugar is dissolved. Stir into cooked greens; remove from heat. Serve immediately. *Makes 4 servings*

Nutrients per Serving

Calories	71	
Total Fat	2	g
Cholesterol	0	mg
Sodium	41	mg

🌶 *Shrimp Okra Gumbo*

Cajun-Style Chicken Soup

1½ pounds chicken thighs
4 cups chicken broth
1 can (8 ounces) tomato sauce
2 ribs celery, sliced
1 medium onion, chopped
2 cloves garlic, minced
2 bay leaves
1 to 1½ teaspoons salt
½ teaspoon ground cumin
¼ teaspoon paprika
¼ teaspoon black pepper
¼ teaspoon ground red pepper
⅛ teaspoon ground white pepper
1 large green bell pepper, chopped
⅓ cup uncooked rice
8 ounces fresh or frozen okra, cut into
    ½-inch slices
    Hot pepper sauce (optional)

1. Place chicken, broth, tomato sauce, celery, onion, garlic, bay leaves, salt, cumin, paprika, black pepper, ground red pepper and ground white pepper in 5-quart Dutch oven. Bring to a boil over high heat. Reduce heat to medium-low. Simmer, uncovered, 1 hour or until chicken is tender, skimming foam that rises to surface.

2. Remove chicken from soup and let cool slightly. Skim fat from soup and discard. Remove chicken meat from bones; discard skin and bones. Cut chicken into bite-sized pieces.

3. Add chicken, bell pepper and rice to soup. Bring to a boil over high heat. Reduce heat to medium-low. Simmer, uncovered, about 12 minutes or until rice is tender. Add okra; simmer 8 minutes or until okra is tender. Discard bay leaves. Ladle soup into bowls. Serve with hot pepper sauce, if desired.

Makes 6 servings

Nutrients per Serving

Calories	363	
Total Fat	18	g
Cholesterol	107	mg
Sodium	1341	mg

Shrimp Okra Gumbo

¼ cup plus 1 tablespoon vegetable oil,
    divided
¼ cup all-purpose flour
1 medium onion, chopped
1 small green bell pepper, chopped
2 cloves garlic, minced
1 can (14½ ounces) tomatoes, cut-up
    and undrained
½ teaspoon dried thyme leaves
½ teaspoon salt
¼ teaspoon ground red pepper
2 bay leaves
8 ounces fresh or frozen okra, cut into
    ¾-inch slices
1 pound medium raw shrimp, peeled
5 cups hot cooked rice

1. To make roux, cook and stir ¼ cup oil and flour in medium saucepan over medium-low heat 20 minutes or until mixture is tannish-brown color; set aside.

2. Heat remaining 1 tablespoon oil in 5-quart Dutch oven or large saucepan over medium-high heat. Add onion, bell pepper and garlic; cook and stir until vegetables are crisp-tender.

3. Stir in 2½ cups water, tomatoes with liquid, thyme, salt, red pepper and bay leaves. Bring to a boil over high heat. Reduce heat to medium-low; simmer, uncovered, 15 minutes.

4. Stir roux and okra into tomato mixture. Bring to a boil over high heat. Reduce heat to medium-low. Simmer, uncovered, 20 minutes, stirring occasionally.

5. Add shrimp to gumbo and cook 5 minutes or until shrimp turn pink and opaque. Discard bay leaf. Serve gumbo over cooked rice. *Makes 5 servings*

Nutrients per Serving

Calories	467	
Total Fat	15	g
Cholesterol	140	mg
Sodium	511	mg

🦐 *Cajun-Style Chicken Soup*

 *Chicken Étouffée*

Chicken Étouffée

Dry Roux (recipe follows)
¾ teaspoon salt
½ teaspoon ground red pepper
¼ teaspoon black pepper
4 skinless chicken breast halves
1 tablespoon vegetable oil
3 cups chopped yellow onions
½ cup chopped green bell pepper
3 large cloves garlic, minced
3 cups reduced-sodium chicken broth
¼ cup chopped green onions
Hot cooked rice

1. Prepare Dry Roux. Combine salt, ground red pepper and black pepper in cup; sprinkle 1 teaspoon mixture over chicken. Heat oil in large heavy skillet over medium heat. Add chicken; cover and cook about 20 minutes or until browned on all sides, draining any liquid from pan halfway through cooking time.

2. Remove chicken from skillet. Add yellow onions and bell pepper; cover and cook 10 to 15 minutes or until onions begin to brown, stirring occasionally. Add ⅓ cup water and increase heat to medium-high. Cook about 10 minutes or until mixture begins to stick and brown again, stirring frequently and watching carefully to prevent burning. Add ⅓ cup water; cook and stir until mixture begins to stick and brown again. Add ⅓ cup water and garlic; cook until mixture begins to stick and brown again, stirring frequently.

3. Stir in broth; bring to a boil over medium-high heat. Quickly whisk in Dry Roux until smooth and well mixed; cook 5 minutes. Add chicken and remaining ½ teaspoon salt mixture to skillet; bring to a boil.

4. Reduce heat to medium-low. Simmer about 15 minutes or until mixture is thickened and chicken is no longer pink in center. Sprinkle with green onions. Serve over rice. Garnish as desired.

Makes 4 servings

Dry Roux

⅓ cup all-purpose flour

Heat medium nonstick skillet over medium-high heat about 3 minutes. Add flour to skillet; cook 10 to 15 minutes or until flour turns the color of peanut butter or light cinnamon, stirring frequently to prevent burning. Sift flour into small bowl; set aside.

Nutrients per Serving

Calories	279
Total Fat	7 g
Cholesterol	73 mg
Sodium	497 mg

Onions Baked in Their Papers

4 medium-size yellow onions (about 2½ inches in diameter)*
1½ teaspoons mixed dry herbs, such as thyme, sage and tarragon leaves
1 teaspoon sugar
½ teaspoon salt
⅛ teaspoon red pepper flakes
¼ cup butter or margarine, melted
½ cup fresh bread crumbs

* Choose onions with skins intact.

1. Preheat oven to 400°F. Line square baking pan with foil; set aside. Slice off stem and root ends of onions. Cut 1½×1½-inch cone-shaped indentation in top of each onion with paring knife. Place onions, root end down, in prepared pan.

2. Stir herbs, sugar, salt and pepper flakes into melted butter. Add bread crumbs; mix until blended. Spoon equal amounts of crumb mixture into indentations in onions.

3. Bake about 1 hour or until fork-tender. Garnish with fresh tarragon sprigs, yellow squash strips, red bell pepper strips and chives, if desired. Serve immediately.

Makes 4 side-dish servings

Nutrients per Serving

Calories	181
Total Fat	12 g
Cholesterol	31 mg
Sodium	416 mg

🖙 *Onions Baked in Their Papers*

Parsnip Patties

1 pound fresh parsnips, peeled and
    cut into ¾-inch pieces
4 tablespoons butter or margarine,
    divided
¼ cup chopped onion
¼ cup all-purpose flour
⅓ cup milk
2 teaspoons chopped chives
    Salt and pepper
¾ cup fresh bread crumbs
2 tablespoons vegetable oil

1. Pour water to depth of 1 inch into
medium saucepan. Bring to a boil over
high heat; add parsnips. Cover; boil 10
minutes or until parsnips are fork-tender.
Drain. Place in large bowl. Coarsely mash
with fork; set aside.

2. Heat 2 tablespoons butter in small
skillet over medium-high heat until
melted and bubbly. Add onion; cook and
stir until transparent. Stir in flour with
wire whisk; heat until bubbly and lightly
browned. Whisk in milk; heat until
thickened. Stir onion mixture and chives
into mashed parsnips; season with salt
and pepper to taste.

3. Form parsnip mixture into 4 patties.
Spread bread crumbs on plate. Dip
patties in bread crumbs to coat sides
evenly. Press crumbs firmly into patties.
Place on waxed paper and refrigerate
2 hours.

4. Heat remaining 2 tablespoons butter
and oil in 12-inch nonstick skillet over
medium-high heat until butter is melted
and bubbly. Add patties; cook about 5
minutes on each side or until browned.
Transfer to warm dish. Garnish as
desired. *Makes 4 side-dish servings*

Nutrients per Serving

Calories	320	
Total Fat	19	g
Cholesterol	32	mg
Sodium	182	mg

🍃 *Beef and Parsnip Stew*

Beef and Parsnip Stew

1¼ pounds beef stew meat
 ½ cup all-purpose flour
 2 tablespoons vegetable oil
4½ cups beef broth
 ½ cup dry red wine
 1 teaspoon salt
 ½ teaspoon dried Italian seasoning
 ⅛ teaspoon black pepper
 8 ounces peeled baby carrots
 2 fresh parsnips
 ¾ cup sugar snap peas

1. Trim meat and discard fat. Cut meat
into ¾-inch cubes; coat with flour. Heat
oil in large saucepan over medium-high
heat. Add beef and any remaining coating
flour; brown, stirring frequently.

2. Stir in broth, wine, salt, Italian
seasoning and pepper. Bring to a boil over
high heat. Reduce heat to medium-low.
Simmer, uncovered, 1 hour.

3. Add carrots. Cook 15 minutes.
Meanwhile, peel parsnips; cut into
⅜-inch slices, halving any large pieces.
Add parsnip slices to stew. Simmer 8
minutes or until vegetables and meat are
tender. Stir in peas. Cook and stir over
medium heat until heated through.
Makes 5 servings

Nutrients per Serving

Calories	368	
Total Fat	12	g
Cholesterol	71	mg
Sodium	1286	mg

Hoppin' John Salad

3 cups dried black-eyed peas
3 cups cooked rice
¼ pound cooked Canadian bacon, finely chopped
1 small red onion, finely chopped
1 rib celery, thinly sliced
2 tablespoons red wine vinegar
1 tablespoon vegetable oil
1 clove garlic, minced
1 teaspoon hot pepper sauce
½ teaspoon salt

1. Rinse peas in colander, picking out any debris. Place 3 quarts water and black-eyed peas in 5-quart Dutch oven; bring to a boil over high heat. Reduce heat to medium-low. Cover; simmer 1 hour or until peas are tender. Rinse with cool water; drain. Cool.

2. Combine peas, rice, bacon, onion and celery in large bowl. Combine vinegar, oil, garlic, hot sauce and salt in small bowl until well blended. Drizzle over pea mixture; toss to coat. Cover; refrigerate 2 hours. Garnish as desired.

Makes 6 servings

Nutrients per Serving

Calories	242
Total Fat	4 g
Cholesterol	7 mg
Sodium	376 mg

🌿 *Hoppin' John Salad*

Green Pea and Potato Soup

1 can (about 14 ounces) fat-free reduced-sodium chicken broth
1 cup diced peeled potato
1 cup fresh or frozen green peas
½ cup sliced green onion tops
2 leaves green leaf lettuce, chopped
1 teaspoon dried dill weed
⅛ teaspoon ground white pepper
1½ cups buttermilk
Dash paprika

1. Combine broth, potato, peas, green onions, lettuce, dill and pepper in medium saucepan. Bring to a boil over high heat. Reduce heat to medium. Cover; cook 10 minutes or until potatoes are just tender. Let cool, uncovered, to room temperature.

2. Place vegetables and cooking liquid in food processor. Process 45 seconds or until almost smooth. Return mixture to saucepan; stir in buttermilk. Cook and stir over low heat 5 minutes or until heated through. Sprinkle with paprika.

Makes 6 servings

Note: Soup may be served cold. Chill at least 8 hours before serving.

Nutrients per Serving

Calories	90
Total Fat	<1 g
Cholesterol	2 mg
Sodium	77 mg

Peas with Cukes 'n' Dill

½ medium cucumber, peeled and cut lengthwise into halves
2 tablespoons butter or margarine
2 pounds fresh peas,* shelled
1 teaspoon dried dill weed
Salt and pepper

* Or, substitute 1 (10-ounce) package frozen, thawed peas for fresh peas.

(continued on page 138)

Peas with Cukes 'n' Dill *(continued from page 137)*

1. Scrape seeds from cucumber with spoon and discard. Cut cucumber into ¼-inch slices.

2. Heat butter in medium skillet over medium-high heat until melted and bubbly. Cook and stir cucumber and peas in hot butter 5 minutes or until vegetables are crisp-tender. Stir in dill weed and season with salt and pepper to taste. Transfer to warm serving dish. Garnish with fresh dill, pineapple and sage leaves, if desired. Serve immediately.
Makes 4 side-dish servings

Nutrients per Serving

Calories	236
Total Fat	6 g
Cholesterol	15 mg
Sodium	65 mg

 *Peas with Cukes 'n' Dill*

Chicken Pot Pie

¾ pound boneless skinless chicken thighs, cut into 1-inch pieces
¾ pound boneless skinless chicken breasts, cut into 1-inch pieces
2 cups sliced carrots
1½ cups cubed potatoes
1 cup cubed turnip
1 cup fresh peas or thawed frozen peas
½ cup chopped onion
3 cloves garlic, sliced
1 teaspoon dried basil leaves
½ teaspoon dried marjoram leaves
½ teaspoon dried oregano leaves
½ teaspoon dried tarragon leaves
¼ teaspoon salt
¼ teaspoon black pepper
1 cup fat-free reduced-sodium chicken broth
3 tablespoons all-purpose flour
3 sheets thawed frozen phyllo pastry

1. Preheat oven to 425°F. Spray large nonstick skillet with nonstick cooking spray; heat over medium heat. Add chicken; cook and stir about 10 minutes or until no longer pink in center. Remove chicken from skillet.

2. Add carrots, potatoes, turnip, peas, onion and garlic to skillet; cook and stir 5 minutes. Sprinkle with basil, marjoram, oregano, tarragon, salt and pepper; cook and stir 1 to 2 minutes. Stir in broth; bring to a boil. Reduce heat to low. Cover; simmer about 10 minutes or until vegetables are tender.

3. Return chicken to skillet; bring to a boil. Combine flour and ⅓ cup water in small bowl until smooth; stir into chicken mixture. Boil 1 minute, stirring constantly. Pour mixture into 1-quart casserole or 10-inch pie plate.

4. Spray 1 sheet phyllo with nonstick cooking spray; top with remaining 2 sheets phyllo, spraying each lightly. Place stack of phyllo on top of casserole; cut edges 1 inch larger than casserole. Fold under edges of phyllo. Bake about 15 minutes or until phyllo is brown and crisp. *Makes 6 servings*

Nutrients per Serving

Calories	266
Total Fat	5 g
Cholesterol	59 mg
Sodium	300 mg

Chicken Pot Pie

 Pad Thai

Pad Thai

8 ounces flat rice noodles
  (⅛- to ¼-inch wide)
3 tablespoons ketchup
3 tablespoons fish sauce
2 tablespoons packed brown sugar
1 tablespoon lime juice
1 jalapeño pepper,* seeded and finely
  chopped
1 teaspoon curry powder
2 tablespoons peanut oil, divided
1 pound medium shrimp, peeled
3 cloves garlic, minced
3 eggs, lightly beaten
2 cups fresh bean sprouts, divided
⅔ cup roasted, skinless peanuts
  (salted or unsalted), chopped
3 green onions, thinly sliced
1 small carrot, shredded
¾ cup shredded red or green cabbage
½ cup cilantro, coarsely chopped
1 lime, cut into wedges

* *Chili peppers can sting and irritate the skin;
wear rubber gloves when handling and do not
touch eyes. Wash hands after handling chili
peppers.*

1. Place noodles in large bowl; cover with hot water. Let stand 10 to 30 minutes or until soft and pliable.

2. Meanwhile for sauce, combine ¼ cup water, ketchup, fish sauce, sugar, lime juice, jalapeño and curry powder in medium bowl; set aside.

3. Heat wok or large skillet over high heat. Add 1 tablespoon oil; heat until hot. Add shrimp; cook and stir 2 minutes or until shrimp turn pink and opaque. Transfer to bowl. Set aside.

4. Reduce heat to medium. Add remaining 1 tablespoon oil and heat 15 seconds. Add garlic; cook and stir 20 seconds or until golden. Add eggs; cook 2 minutes or just until set, turning and stirring every 30 seconds to scramble. Stir in sauce.

5. Increase heat to high. Add noodles; stir to coat with sauce. Cook 2 to 4 minutes, stirring often, until noodles are tender. (Add water, 1 tablespoon at a time, if sauce is absorbed and noodles are still dry.)

6. Add cooked shrimp, 1½ cups bean sprouts, peanuts and green onions; cook and stir 1 to 2 minutes or until heated through. Transfer mixture to large serving platter. Pile remaining ½ cup sprouts, carrot, cabbage, cilantro and lime wedges around noodles. Squeeze lime over noodles before eating.

Makes 4 servings

Nutrients per Serving

Calories	639	
Total Fat	24	g
Cholesterol	335	mg
Sodium	1309	mg

Curried Turkey Stew
with Dumplings

2 pounds turkey thighs
1 medium onion, chopped
1 teaspoon salt
1 teaspoon dried thyme leaves
⅛ teaspoon black pepper
¼ cup cornstarch
1 teaspoon curry powder
2 cups frozen mixed broccoli, cauliflower and carrots
1 large tart apple, peeled, cored and coarsely chopped
¾ cup all-purpose flour
1¼ teaspoons baking powder
¼ teaspoon onion salt
1 tablespoon chopped fresh parsley
2 tablespoons shortening
¼ cup milk
  Paprika
¼ cup chopped peanuts

1. Place turkey, onion, 4 cups water, salt, thyme and pepper in Dutch oven. Bring to a boil over high heat. Reduce heat to medium-low. Simmer, uncovered, 1¾ hours or until turkey is tender.

2. Remove turkey from soup and let cool slightly. Skim fat from soup. Remove turkey meat from bones; discard skin and bones. Cut turkey into bite-sized pieces.

3. Stir ¾ cup cold water into cornstarch and curry in small bowl until smooth. Stir into broth. Cook and stir over medium heat until mixture comes to a boil and thickens. Stir in frozen vegetables, turkey and apple. Bring to a boil over high heat, stirring occasionally.

4. For dumplings, combine flour, baking powder, onion salt and parsley in medium bowl. Cut in shortening using pastry blender or 2 knives until mixture forms pea-sized pieces. Stir in milk until just combined; don't overmix.

5. Drop dough in six mounds over stew. Cover; simmer over medium-low heat about 15 minutes or until dumplings test done with toothpick.

6. Sprinkle dumplings with paprika. Spoon stew into bowls placing dumpling on top of each serving; sprinkle with peanuts. Garnish with fresh herb sprig, if desired. *Makes 6 servings*

Nutrients per Serving

Calories	432	
Total Fat	20	g
Cholesterol	94	mg
Sodium	1294	mg

Curried Turkey Stew with Dumplings

🍂 *Chicken Chili*

Chicken Chili

1 tablespoon vegetable oil
1 medium onion, chopped
1 medium green bell pepper, seeded
   and chopped
1 pound ground chicken or turkey
2 fresh jalapeño peppers,* chopped
1 can (28 ounces) tomatoes, cut-up,
   undrained
1 can (15½ ounces) kidney beans,
   rinsed and drained
1 can (8 ounces) tomato sauce
1 tablespoon chili powder
1 teaspoon salt
1 teaspoon dried oregano leaves
1 teaspoon ground cumin
¼ teaspoon ground red pepper
½ cup (2 ounces) shredded Cheddar
   cheese

Chili peppers can sting and irritate the skin; wear rubber gloves when handling and do not touch eyes. Wash hands after handling chili peppers.

1. Heat oil in 5-quart Dutch oven or large saucepan over medium-high heat. Cook onion, bell pepper and chicken in hot oil until chicken is no longer pink and onion is crisp-tender, stirring frequently to break up chicken.

2. Stir in jalapeño peppers, tomatoes with juice, beans, tomato sauce, chili powder, salt, oregano, cumin and red pepper. Bring to a boil over high heat. Reduce heat to medium-low. Simmer, uncovered, 45 minutes. Spoon into bowls and top with cheese.   *Makes 6 servings*

Nutrients per Serving

Calories	233
Total Fat	8 g
Cholesterol	34 mg
Sodium	1140 mg

Three Bean Chili

⅔ cup dried kidney beans
⅔ cup dried navy beans
⅔ cup black beans
1 medium onion, chopped
3 medium carrots, sliced
2 teaspoons chili powder
½ teaspoon ground cumin
1 bay leaf
1 teaspoon salt
1 fresh jalapeño pepper,* chopped
1 can (28 ounces) tomatoes, cut-up,
   drained
⅓ cup tomato paste
2 cups hot cooked rice

Chili peppers can sting and irritate the skin; wear rubber gloves when handling and do not touch eyes. Wash hands after handling chili peppers.

1. Rinse beans in colander, picking out any debris. Cover beans with 6 cups water in large bowl; soak overnight. Drain beans, discarding soaking water. Combine beans, 4 cups water, onion, carrots, chili powder, cumin, bay leaf and salt in 5-quart Dutch oven. Bring to a boil over high heat. Reduce heat to medium-low. Simmer, uncovered, 1½ hours, stirring occasionally.

2. Remove bay leaf and discard. Stir in jalapeño, tomatoes and tomato paste. Bring to a boil over high heat. Reduce heat to medium-low. Simmer, uncovered, 15 minutes, stirring occasionally. Serve over rice.   *Makes 8 servings*

Nutrients per Serving

Calories	374
Total Fat	2 g
Cholesterol	0 mg
Sodium	780 mg

Roasted Sweet Pepper Tapas

2 medium red bell peppers
1 clove garlic, minced
1 teaspoon chopped fresh oregano *or*
   ½ teaspoon dried oregano leaves
2 tablespoons olive oil
   Garlic bread (optional)

1. Cover broiler pan with foil. Set broiler pan about 4 inches from heat. Preheat broiler. Place peppers on foil. Broil 15 to 20 minutes or until blackened on all sides, turning peppers every 5 minutes with tongs.

2. To peel peppers, place blackened peppers in paper bag. Close bag; set aside to cool about 15 to 20 minutes. Cut around each core, twist and remove. Cut peppers into halves. Place pepper halves on cutting board. Peel off skins with paring knife; rinse under cold water to remove seeds.

3. Lay pepper halves flat and slice lengthwise into ¼-inch strips with chef's knife. Transfer pepper strips to glass jar. Add garlic, oregano and oil. Close lid; shake to blend. Marinate at least 1 hour. Serve on plates with garlic bread, if desired. Or, refrigerate in jar up to 1 week. Garnish as desired.
Makes 6 appetizer servings

Tip: Use this roasting technique for all types of sweet and hot peppers. Broiling time will vary depending on size of pepper. When handling hot peppers, such as Anaheim, jalapeño, poblano or serrano, wear disposable plastic gloves and use caution to prevent irritation of skin or eyes.

Nutrients per Serving

Calories	47
Total Fat	4 g
Cholesterol	0 mg
Sodium	<1 mg

🌿 *Oriental Chicken Kabobs*

Oriental Chicken Kabobs

1 pound boneless skinless chicken
  breasts
2 small zucchini or yellow squash, cut
  into 1-inch slices
8 large fresh mushrooms
1 cup red, yellow or green bell pepper
  pieces
2 tablespoons reduced-sodium soy
  sauce
2 tablespoons dry sherry
1 teaspoon Oriental sesame oil
2 cloves garlic, minced
2 large green onions, cut into 1-inch
  pieces

1. Cut chicken into 1½-inch pieces; place
in large resealable plastic food storage
bag. Add zucchini, mushrooms and bell
pepper to bag.

2. Combine soy sauce, sherry, oil and
garlic in cup; pour over chicken and

vegetables. Close bag securely; turn to
coat. Refrigerate at least 30 minutes or
up to 4 hours.

3. Soak 4 (12-inch) skewers in enough
water to cover 20 minutes. Preheat
broiler. Drain chicken and vegetables;
reserve marinade. Alternately thread
chicken, vegetables and onions onto
skewers.

4. Place on rack of broiler pan. Brush
with half of reserved marinade. Broil
5 to 6 inches from heat 5 minutes. Turn
kabobs over; brush with remaining
marinade. Broil 5 minutes or until
chicken is no longer pink. Garnish with
green onion brushes, if desired.
Makes 4 servings

Nutrients per Serving

Calories	135
Total Fat	3 g
Cholesterol	46 mg
Sodium	307 mg

Chicken Fajitas

1 pound chicken tenders
¼ cup lime juice
4 cloves garlic, minced, divided
1 cup sliced red bell peppers
1 cup sliced green bell peppers
1 cup sliced yellow bell peppers
¾ cup onion slices
½ teaspoon ground cumin
¼ teaspoon salt
¼ teaspoon ground red pepper
8 teaspoons low-fat sour cream
8 flour tortillas (6-inch), warm
  Green onion tops and salsa
  (optional)

1. Arrange chicken in 11×7-inch glass
baking dish; add lime juice and 2 cloves
minced garlic. Toss to coat. Cover;
refrigerate 30 minutes, stirring
occasionally.

2. Spray large nonstick skillet with
nonstick cooking spray; heat over
medium heat until hot. Add chicken
mixture; cook and stir 5 to 7 minutes or
until browned and no longer pink in
center. Remove chicken from skillet.
Drain excess liquid from skillet, if
necessary.

3. Add bell peppers, onion and remaining
garlic to skillet; cook and stir about 5
minutes or until tender. Sprinkle with
cumin, salt and ground red pepper.
Return chicken to skillet. Cook and stir
1 to 2 minutes.

4. Spread 1 teaspoon sour cream on
1 side of each tortilla. Spoon chicken and
pepper mixture over sour cream; roll up
tortillas. Tie each tortilla with green
onion top, if desired. Serve with salsa, if
desired. *Makes 4 servings*

Nutrients per Serving

Calories	382
Total Fat	7 g
Cholesterol	2 mg
Sodium	421 mg

Zesty Lentil Stew

1 cup dried lentils
2 cups chopped peeled potatoes
1 can (14½ ounces) fat-free
reduced-sodium chicken broth
1½ cups chopped seeded tomatoes
1 can (11½ ounces) no-salt-added
spicy vegetable juice cocktail
1 cup chopped onion
½ cup chopped carrot
½ cup chopped celery
2 tablespoons chopped fresh basil *or*
2 teaspoons dried basil leaves
2 tablespoons chopped fresh oregano
or 2 teaspoons dried oregano
leaves
1 to 2 tablespoons finely chopped
jalapeño pepper*
¼ teaspoon salt

* Chili peppers can sting and irritate the skin; wear rubber gloves when handling and do not touch eyes. Wash hands after handling chili peppers.

1. Rinse lentils under cold water; drain. Combine lentils, potatoes, broth, 1⅔ cups water, tomatoes, vegetable juice cocktail, onion, carrot, celery, basil, oregano, jalapeño pepper and salt in 3-quart saucepan.

2. Bring to a boil over high heat. Reduce heat to medium-low. Cover; simmer 45 to 50 minutes or until lentils are tender, stirring occasionally.

Makes 4 servings

Nutrients per Serving

Calories	369
Total Fat	1 g
Cholesterol	0 mg
Sodium	620 mg

Low-Fat Cajun Wedges

Russet potatoes
Nonstick cooking spray
Cajun seasoning or other seasoning,
such as paprika

1. Preheat oven to 400°F. Scrub potatoes under running water with soft vegetable brush; rinse. Dry well. *Do not peel.* Line baking sheet with foil and spray with nonstick cooking spray.

2. Cut potatoes into halves lengthwise with chef's knife; then cut each half lengthwise into 3 wedges. Place potatoes, skin sides down, in single layer on prepared baking sheet. Spray potatoes lightly with nonstick cooking spray and sprinkle with seasoning.

3. Bake 25 minutes or until browned and fork-tender. Garnish with purple kale and fresh sage leaves, if desired. Serve immediately.

Makes about 1 serving per potato

Nutrients per Serving

Calories	220
Total Fat	<1 g
Cholesterol	0 mg
Sodium	62 mg

Low-Fat Cajun Wedges

Potato Pancakes

1½ pounds russet potatoes, grated
½ cup onion, grated
2 tablespoons chopped chives
¼ teaspoon salt
¼ teaspoon black pepper
½ cup applesauce

1. Combine potatoes, onion, chives, salt and pepper in medium bowl; mix well.

2. Spray large nonstick skillet with nonstick cooking spray. Heat over medium heat until water droplets sprinkled on skillet bounce off surface.

3. Drop potato mixture by ⅓ cupfuls into skillet; flatten with spatula. Cook over medium-high heat 4 to 5 minutes on each side or until pancakes are cooked through. Serve with applesauce.

Makes 6 servings

Nutrients per Serving

Calories	126
Total Fat	<1 g
Cholesterol	0 mg
Sodium	97 mg

Microwave Sweet Potato Chips

2 cups thinly sliced sweet potatoes
1 tablespoon packed brown sugar
2 teaspoons margarine

1. Place sweet potatoes, in single layer, in microwavable dish. Sprinkle with water.

2. Microwave at HIGH (100% power) 5 minutes. Stir in brown sugar and margarine; microwave at HIGH 2 to 3 minutes. Let stand a few minutes before serving. *Makes 4 servings*

Nutrients per Serving

Calories	98
Total Fat	2 g
Cholesterol	0 mg
Sodium	30 mg

*Favorite recipe from **The Sugar Association, Inc.***

Sweet Potato Bisque

1 pound sweet potatoes, peeled and coarsely chopped
2 teaspoons margarine
½ cup minced onion
1 teaspoon curry powder
½ teaspoon ground coriander
¼ teaspoon salt
⅔ cup unsweetened apple juice
1 cup low-fat buttermilk

1. Bring 2 quarts water and potatoes to a boil in large saucepan over high heat. Cook, uncovered, 40 minutes or until potatoes are fork-tender. Drain; rinse under cold water until cool enough to handle.

2. Meanwhile, melt margarine in small saucepan over medium heat. Add onion; cook and stir 2 minutes. Stir in curry, coriander and salt; cook and stir about 45 seconds. Remove from heat; stir in apple juice. Set aside until potatoes have cooled.

3. Place potatoes, buttermilk and onion mixture in food processor or blender; process until smooth.

4. Pour soup back into large saucepan; stir in ¼ cup water to thin to desired consistency. (If soup is too thick, add 1 to 2 more tablespoons water.) Cook and stir over medium heat until heated through. *Do not boil.* Garnish each serving with dollop of plain low-fat yogurt, if desired.

Makes 4 servings

Nutrients per Serving

Calories	159
Total Fat	3 g
Cholesterol	2 mg
Sodium	230 mg

Microwave Sweet Potato Chips

Turkey, Corn and Sweet Potato Soup

Turkey, Corn and Sweet Potato Soup

- 1 teaspoon margarine
- ½ cup chopped onion
- 1 small jalapeño pepper,* minced
- 5 cups turkey broth *or* reduced-sodium chicken bouillon
- 1½ pounds sweet potatoes, peeled and cut into 1-inch cubes
- 2 cups cooked turkey, cut into ½-inch cubes
- ½ teaspoon salt
- 1½ cups frozen corn

* Chili peppers can sting and irritate the skin; wear rubber gloves when handling and do not touch eyes. Wash hands after handling chili peppers.

1. Melt margarine in 5-quart saucepan over medium-high heat. Add onion and jalapeño pepper; cook and stir 5 minutes or until onion is soft.

2. Add broth, potatoes, turkey and salt; bring to a boil. Reduce heat to low. Cover; simmer 20 to 25 minutes or until potatoes

are tender. Stir in corn. Increase heat to medium and cook 5 to 6 minutes. Garnish with cilantro, if desired.

Makes 8 servings

Nutrients per Serving

Calories	155	
Total Fat	1	g
Cholesterol	24	mg
Sodium	254	mg

Favorite recipe from **National Turkey Federation**

Japanese Steak Salad

Sesame Marinade and Dressing (recipe follows)
- 1 pound trimmed beef top sirloin steak, cut 1 inch thick
- 3 cups sliced napa cabbage
- 3 cups torn romaine lettuce
- ½ cup diagonally sliced carrots
- ½ cup thinly sliced radishes
- ½ cup thinly sliced cucumber
- 1 cup cooked rice
- 24 pea pods, blanched

1. Prepare Sesame Marinade and Dressing.

2. Place beef in resealable plastic food storage bag. Add ⅓ cup Sesame Marinade; close bag securely. Turn to coat. Marinate in refrigerator 2 hours, turning once.

3. Preheat broiler. Remove steak from marinade; discard marinade. Place on rack in broiler pan. Broil steak 3 to 4 inches from heat, 14 to 16 minutes, turning once. Let stand 5 minutes. Carve steak into thin slices.

4. Combine cabbage, lettuce, carrots and radishes in large bowl; divide evenly between 4 individual plates. Arrange equal numbers of cucumber slices in a circle at top of salad greens on each plate.

5. Mound ¼ cup rice over each cucumber circle. Fan pea pods around both sides of rice. Arrange steak slices in spoke fashion over salad greens, radiating down from rice. Serve with ¾ cup Sesame Dressing. *Makes 4 servings*

Sesame Marinade and Dressing

- 3 tablespoons *each* dry sherry, reduced-sodium soy sauce and rice wine vinegar
- 2 tablespoons hoisin sauce
- ½ teaspoon grated fresh ginger root
- 2 tablespoons chopped green onion
- 1 tablespoon *each* sugar and Oriental sesame oil

Combine sherry, soy sauce, vinegar, hoisin sauce and ginger in small bowl. Reserve ⅓ cup for marinade. Combine remaining sherry mixture with ¼ cup water, onion, sugar and sesame oil.

Makes ⅓ cup marinade and ¾ cup dressing

Nutrients per Serving

Calories	308	
Total Fat	10	g
Cholesterol	57	mg
Sodium	527	mg

Favorite recipe from **National Cattlemen's Beef Association**

Rhubarb and Strawberry Sauce

1 cup rhubarb, cut into ½-inch slices
½ teaspoon ground cinnamon
½ cup sliced strawberries
3 to 4 tablespoons sugar

1. Bring rhubarb, 2 tablespoons water and cinnamon to a boil in small saucepan over high heat. Reduce heat to low. Simmer, uncovered, about 10 minutes or until rhubarb is soft.

2. Stir in strawberries and sugar; cook 1 to 2 minutes or until sugar is dissolved. Serve sauce warm or chilled over vanilla low-fat yogurt, fruit or angel food cake.
Makes 8 servings
(about 2 tablespoons per serving)

Nutrients per Serving

Calories	23	
Total Fat	1	g
Cholesterol	0	mg
Sodium	<1	mg

Rhubarb Chutney

1 cup coarsely chopped peeled apple
½ cup sugar
¼ cup raisins
1 teaspoon grated lemon peel
2 cups rhubarb, cut into ½-inch slices
3 tablespoons coarsely chopped pecans
2 to 3 teaspoons distilled white vinegar
¾ teaspoon ground cinnamon (optional)

1. Heat apple, sugar, ¼ cup water, raisins and lemon peel in medium saucepan over medium heat until sugar is dissolved, stirring constantly. Reduce heat to low. Simmer, uncovered, about 5 minutes or until apple is almost tender.

2. Stir rhubarb and pecans into apple mixture; bring to a boil over high heat. Reduce heat to low. Simmer, uncovered, 8 to 10 minutes or until mixture is reduced to 1 cup, stirring occasionally.

3. Stir vinegar and cinnamon into apple mixture during last 2 to 3 minutes of cooking. Remove from heat; cool to room temperature. Refrigerate, covered, until ready to serve.
Makes 8 servings
(2 tablespoons per serving)

Nutrients per Serving

Calories	91	
Total Fat	2	g
Cholesterol	0	mg
Sodium	2	mg

Mashed Rutabagas and Potatoes

1 pound rutabagas, peeled and cut into ½-inch pieces
½ pound potatoes, peeled and cut into ½-inch pieces
¼ cup milk
¼ teaspoon ground nutmeg
1 tablespoon chopped fresh parsley

1. Place rutabagas and potatoes in large saucepan; add enough water to cover. Bring to a boil over high heat. Cook, uncovered, 15 minutes or until vegetables are fork-tender. Drain well; transfer to medium bowl.

2. Mash vegetables with potato masher or electric mixer. Blend in milk and nutmeg until smooth. Stir in parsley before serving.
Makes 4 servings

Nutrients per Serving

Calories	92	
Total Fat	<1	g
Cholesterol	1	mg
Sodium	30	mg

Rutabaga "Fries"

Nonstick cooking spray
2 pounds rutabagas, peeled
Dash paprika

1. Preheat oven to 450°F. Spray jelly-roll pan with nonstick cooking spray. Cut rutabagas lengthwise into ½-inch-thick slices; cut slices crosswise into ½-inch-wide sticks.

2. Arrange rutabagas in single layer in prepared pan. Spray lightly with cooking spray; sprinkle with paprika and toss to coat.

3. Bake about 20 minutes or until rutabagas are lightly browned and crisp, turning once during baking.
Makes 4 servings

Nutrients per Serving

Calories	71	
Total Fat	<1	g
Cholesterol	0	mg
Sodium	38	mg

Steak Frite

1 pound boneless beef eye of round steak, trimmed
2 medium cloves garlic, minced
1 teaspoon salt, divided
½ teaspoon black pepper, divided
4 medium russet potatoes
Nonstick cooking spray
½ teaspoon paprika
¼ cup thinly sliced shallots or sweet onions

1. Pound beef with meat mallet until ½ inch thick. Rub both sides of beef with garlic, ½ teaspoon salt and ¼ teaspoon pepper. Place in glass baking dish; cover. Refrigerate 20 to 30 minutes.

2. Preheat oven to 400°F. Cut potatoes lengthwise into ¼-inch-thick slices; cut slices lengthwise into ¼-inch-wide sticks. Arrange potatoes in single layer in jelly-roll pan. Spray with nonstick cooking spray; sprinkle with paprika and toss to coat.

3. Bake about 25 minutes or until potatoes are lightly browned and crisp, turning 1 or 2 times during baking. Sprinkle with remaining ½ teaspoon salt and ¼ teaspoon pepper.

4. Spray medium nonstick skillet with cooking spray; heat over medium heat. Add shallots; cook and stir about 3 minutes or until tender. Remove shallots; set aside until ready to serve.

5. Add beef to skillet; cook over medium-high heat about 5 minutes on each side for medium or to desired doneness. Serve with shallots and potatoes.

Makes 4 servings

Snapper Fillets with Orange-Shallot Sauce

    2 oranges, peeled
    6 fish fillets (red snapper, flounder,
         grouper or scrod)
    1 tablespoon olive oil
    1 cup finely chopped shallots
    2 cloves garlic, minced
    3 tablespoons all-purpose flour
    1 cup chicken broth
    1 cup orange juice
    2 tablespoons cooking sherry
    1 tablespoon grated orange peel
 1½ teaspoons dried oregano leaves

1. Preheat broiler. Thinly slice oranges; set aside. Place fillets, skin side down, on nonstick jelly-roll pan. Broil about 4 inches from heat 5 to 8 minutes or until fish flakes easily with fork. Remove from broiler; set aside.

2. Meanwhile, heat oil in large nonstick skillet over medium-high heat until hot. Add shallots and garlic; cook and stir 3 to 4 minutes or until shallots begin to brown. Add flour; cook and stir about 30 seconds.

3. Stir broth, orange juice, sherry, orange peel, oregano and salt and pepper to taste into skillet. Bring to a boil, stirring constantly and cook until slightly thickened.

4. Add orange slices and fish fillets, skin side up, to skillet. Cook 1 to 2 minutes or until fish is heated through and orange slices are slightly softened. Garnish with chopped fresh parsley, if desired. Serve immediately.   *Makes 6 servings*

Wilted Spinach Mandarin

  ½ pound fresh spinach
    1 tablespoon vegetable oil
    1 cup bean sprouts
    1 can (11 ounces) mandarin oranges,
         drained
    2 tablespoons reduced-sodium soy
         sauce
    2 tablespoons orange juice

1. Separate spinach into leaves. Swish in cold water. Repeat several times with fresh cold water to remove sand and grit. Pat dry with paper towels. Remove stems from spinach and discard.

2. Heat oil in wok or large nonskillet over medium-high heat. Add spinach, bean sprouts and mandarin oranges to wok; cook and stir 1 to 2 minutes *just* until spinach wilts. Transfer to serving dish.

3. Heat soy sauce and orange juice in wok; pour over spinach and toss gently to coat. Garnish with quartered orange slices, if desired. Serve immediately.

Makes 4 side-dish servings

Wilted Spinach Mandarin

Roman Spinach Soup

6 cups fat-free reduced-sodium chicken broth
1 cup cholesterol-free egg substitute
¼ cup minced fresh basil
3 tablespoons freshly grated Parmesan cheese
2 tablespoons lemon juice
1 tablespoon minced fresh parsley
¼ teaspoon ground white pepper
⅛ teaspoon ground nutmeg
8 cups fresh spinach, washed, stemmed and chopped

1. Bring broth to a boil in 4-quart saucepan over medium heat.

2. Combine egg substitute, basil, cheese, lemon juice, parsley, ground white pepper and nutmeg in small bowl. Set aside.

3. Stir spinach into broth; simmer 1 minute. Slowly pour egg mixture into broth mixture, whisking constantly so egg threads form. Simmer 2 to 3 minutes or until egg is cooked. Garnish with lemon slices, if desired. Serve immediately.
Makes 8 (¾-cup) servings

Note: Soup may look curdled.

Nutrients per Serving

Calories	46	
Total Fat	1	g
Cholesterol	2	mg
Sodium	153	mg

Greek Pasta and Vegetable Salad

⅔ cup corkscrew macaroni
⅓ cup lime juice
2 tablespoons honey
1 tablespoon olive oil
1 clove garlic, minced
4 cups torn washed stemmed spinach
1 cup sliced cucumber
½ cup thinly sliced carrot
¼ cup sliced green onions
2 tablespoons crumbled feta cheese
2 tablespoons sliced pitted ripe olives

1. Prepare macaroni according to package directions; drain. Rinse under cold water; drain again.

2. Combine lime juice, honey, oil and garlic in large bowl. Stir in macaroni. Cover; refrigerate 2 to 24 hours.

3. Combine spinach, cucumber, carrot, onions, cheese and olives in large bowl. Add macaroni mixture to salad; toss to combine. *Makes 4 servings*

Nutrients per Serving

Calories	188	
Total Fat	6	g
Cholesterol	3	mg
Sodium	230	mg

Vegetable-Barley Pilaf

¾ cup chopped onion
¾ cup chopped celery
¾ cup sliced mushrooms
¾ cup sliced yellow summer squash
½ cup quick-cooking barley
½ cup sliced carrot
¼ cup chopped fresh parsley
2 teaspoons chopped fresh basil *or*
    ½ teaspoon dried basil leaves
½ teaspoon chicken bouillon granules
⅛ teaspoon black pepper

1. Spray large nonstick skillet with nonstick cooking spray. Add onion, celery and mushrooms; cook and stir over medium heat until vegetables are tender.

2. Stir in 1 cup water, squash, barley, carrot, parsley, basil, bouillon granules and pepper. Bring to a boil over high heat. Reduce heat to medium-low. Cover; simmer 10 to 12 minutes or until barley and vegetables are tender.
Makes 4 servings

Nutrients per Serving

Calories	111	
Total Fat	1	g
Cholesterol	0	mg
Sodium	147	mg

Greek Pasta and Vegetable Salad

Crisp Zucchini Ribbons

Butternut Squash in Coconut Milk

2 teaspoons vegetable oil
½ small onion, finely chopped
2 cloves garlic, minced
1 cup unsweetened coconut milk *or* 1 cup water *plus* 1 teaspoon coconut extract
¼ cup packed brown sugar
1 tablespoon fish sauce
⅛ to ¼ teaspoon red pepper flakes
1 butternut squash, peeled, seeded and cut into 2-inch pieces
⅓ cup sweetened flaked coconut, toasted
1 tablespoon chopped fresh cilantro

1. Heat oil in large saucepan over medium-high heat. Add onion and garlic; cook and stir 3 minutes or until tender. Add coconut milk, sugar, fish sauce and pepper flakes; stir until sugar is dissolved.

2. Bring mixture to a boil; add squash. Reduce heat to medium. Cover; simmer 30 minutes or until squash is fork-tender. Transfer squash to serving bowl.

3. Increase heat to high; boil remaining liquid until thick, stirring constantly. (If water was used in place of coconut milk, sauce will not thicken.) Pour liquid over squash in bowl. Sprinkle with toasted coconut and chopped cilantro. Garnish with cilantro and purple kale, if desired.
Makes 4 side-dish servings

Nutrients per Serving

Calories	289	
Total Fat	**19**	**g**
Cholesterol	**0**	**mg**
Sodium	**245**	**mg**

Crisp Zucchini Ribbons

3 small zucchini
2 tablespoons olive oil
1 tablespoon white wine vinegar
2 teaspoons chopped fresh basil *or* ½ teaspoon dried basil leaves
½ teaspoon red pepper flakes
¼ teaspoon ground coriander
Salt and black pepper

1. Cut tip and stem ends from zucchini. Using vegetable peeler, begin at stem end and make continuous ribbons down length of each zucchini.

2. Place steamer basket in large saucepan; add water to 1 inch depth. (Water should not touch bottom of basket.) Place zucchini ribbons in steamer basket; cover. Bring to a boil over high heat. Steam zucchini 3 to 5 minutes or until crisp-tender. Transfer zucchini to warm serving dish.

3. Combine oil, vinegar, basil, pepper flakes and coriander in small glass bowl, whisking until thoroughly blended.

4. Pour dressing mixture over zucchini ribbons; toss gently to coat. Season to taste with salt and black pepper. Garnish with chopped green onions and carrot strips, if desired. Serve immediately or refrigerate up to 2 days.
Makes 4 side-dish servings

Nutrients per Serving

Calories	74	
Total Fat	**7**	**g**
Cholesterol	**0**	**mg**
Sodium	**3**	**mg**

🍃 *Butternut Squash in Coconut Milk*

Spicy Zucchini-Pepper Stew

2 tablespoons olive oil
1 large onion, chopped
3 cloves garlic, chopped
1 to 2 teaspoons minced seeded
jalapeño pepper*
2 jars (12 ounces each) roasted red
peppers, drained
2 large tomatoes, diced
2 cups thin zucchini slices
Grated peel of 1 lemon
1 teaspoon dried oregano leaves
1 teaspoon dried thyme leaves
½ teaspoon salt
¼ to ½ teaspoon saffron
Black pepper
2½ cups chicken broth or water
3 tablespoons cornstarch
Hot cooked rice

*Chili peppers can sting and irritate the skin;
wear rubber gloves when handling and do not
touch eyes. Wash hands after handling chili
peppers.*

1. Heat oil in 5-quart Dutch oven over
medium-high heat. Add onion, garlic and
jalapeño; cook and stir until onion is soft.
Add red peppers, tomatoes, zucchini,
lemon peel, oregano, thyme, salt, saffron
and black pepper. Cook and stir 5
minutes; add broth. Bring to a boil over
high heat. Reduce heat to low. Cover and
simmer 35 minutes.

2. Blend water into cornstarch in small
cup until smooth; stir into stew. Cook and
stir until stew boils and sauce is slightly
thickened. Serve over rice.

Makes 4 to 6 servings

Nutrients per Serving

Calories	179
Total Fat	9 g
Cholesterol	11 mg
Sodium	909 mg

🍂 *Chutney-Squash Circles*

Chutney-Squash Circles

2 acorn squash (1 pound each)
2 tablespoons butter or margarine
½ cup prepared chutney

1. Preheat oven to 400°F. Slice tip and
stem ends from squash; cut squash
crosswise into ¾-inch circles. Scoop out
seeds with spoon.

2. Tear off 18-inch square of heavy-duty
foil. Center foil in 13×9-inch baking dish.
Dot foil with butter and place squash on
butter, slightly overlapping circles. Spoon
chutney over slices and sprinkle with 2
tablespoons water.

3. Bring foil on long sides of pan together
in center, folding over to make tight
seam. Crimp ends to form tight seal.

4. Bake 20 to 30 minutes or until squash
is fork-tender. Transfer squash to warm
serving plate. Pour pan drippings over
squash. Garnish with purple kale and
scented geranium leaves,* if desired.

Makes 4 side-dish servings

Be sure to use only nontoxic leaves.

Nutrients per Serving

Calories	203
Total Fat	7 g
Cholesterol	15 mg
Sodium	68 mg

Baked Acorn Squash with Apples and Raisins

2 medium acorn squash (about 2¼ pounds)
⅓ cup reduced-calorie pancake syrup
1 Granny Smith apple, peeled, cored and coarsely chopped
¼ cup seedless raisins
⅛ teaspoon ground nutmeg
1½ teaspoons cornstarch

1. Preheat oven to 400°F. Cut squash into halves. Scoop out and discard seeds. Place squash, cut side down, in 13×9-inch baking dish. Add 1 cup water to baking dish; bake 35 to 45 minutes or until fork-tender. Turn squash cut side up.

2. Meanwhile, heat pancake syrup in medium saucepan over medium heat. Add apple, raisins and nutmeg; cook and stir about 8 minutes or until apples are almost crisp-tender.

3. Combine cornstarch and 2 tablespoons water in small cup until smooth; stir into saucepan. Bring to a boil over medium-high heat, stirring constantly. Cook and stir 2 minutes. Divide mixture evenly among squash halves. Return squash to oven; bake 10 minutes or until heated through. *Makes 4 servings*

Nutrients per Serving

Calories	196	
Total Fat	<1	**g**
Cholesterol	0	**mg**
Sodium	152	**mg**

Chile Verde

½ to ¾ pound boneless lean pork, trimmed and cut into 1-inch cubes
1 large onion, halved, thinly sliced
4 cloves garlic, chopped or sliced
1 pound fresh tomatillos
1 can (14½ ounces) fat-free reduced-sodium chicken broth
1 can (4 ounces) diced mild green chilies
1 teaspoon ground cumin
1½ cups cooked navy or Great Northern beans *or* 1 can (15 ounces) Great Northern beans, rinsed and drained
½ cup lightly packed fresh cilantro, chopped
Nonfat plain yogurt (optional)

1. Place pork, onion, garlic and ½ cup water in large saucepan; cover. Simmer over medium-low heat, stirring occasionally, 30 minutes (add more water, if necessary). Uncover; boil over medium-high heat until liquid evaporates and meat browns.

2. Add tomatillos and broth to pork mixture; stir. Cover; simmer over medium heat 20 minutes or until tomatillos are tender. Tear tomatillos apart with 2 forks.

3. Add chilies and cumin to pork mixture; cover. Simmer over medium-low heat 45 minutes or until meat is tender and tears apart easily (add more water or broth to keep liquid level the same). Add beans; simmer 10 minutes or until heated through. Stir in cilantro. Serve with yogurt, if desired. *Makes 4 servings*

Nutrients per Serving

Calories	311	
Total Fat	5	**g**
Cholesterol	40	**mg**
Sodium	51	**mg**

 Chile Verde

🐚 Corn and Tomatillo Salsa

Corn and Tomatillo Salsa

4 ears fresh corn, shucked
½ pound fresh tomatillos or tomatoes, cored and chopped
½ red or green bell pepper, cored and chopped*
2 jalapeño peppers, seeded and minced**
2 green onions, thinly sliced
2 tablespoons lime or lemon juice
½ teaspoon ground coriander
2 tablespoons chopped fresh cilantro
Tortilla chips (optional)

Use red bell pepper if using tomatillos and green bell pepper if using tomatoes for variety in color.

**Chili peppers can sting and irritate the skin; wear rubber gloves with handling and do not touch eyes. Wash hands after handling chili peppers.*

1. Combine corn, tomatillos, bell pepper, jalapeño peppers, onions, lime juice, 2 tablespoons water and coriander in large skillet; cover. Bring to a boil over high heat. Reduce heat to medium-low; simmer 5 minutes, stirring halfway through cooking. Cool.

2. Stir in cilantro. Store in refrigerator. Serve with tortilla chips. Garnish with lime slices, red chili pepper slices and cilantro leaves, if desired.

Makes 3 cups salsa
(½ cup per serving)

Nutrients per Serving

Calories	77	
Total Fat	1	g
Cholesterol	0	mg
Sodium	31	mg

🌶 *Fresh Tomato Pasta Soup*

Fresh Tomato Pasta Soup

1 tablespoon olive oil
½ cup chopped onion
1 clove garlic, minced
3 pounds fresh tomatoes, coarsely chopped
3 cups fat-free reduced-sodium chicken broth
1 tablespoon minced fresh basil
1 tablespoon minced fresh marjoram
1 tablespoon minced fresh oregano
1 teaspoon fennel seeds
½ teaspoon black pepper
¾ cup uncooked rosamarina or other small pasta
½ cup (2 ounces) shredded part-skim mozzarella cheese

1. Heat oil in large saucepan over medium heat. Add onion and garlic; cook and stir until onion is tender. Add tomatoes, broth, basil, marjoram, oregano, fennel seeds and pepper. Bring to a boil; reduce heat. Cover; simmer 25 minutes. Remove from heat; cool slightly.

2. Puree tomato mixture in food processor or blender in batches. Return to saucepan; bring to a boil. Add pasta; cook 7 to 9 minutes or until tender. Transfer to serving bowls. Sprinkle with mozzarella. Garnish with marjoram sprigs, if desired.

Makes 8 (¾-cup) servings

Nutrients per Serving

Calories	116	
Total Fat	4	g
Cholesterol	4	mg
Sodium	62	mg

Ragoût of Tuna

3 cloves garlic, minced and divided
1 to 2 sprigs fresh mint, chopped *or*
    1 teaspoon dried mint leaves
½ to 1 teaspoon salt, divided
    Black pepper
2 to 2½ pounds fresh tuna or
    swordfish steaks
2 teaspoons olive oil
½ cup dry white wine
2 medium onions, thinly sliced
1 teaspoon sugar
1 pound ripe tomatoes, coarsely
    chopped
1 cup hot water
4 cups hot cooked noodles or rice
    (optional)

1. Combine 1 clove minced garlic, mint, ½ teaspoon salt and pepper to taste in small bowl. Make about 12 equal cuts into sides of fish. Insert garlic mixture into each cut.

Ragoût of Tuna

2. Heat oil in large nonstick skillet over medium-high heat. Add fish and brown on both sides. Pour wine over fish; continue cooking, basting with liquid, about 5 minutes or until wine has completely evaporated. Remove fish to warm casserole.

3. Add remaining 2 cloves minced garlic and onions to skillet; sprinkle with sugar and remaining ½ teaspoon salt. Cook over low heat, about 5 minutes. Return fish to skillet; add tomatoes and hot water. Simmer until fish is cooked through and sauce thickens. To serve, pour sauce over fish and serve remaining sauce with noodles or rice, if desired.

Makes 6 servings

Nutrients per Serving

Calories	224
Total Fat	3 g
Cholesterol	69 mg
Sodium	243 mg

Favorite recipe from **The Sugar Association, Inc.**

Tabbouleh in Tomato Cups

4 large firm, ripe tomatoes
4 green onions, sliced diagonally
2 tablespoons olive oil
1 cup bulgur wheat
2 tablespoons lemon juice
1 tablespoon chopped fresh mint
    leaves *or* ½ teaspoon dried mint
    leaves
    Salt and black pepper

1. To prepare tomato cups, remove stems. Cut tomatoes in half crosswise. Carefully loosen pulp from shell with spoon. Scoop pulp and seeds out of tomatoes into medium bowl, leaving shells intact.

2. Invert tomatoes onto paper towel-lined plate; drain 20 minutes. Meanwhile, chop tomato pulp. Set aside.

3. Heat oil in 2-quart saucepan over medium-high heat. Add white parts of onions; cook and stir 1 to 2 minutes or until wilted. Stir in bulgur; cook 3 to 5 minutes or until browned.

4. Add reserved tomato pulp, 1 cup water, lemon juice and mint to bulgur mixture. Bring to a boil over high heat. Reduce heat to medium-low. Cover; simmer 15 to 20 minutes or until liquid is absorbed.

5. Reserve a few sliced green onion tops for garnish; stir remaining green onions into bulgur mixture. Season to taste with salt and pepper. Spoon mixture into tomato cups.*

6. Preheat oven to 400°F. Place filled cups in 13×9-inch baking dish. Bake 15 minutes or until heated through. Top with reserved onion tops. Garnish with lemon peel and mint leaves, if desired. Serve immediately.

*Makes 4 main-dish or
8 side-dish servings*

* *Tomato cups may be covered and refrigerated at this point up to 24 hours.*

Nutrients per Serving

Calories	48
Total Fat	1 g
Cholesterol	0 mg
Sodium	71 mg

Tabbouleh in Tomato Cups

Turnip Shepherd's Pie

Turnip Shepherd's Pie

1 pound small turnips, peeled and cut into ½-inch cubes
1 pound lean ground turkey
⅓ cup dry bread crumbs
¼ cup chopped onion
¼ cup ketchup
1 egg
½ teaspoon *each* salt, black pepper and beau monde seasoning
⅓ cup half-and-half
1 tablespoon butter or margarine
 Additional salt and black pepper
1 tablespoon chopped fresh parsley
¼ cup (1 ounce) shredded sharp Cheddar cheese

1. Preheat oven to 400°F. Place turnips in large saucepan; cover with water. Cover; bring to a boil over high heat. Reduce heat to medium-low. Simmer 20 minutes or until fork-tender.

2. Mix turkey, bread crumbs, onion, ketchup, egg, salt, pepper and seasoning in large bowl. Press into bottom and up side of 9-inch pie plate.

3. Bake 20 to 30 minutes or until turkey is no longer pink. Pat with paper towel to remove any liquid.

4. Drain cooked turnips. Mash turnips with electric mixer until smooth, blending in half-and-half and butter. Season to taste with salt and pepper. Fill meat shell with turnip mixture; sprinkle with parsley and cheese. Return to oven until cheese melts. Garnish as desired.
Makes 4 main-dish servings

Nutrients per Serving

Calories	365	
Total Fat	20	g
Cholesterol	132	mg
Sodium	832	mg

Herbed Duchess Turnips

2 cups peeled turnip cubes
1½ cups peeled potato slices
1 cup carrot slices
2 egg whites
2 teaspoons reduced-calorie margarine
1 teaspoon onion powder
½ teaspoon dried marjoram leaves
¼ teaspoon salt
⅛ teaspoon black pepper

1. Bring 2 cups water to a boil in medium saucepan over high heat. Add turnips, potatoes and carrots; return to a boil. Reduce heat to medium-low. Cover; simmer 30 to 35 minutes or until vegetables are very tender. Drain well; transfer vegetables to large bowl.

2. Preheat oven to 375°F. Spray baking sheet with nonstick cooking spray; set aside. Beat vegetables with electric mixer at medium-low speed until mashed. Add egg whites, margarine, onion powder, marjoram, salt and pepper. Beat at medium speed until mixture is nearly smooth. (Mixture should have consistency of mashed potatoes.)

3. Spoon mixture into pastry bag with large open star tip. Pipe mixture into 12 mounds on prepared baking sheet.* Bake 12 to 14 minutes or until heated through. *Makes 4 servings*

* *Or, spoon mixture into mounds onto prepared baking sheet. Bake as directed above.*

Nutrients per Serving

Calories	119	
Total Fat	1	g
Cholesterol	0	mg
Sodium	235	mg

Sweet-Sour Turnip Green Salad

2 cups shredded stemmed washed turnip greens
2 cups washed mixed salad greens
1 cup sliced plum tomatoes or quartered cherry tomatoes
½ cup shredded carrot
⅓ cup sliced green onions
2 teaspoons all-purpose flour
1 tablespoon packed brown sugar
½ teaspoon celery seeds
 Dash black pepper
1 tablespoon white wine vinegar

1. Combine turnip greens, salad greens, tomatoes and carrot in salad bowl; set aside.

2. Combine green onions and 2 tablespoons water in small saucepan. Bring to a boil over high heat. Reduce heat to medium. Cover; cook 2 to 3 minutes or until onions are tender.

3. Mix 6 tablespoons water and flour in small bowl until smooth. Stir into green onions in saucepan. Add brown sugar, celery seeds and pepper; cook and stir until mixture boils and thickens. Cook and stir 1 minute. Stir in vinegar. Pour hot dressing over salad; toss to coat. Serve immediately.
Makes 4 servings

Nutrients per Serving

Calories	48	
Total Fat	<1	g
Cholesterol	0	mg
Sodium	40	mg

Sun Country Chicken Salad

1 large cantaloupe
2 cups cubed cooked chicken
1 cup cucumber slices
1 cup green grapes
½ cup chopped green onions
2 tablespoons chopped fresh parsley
1 cup plain nonfat yogurt
3 tablespoons prepared chutney
¼ teaspoon grated lemon peel
1 tablespoon lemon juice
¼ cup whole blanched almonds, toasted*
1 large bunch watercress

To toast almonds, spread in single layer on baking sheet. Toast at 350°F 5 to 8 minutes, stirring occasionally, until lightly browned. Cool.

1. Cut cantaloupe into 12 wedges, removing seeds and peel.

2. Combine chicken, cucumber, grapes, onions and parsley in large bowl. Blend together yogurt, chutney, lemon peel and lemon juice in small bowl; toss lightly with chicken mixture. Fold in almonds.

3. Arrange watercress on 4 salad plates. Stand 3 wedges of cantaloupe on each plate. Spoon chicken salad mixture over cantaloupe.   *Makes 4 servings*

Nutrients per Serving

Calories	356
Total Fat	9 g
Cholesterol	49 mg
Sodium	154 mg

*Favorite recipe from **Almond Board of California***

Spicy Grapefruit Salad with Raspberry Dressing

2 cups washed watercress
2 cups washed mixed salad greens
3 medium grapefruits, peeled, sectioned and seeded
½ pound jicama, julienned
1 cup fresh or frozen thawed raspberries
2 tablespoons chopped green onion
1 teaspoon balsamic vinegar
1 tablespoon honey
½ to ¾ teaspoon dry mustard

1. Combine watercress and salad greens in large bowl. Divide watercress mixture evenly between 4 salad plates. Arrange grapefruit and jicama over watercress mixture.

2. Reserve 12 raspberries for garnish. For dressing, combine remaining raspberries, green onion, vinegar, honey and mustard in food processor or blender; process until smooth. Drizzle dressing over salads. Garnish with reserved raspberries.   *Makes 4 servings*

Nutrients per Serving

Calories	113
Total Fat	<1 g
Cholesterol	0 mg
Sodium	16 mg

Citrus Salad with Bibb Lettuce, Watercress and Balsamic Dressing

1 medium pink grapefruit, peeled, white pith removed and sectioned
2 large oranges, peeled, white pith removed and sectioned
2 tangerines, peeled and sectioned
1 bunch watercress, rinsed and patted dry
3 tablespoons orange juice
1 tablespoon balsamic vinegar
¼ teaspoon salt
1 tablespoon vegetable oil
1 large head Bibb lettuce, separated, rinsed and patted dry

1. Combine grapefruit, oranges, tangerines and watercress in medium bowl. Combine orange juice, vinegar and salt in small bowl. Add oil; whisk until combined. Pour over fruit and watercress; gently toss to combine.

2. Line four serving plates with lettuce. Divide fruit mixture among plates. Garnish each with thin strips of orange peel, if desired.   *Makes 4 servings*

Nutrients per Serving

Calories	113
Total Fat	4 g
Cholesterol	0 mg
Sodium	140 mg

❧ *Sun Country Chicken Salad*

Fresh Fruit with Creamy Lime Dipping Sauce

Creamy Lime Dipping Sauce (recipe follows)

2 tablespoons lime juice

1 small jicama, peeled, cut into ½-inch-thick strips

2 pounds watermelon, peel removed and fruit cut into ½-inch-thick wedges 2 to 3 inches wide

½ small pineapple, peeled, halved lengthwise and cut crosswise into wedges

1 ripe papaya, peeled, seeded and sliced crosswise

1. Prepare Creamy Lime Dipping Sauce. Combine lime juice and jicama in large bowl; toss to coat. Drain.

2. Arrange jicama, watermelon, pineapple and papaya on large platter. Serve with Creamy Lime Dipping Sauce.

Makes 12 servings

Creamy Lime Dipping Sauce

1 carton (6 ounces) nonfat vanilla yogurt

2 tablespoons minced fresh cilantro

2 tablespoons lime juice

1 tablespoon minced jalapeño pepper*

* Chili peppers can sting and irritate the skin; wear rubber gloves when handling and do not touch eyes. Wash hands after handling chili peppers.

Combine all ingredients in small bowl.

Makes about 1 cup sauce

Nutrients per Serving

Calories	65
Total Fat	<1 g
Cholesterol	<1 mg
Sodium	23 mg

🍂 *Chicken Breast with Orange-Basil Pesto*

164

Basil-Pecan Shells with Smoked Salmon

1 cup fresh basil, stems removed
¼ cup freshly grated Parmesan cheese
2 cloves garlic
1 tablespoon olive oil
¾ cup plain nonfat yogurt
⅓ cup skim milk
12 ounces uncooked medium-sized
    pasta shells or conchiglie
8 ounces smoked salmon, cut into
    bite-sized pieces
4 tablespoons chopped pecans,
    toasted

1. Place basil, cheese, garlic and oil in food processor or blender; process until finely chopped. Set aside. Combine yogurt and milk in small bowl; set aside.

2. Cook pasta according to package directions. Drain well. Transfer to large serving bowl. Add basil mixture, yogurt mixture, salmon and pecans; mix well. Garnish as desired. Serve immediately.

Makes 4 servings

Nutrients per Serving

Calories	497
Total Fat	15 g
Cholesterol	19 mg
Sodium	600 mg

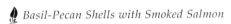

Basil-Pecan Shells with Smoked Salmon

Chicken Breasts with Orange-Basil Pesto

½ cup fresh basil
2 tablespoons grated orange peel
2 cloves garlic
2 teaspoons olive oil
3 tablespoons orange juice
1 tablespoon Dijon mustard
    Salt and black pepper
6 chicken breast halves

1. Preheat broiler. Add basil, orange peel and garlic to food processor; process until finely chopped. Add oil, orange juice and mustard. Season to taste with salt and pepper. Process few seconds or until paste forms.

2. Spread equal amounts of mixture under skin and on bone side of each chicken breast. Place chicken, skin side down, on broiler pan. Broil 4 inches from heat 10 minutes. Turn chicken over; broil 10 to 12 minutes or until chicken is no longer pink in center. If chicken browns too quickly, cover with foil. Remove skin from chicken before serving.

Makes 6 servings

Nutrients per Serving

Calories	206
Total Fat	6 g
Cholesterol	91 mg
Sodium	113 mg

*Favorite recipe from **Florida Department of Citrus***

Fruited Lamb Stew

2 tablespoons all-purpose flour
½ teaspoon salt
  Dash ground red pepper
1 pound boneless lamb, cut into
    ¾-inch cubes
2 tablespoons vegetable oil
1 small leek, sliced
3 cups chicken broth
½ teaspoon grated fresh ginger root
8 ounces peeled baby carrots
½ cup frozen peas
¾ cup chopped mixed dried fruit
    (½ of 8-ounce package)
  Black pepper
1⅓ cups hot cooked couscous

1. Preheat oven to 350°F. Combine flour, salt and red pepper in medium bowl. Add lamb to flour mixture; toss well.

2. Heat oil in 5-quart ovenproof Dutch oven over medium-high heat. Add lamb; brown, stirring frequently. Add leek, broth and ginger to Dutch oven. Bring to a boil over high heat.

3. Cover; remove to oven. Bake 45 minutes. Stir in carrots. Cover; bake 30 minutes or until lamb and carrots are almost tender.

4. Stir peas and fruit into stew. Cover; bake 10 minutes. If necessary, skim off fat with large spoon. Season to taste with pepper.

5. Serve stew in bowls; top with couscous. Garnish with fresh chervil, if desired.
Makes 4 servings

Nutrients per Serving

Calories	480
Total Fat	17 g
Cholesterol	91 mg
Sodium	1151 mg

Chive Whole Wheat Drop Biscuits

1¼ cups whole wheat flour
¾ cup all-purpose flour
3 tablespoons toasted wheat germ,
    divided
1 tablespoon baking powder
1 tablespoon chopped fresh chives *or*
    1 teaspoon dried chives
2 teaspoons sugar
3 tablespoons margarine
1 cup skim milk
½ cup (2 ounces) shredded low-fat
    process American cheese

1. Preheat oven to 450°F. Spray baking sheet with nonstick cooking spray. Combine both flours, 2 tablespoons wheat germ, baking powder, chives and sugar in medium bowl. Cut in margarine with pastry blender or 2 knives until mixture resembles coarse crumbs. Add milk and cheese; stir until just combined.

2. Drop dough by rounded teaspoonfuls onto prepared baking sheet about 1 inch apart. Sprinkle with remaining 1 tablespoon wheat germ. Bake 10 to 12 minutes or until golden brown. Remove immediately from baking sheet. Serve warm.
Makes 12 servings

Nutrients per Serving

Calories	125
Total Fat	4 g
Cholesterol	2 mg
Sodium	152 mg

Chive Whole Wheat Drop Biscuits

🍂 *Fruited Lamb Stew*

🍲 *Chilly Vichyssoise with Cheese*

Chilly Vichyssoise with Cheese

2 tablespoons butter or margarine
2 small leeks, sliced
4 medium potatoes, peeled and cubed
2 cups chicken broth
1 package (3 ounces) cream cheese, cut into 1-inch pieces
2 cups milk
1 cup half-and-half
½ teaspoon seasoned salt
⅛ teaspoon black pepper

1. Melt butter in large saucepan over medium heat. Add leeks; cook and stir until soft. Add potatoes and broth to saucepan. Bring to a boil over high heat. Reduce heat to medium-low; simmer, uncovered, 15 minutes or until potatoes are tender.

2. Add cream cheese to potato mixture; melt over low heat, stirring constantly.

3. Place soup in batches in food processor or blender; process until smooth. Return soup to saucepan. Stir in milk, half-and-half, salt and pepper.

4. Sprinkle each serving with chopped chives. Garnish as desired.

Makes 8 servings

Note: To serve soup hot, cook soup over medium-high heat until bubbly; serve immediately. To serve soup cold, pour into large bowl; refrigerate at least 6 hours or overnight. Serve chilled.

Nutrients per Serving

Calories	217	
Total Fat	12	g
Cholesterol	39	mg
Sodium	494	mg

Grilled Scallops and Vegetables with Cilantro Sauce

1 teaspoon hot chili oil
1 teaspoon sesame oil
1 green onion, chopped
1 tablespoon finely chopped fresh ginger root
1 cup reduced-sodium chicken broth
1 cup chopped fresh cilantro
1 pound raw sea scallops
2 medium zucchini, cut into ½-inch slices
2 medium yellow squash, cut into ½-inch slices
1 medium yellow onion, cut into wedges
8 large mushrooms, wiped clean

1. Spray grid with nonstick cooking spray. Preheat grill to medium-high heat. Heat chili oil and sesame oil in small saucepan over medium-low heat. Add green onion; cook about 15 seconds or just until fragrant. Add ginger; cook 1 minute.

2. Add broth; bring to a boil. Cook until liquid is reduced by half. Place broth mixture in blender or food processor; add cilantro. Blend until smooth. Set aside.

3. Thread scallops and vegetables onto skewers. Grill about 8 minutes per side or until scallops turn opaque. Serve hot with cilantro sauce. Garnish as desired.

Makes 4 servings

Nutrients per Serving

Calories	171	
Total Fat	4	g
Cholesterol	48	mg
Sodium	258	mg

Grilled Scallops and Vegetables with Cilantro Sauce

Cherry Salsa

¾ pound dark or light sweet cherries
¼ cup finely chopped red onion
1 tablespoon chopped cilantro
2 teaspoons lime juice
2 teaspoons minced jalapeño pepper*
1 teaspoon minced fresh ginger root

Chili peppers can sting and irritate the skin; wear rubber gloves when handling and do not touch eyes. Wash hands after handling chili peppers.

1. Remove stems and pits from cherries. Cut cherries into halves (about 2¼ cups). Combine cherries, onion, cilantro, lime juice, jalapeño and ginger in medium bowl.

2. Cover; refrigerate at least 1 hour before serving. Stir before serving.

Makes 4 servings

Note: Serve salsa with baked or grilled chicken breasts, pork tenderloin or hearty fish, such as tuna, mackerel or catfish.

Nutrients per Serving

Calories	66	
Total Fat	<1	g
Cholesterol	0	mg
Sodium	21	mg

Black Bean and Tempeh Burritos with Sauce

2 teaspoons olive oil
½ cup chopped onion
½ cup chopped green bell pepper
2 cloves garlic, minced
2 teaspoons chili powder
1 teaspoon dried oregano leaves
½ teaspoon dried coriander leaves
2 cans (14½ ounces each) no-salt-added stewed tomatoes, undrained
1 can (15 ounces) black beans, rinsed and drained
¼ pound tempeh, diced
¼ cup minced onion
¼ teaspoon black pepper
½ teaspoon ground cumin
8 flour tortillas (6-inch)

1. For sauce, heat oil in large nonstick skillet over medium heat. Add ½ cup chopped onion, bell pepper and garlic; cook and stir 5 minutes or until onion is tender. Add chili powder; cook 1 minute. Add oregano, coriander and tomatoes with liquid; cook and stir over medium heat 15 minutes.

2. Preheat oven to 350°F. Place beans in medium bowl; mash well with fork. Mix in tempeh, ¼ cup minced onion, black pepper and cumin. Stir in ¼ cup sauce.

3. Soften tortillas, if necessary.* Spread ⅓ cup bean mixture in center of each tortilla. Roll up tortillas; place in single layer in shallow baking dish. Pour remaining sauce over burritos. Bake 15 minutes or until heated through.

Makes 4 servings

To soften tortillas, wrap stack of tortillas in foil. Heat in preheated 350°F oven about 10 minutes or until softened.

Nutrients per Serving

Calories	440	
Total Fat	10	g
Cholesterol	0	mg
Sodium	620	mg

Curried Cauliflower Rice & Vermicelli

1 teaspoon vegetable oil
½ cup finely chopped onion
1 large clove garlic, minced
1 teaspoon curry powder
½ teaspoon ground coriander
¼ teaspoon salt
⅓ cup uncooked long-grain rice
⅓ cup uncooked vermicelli broken into 1-inch pieces
1 cup apple juice
3 cups cauliflower florets
3 tablespoons golden raisins

1. Heat oil in large nonstick skillet over medium heat. Add onion and garlic; cook and stir 2 minutes. Add curry powder, coriander and salt; cook and stir 1 minute. Stir in rice and vermicelli until well coated. Remove pan from heat.

2. Bring apple juice and ½ cup water to a boil in small saucepan over high heat; pour over rice and vermicelli mixture. Bring mixture to a boil over high heat. Reduce heat to low. Simmer, covered, 15 minutes.

3. Place cauliflower florets and raisins over rice mixture. Cover; simmer about 7 minutes or until water is absorbed. Stir cauliflower florets and raisins into rice mixture. Remove from heat; let stand, covered, 5 minutes or until cauliflower is crisp-tender. Fluff with fork before serving.

Makes 4 servings

Nutrients per Serving

Calories	206	
Total Fat	4	g
Cholesterol	0	mg
Sodium	187	mg

Chicken Fricassee

3 pounds chicken pieces (breasts, legs, thighs)
All-purpose flour
3 cups fat-free reduced-sodium chicken broth
1 bay leaf
1 pound whole baby carrots
¾ cup onion wedges (about 1 medium)
1 tablespoon margarine
3 tablespoons all-purpose flour
¾ cup skim milk
1 tablespoon lemon juice
3 tablespoons minced fresh dill *or* 2 teaspoons dried dill weed
1 teaspoon sugar
½ teaspoon salt
6 cups hot cooked noodles

1. Coat chicken pieces very lightly with flour. Spray large nonstick skillet with cooking spray; heat over medium heat until hot. Add chicken; cook 10 to 15 minutes or until browned. Drain fat from skillet.

2. Add broth and bay leaf to skillet; bring to a boil. Cover; reduce heat to low. Simmer about 1 hour or until chicken is no longer pink in center and juices run clear, adding carrots and onion during last 20 minutes of cooking.

(continued on page 172)

Chicken Fricassee

Chicken Fricassee *(continued from page 170)*

3. Transfer chicken and vegetables with slotted spoon to platter; keep warm. Bring broth to a boil; cook until broth is reduced to 1 cup. Remove and discard bay leaf.

4. Melt margarine in small saucepan over low heat; stir in 3 tablespoons flour. Cook and stir 1 to 2 minutes. Stir in broth, milk and lemon juice; bring to a boil. Boil until thickened, stirring constantly. Stir in dill, sugar and salt. Arrange chicken and vegetables over noodles on serving plates; top with sauce. Garnish as desired.

Makes 6 servings

Nutrients per Serving

Calories	565
Total Fat	19 g
Cholesterol	158 mg
Sodium	357 mg

Dilled Tuna Sandwiches

1	can (12½ ounces) chunk light tuna in water, drained
¼	cup thinly sliced green onions
¼	cup chopped seeded cucumber
3	tablespoons reduced-calorie mayonnaise
1½	teaspoons drained capers
1	teaspoon Dijon mustard
½	to 1 teaspoon lemon juice
¾	teaspoon dried dill weed
	Ground white pepper
4	slices multigrain bread, toasted

1. Break tuna into chunks in small bowl; add green onions and chopped cucumber. Stir in mayonnaise, capers, mustard, lemon juice and dill weed; season to taste with pepper.

2. Spread tuna mixture over toasted bread slices. Garnish as desired.

Makes 4 servings

Nutrients per Serving

Calories	200
Total Fat	6 g
Cholesterol	20 mg
Sodium	180 mg

Favorite recipe from **Canned Food Information Council**

Brussels Sprouts with Lemon-Dill Glaze

1	pound Brussels sprouts
2	teaspoons cornstarch
½	teaspoon dried dill weed
½	cup fat-free reduced-sodium chicken broth
3	tablespoons lemon juice
½	teaspoon grated lemon peel

1. Trim Brussels sprouts. Cut an "X" in stem ends. Bring 1 cup water to a boil in large saucepan over high heat. Add Brussels sprouts; return to a boil. Reduce heat to medium-low. Cover; simmer 10 minutes or until just tender. Drain well; return to pan. Set aside.

2. Meanwhile, combine cornstarch and dill weed in small saucepan. Blend in broth and lemon juice until smooth. Stir in lemon peel. Cook and stir over medium heat 5 minutes or until mixture boils and thickens. Cook and stir 1 minute more.

3. Pour glaze over Brussels sprouts; toss gently to coat. Serve hot.

Makes 4 servings

Nutrients per Serving

Calories	58
Total Fat	<1 g
Cholesterol	0 mg
Sodium	30 mg

Fennel with Parmesan Bread Crumbs

2	large fennel bulbs
½	cup dry bread crumbs
¼	cup lemon juice
1	tablespoon freshly grated Parmesan cheese
1	tablespoon capers
2	teaspoons olive oil
⅛	teaspoon black pepper
½	cup reduced-sodium chicken broth

1. Preheat oven to 375°F. Spray 9-inch square baking dish with nonstick cooking spray; set aside.

2. Remove outer leaves and wide base from fennel bulbs. Slice bulbs crosswise.

3. Combine fennel and ¼ cup water in medium nonstick skillet with tight-fitting lid. Bring to a boil over high heat. Reduce heat to medium. Cover; steam 4 minutes or until fennel is crisp-tender. Cool slightly; arrange in prepared baking pan.

4. Combine bread crumbs, lemon juice, cheese, capers, oil and pepper in small bowl. Sprinkle bread crumb mixture over fennel; pour broth over top.

5. Bake, uncovered, 20 to 25 minutes or until golden brown. Garnish with minced fennel leaves and red bell pepper strips, if desired. *Makes 4 servings*

Nutrients per Serving

Calories	113
Total Fat	4 g
Cholesterol	1 mg
Sodium	213 mg

Fennel with Parmesan Bread Crumbs

 Garden Greens with Fennel Dressing

174

Garden Greens with Fennel Dressing

Dressing

- ½ teaspoon unflavored gelatin
- 2 tablespoons cold water
- ¼ cup boiling water
- ½ teaspoon salt
- ½ teaspoon sugar
- ¼ teaspoon dry mustard
- ⅛ teaspoon black pepper
- ¼ teaspoon anise extract or ground fennel seeds
- 1 tablespoon fresh lemon juice
- ¼ cup raspberry or wine vinegar
- 1¼ teaspoons walnut or vegetable oil

Salad

- 1 head (10 ounces) Bibb lettuce, washed and torn into bite-sized pieces
- 1 head (10 ounces) radicchio, washed and torn into bite-sized pieces
- 1 bunch arugula (3 ounces), washed and torn into bite-sized pieces
- 1 cup mâche or spinach leaves, washed and torn into bite-sized pieces
- 1 fennel bulb (8 ounces), finely chopped
- 1 tablespoon pine nuts, toasted

1. To prepare dressing, sprinkle gelatin over cold water in small bowl; let stand 1 minute to soften. Add boiling water; stir 2 minutes or until gelatin is completely dissolved. Add salt and sugar; stir until sugar is completely dissolved. Add mustard, pepper, anise extract, lemon juice and vinegar; mix well.

2. Slowly whisk in oil until well blended. Cover; refrigerate 2 hours or overnight. Shake well before using.

3. To prepare salad, place lettuce, radicchio, arugula, mâche and fennel in large bowl. Add dressing; toss until well coated. Divide salad among 6 salad plates. Top each serving with ½ teaspoon pine nuts. Garnish with sprig of fennel fern, if desired. *Makes 6 servings*

Nutrients per Serving

Calories	60
Total Fat	2 g
Cholesterol	0 mg
Sodium	226 mg

Kasha and Bow Tie Pasta with Mushrooms and Broccoli

- 2 cups broccoli florets
- 2½ cups small bow tie pasta
- 2 teaspoons olive oil
- ½ pound fresh mushrooms, wiped clean and sliced ¼ inch thick
- ½ cup chopped onion
- 3 cloves garlic, minced
- ¾ cup uncooked kasha
- 1 egg
- 1½ cups fat-free reduced-sodium chicken broth
- 1 teaspoon dried marjoram leaves
- ¼ teaspoon black pepper

1. Bring 3 quarts water to a boil in large saucepan over high heat. Add broccoli; return to a boil. Cook, uncovered, over medium-high heat 2 minutes or until crisp-tender. Remove broccoli to large bowl with slotted spoon, reserving water.

2. Return water to a boil. Add pasta; cook, uncovered, 5 minutes or until just tender. *Do not overcook.* Drain; add pasta to broccoli and mix gently. Set aside.

3. Wipe saucepan with paper towel. Add oil, mushrooms, onion and garlic to saucepan; cook and stir 5 minutes or until onion is soft. Stir into broccoli mixture.

4. Add kasha and egg to saucepan; stir until blended. Cook and stir over medium heat 3 minutes or until kasha is dry and grains are separated. Stir in broth, marjoram and pepper. Bring to a boil over medium-high heat. Reduce heat to low. Cover; cook 10 minutes, stirring occasionally. Remove from heat; let stand, covered, 10 minutes. Gently mix with pasta mixture. Garnish each serving with chopped red bell pepper, if desired. *Makes 4 servings*

Nutrients per Serving

Calories	278
Total Fat	6 g
Cholesterol	76 mg
Sodium	51 mg

Beef Barley Soup

- ¾ pound boneless beef top round, trimmed, cut into ½-inch pieces
- 3 cans (14 ounces each) fat-free reduced-sodium beef broth
- 1 can (14½ ounces) no-salt-added tomatoes, undrained
- 2 cups cubed unpeeled potatoes
- 1½ cups thinly sliced green beans
- 1 cup chopped onion
- 1 cup sliced carrots
- ½ cup pearled barley
- 1 tablespoon cider vinegar
- 2 teaspoons caraway seeds, lightly crushed
- 2 teaspoons dried marjoram leaves
- 2 teaspoons dried thyme leaves
- ½ teaspoon salt
- ½ teaspoon black pepper

1. Spray large saucepan with nonstick cooking spray; heat over medium heat. Add beef; cook and stir until browned.

2. Add remaining ingredients; bring to a boil over high heat. Reduce heat to low. Cover; simmer about 2 hours or until beef is fork-tender, uncovering saucepan during last 30 minutes of cooking. *Makes 4 servings*

Nutrients per Serving

Calories	447
Total Fat	5 g
Cholesterol	76 mg
Sodium	431 mg

🌶 *Mediterranean Sandwiches*

Bean & Mushroom Salad with Fresh Herb Dressing

1 can (16 ounces) red kidney beans, rinsed and drained
1 can (16 ounces) lima beans, rinsed and drained
1 cup sliced mushrooms
1 cup chopped green bell pepper
¼ cup chopped green onions, including tops
  Fresh Herb Dressing (recipe follows)
1 cup cherry tomatoes, halved
10 leaves romaine lettuce (optional)

1. Combine beans, mushrooms, bell pepper and onions in large bowl. Prepare Fresh Herb Dressing. Add dressing to vegetable mixture. Cover; refrigerate 2 to 3 hours or overnight.

2. Add tomatoes to bean mixture; mix well. Serve on lettuce-lined plates, if desired. *Makes 10 servings*

Fresh Herb Dressing

½ cup red wine vinegar
2 tablespoons olive oil
1 clove garlic, crushed
1 tablespoon chopped fresh oregano
1 tablespoon chopped fresh marjoram
½ teaspoon sugar
⅛ teaspoon black pepper

Combine all ingredients in small bowl; mix well.

Nutrients per Serving

Calories	111
Total Fat	3 g
Cholesterol	0 mg
Sodium	273 mg

Mediterranean Sandwiches

1¼ pounds chicken tenders, cut crosswise in half
1 large tomato, cut into bite-sized pieces
½ small cucumber, seeded and sliced
½ cup sweet onion slices
2 tablespoons cider vinegar
1 tablespoon olive oil
3 teaspoons minced fresh oregano *or* 1 teaspoon dried oregano leaves
2 teaspoons minced fresh mint *or* ¼ teaspoon dried mint leaves
¼ teaspoon salt
12 lettuce leaves (optional)
6 whole wheat pita breads, cut into halves crosswise

1. Spray large nonstick skillet with nonstick cooking spray; heat over medium heat until hot. Add chicken; cook and stir 7 to 10 minutes or until browned and no longer pink in center. Cool slightly.

2. Combine chicken, tomato, cucumber and onion in medium bowl. Drizzle with vinegar and oil; toss to coat. Sprinkle with oregano, mint and salt; toss to combine.

3. Place 1 lettuce leaf in each pita bread half, if desired. Divide chicken mixture evenly; spoon into pita bread halves. *Makes 6 servings*

Nutrients per Serving

Calories	242
Total Fat	6 g
Cholesterol	50 mg
Sodium	353 mg

🍃 Bean & Mushroom Salad with Fresh Herb Dressing

Pork and Vegetable Stew with Noodles

Pepperoni-Oregano Focaccia

1 tablespoon cornmeal
1 package (10 ounces) refrigerated pizza crust dough
½ cup finely chopped pepperoni (3 to 3½ ounces)
1½ teaspoons finely chopped fresh oregano *or* ½ teaspoon dried oregano leaves
2 teaspoons olive oil

1. Preheat oven to 425°F. Grease large baking sheet; sprinkle with cornmeal. Set aside.

2. Unroll dough onto lightly floured surface. Pat dough into 12×9-inch rectangle. Sprinkle half of the pepperoni and half of the oregano over one side of dough. Fold dough making 6×4½-inch rectangle.

3. Roll dough into 12×9-inch rectangle. Place on prepared baking sheet. Prick dough with fork at 2-inch intervals, about 30 times. Brush with oil; sprinkle with remaining pepperoni and oregano.

4. Bake 12 to 15 minutes or until golden brown. (Prick dough several more times if dough puffs as it bakes.) Cut into squares. *Makes 12 servings*

Nutrients per Serving

Calories	104
Total Fat	4 g
Cholesterol	0 mg
Sodium	258 mg

Pork and Vegetable Stew with Noodles

2 tablespoons vegetable oil
1 pound lean boneless pork, cut into ¾-inch cubes
3 cups canned beef broth
3 tablespoons chopped fresh parsley, divided
1 can (14½ ounces) stewed tomatoes, undrained
1 large carrot, sliced
3 green onions, sliced
2 teaspoons Dijon mustard
¼ teaspoon rubbed sage
⅛ teaspoon black pepper
3 cups uncooked noodles
1 teaspoon butter or margarine
2 tablespoons all-purpose flour

1. Heat oil in large saucepan over medium-high heat. Add pork; brown, stirring frequently.

2. Carefully add broth. Stir in 1 tablespoon parsley, tomatoes, carrot, onions, mustard, sage and pepper. Bring to a boil over high heat. Reduce heat to medium-low; simmer, uncovered, 30 minutes.

3. Meanwhile, cook noodles according to package directions; drain. Add remaining 2 tablespoons parsley and butter; toss lightly. Keep warm.

4. Stir flour into ⅓ cup cold water in cup until smooth. Stir into stew. Cook and stir over medium heat until slightly thickened.

5. Divide noodles between 4 plates. Ladle stew over noodles. Garnish as desired. *Makes 4 servings*

Nutrients per Serving

Calories	372
Total Fat	16 g
Cholesterol	79 mg
Sodium	967 mg

Tabbouleh

½ cup uncooked bulgur
¾ cup boiling water
¼ teaspoon salt
5 teaspoons lemon juice
2 teaspoons olive oil
½ teaspoon dried basil leaves
¼ teaspoon black pepper
1 green onion, thinly sliced
½ cup chopped cucumber
½ cup chopped green bell pepper
½ cup chopped tomato
¼ cup chopped fresh parsley
2 teaspoons chopped mint

1. Rinse bulgur thoroughly under cold water, picking out any debris. Drain well; transfer to medium heat-proof bowl. Stir in boiling water and salt. Cover; let stand 30 minutes. Drain well.

2. Combine lemon juice, oil, basil and black pepper in small bowl. Pour over bulgur; mix well. Layer bulgur, onion, cucumber, bell pepper and tomato in clear glass bowl; sprinkle with parsley and mint.

3. Cover; refrigerate at least 2 hours before serving. Serve layered or toss before serving. *Makes 8 servings*

Nutrients per Serving

Calories	48
Total Fat	1 g
Cholesterol	0 mg
Sodium	71 mg

Spicy Parsley Sauce with Angel Hair Pasta

1 cup chopped fresh parsley
2 fresh red chili peppers, seeded and chopped*
  Dash hot red pepper sauce
1 clove garlic, minced
2 tablespoons lemon juice
1 teaspoon grated lemon peel
⅛ teaspoon black pepper
4 teaspoons olive oil
¼ cup slivered almonds
1 teaspoon cornstarch
½ cup reduced-sodium chicken broth
½ pound uncooked angel hair pasta

Chili peppers can sting and irritate the skin; wear rubber gloves when handling and do not touch eyes. Wash hands after handling chili peppers.

1. Combine parsley, chili peppers, hot pepper sauce, garlic, lemon juice, lemon peel and black pepper in medium bowl. Blend well. Mix in oil and almonds.

2. Combine cornstarch and broth in small saucepan. Cook and stir over low heat 3 to 5 minutes or until thickened. Remove from heat; add to parsley mixture.

3. Cook pasta according to package directions. Drain well. Transfer to large serving bowl. Pour parsley sauce over pasta; mix well. Garnish as desired.

Makes 8 servings

Nutrients per Serving

Calories	146
Total Fat	5 g
Cholesterol	0 mg
Sodium	11 mg

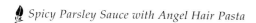
Spicy Parsley Sauce with Angel Hair Pasta

Roasted Rosemary-Lemon Chicken

1 whole chicken (about 3 pounds)
½ teaspoon black pepper
1 lemon, cut into eighths
¼ cup fresh parsley
4 sprigs fresh rosemary
3 fresh sage leaves
2 sprigs fresh thyme
1 can (14 ounces) reduced-sodium chicken broth
1 cup sliced onions
4 cloves garlic
1 cup thinly sliced carrots
1 cup thinly sliced zucchini

1. Preheat oven to 350°F. Trim fat from chicken, leaving skin on. Rinse chicken and pat dry with paper towels. Fill cavity of chicken with pepper, lemon, parsley, rosemary, sage and thyme. Close cavity with skewers.

2. Combine broth, onions and garlic in heavy roasting pan. Place chicken in broth. Bake 1½ hours or until juices run clear when pierced with fork. Remove chicken to serving plate.

3. Combine carrots and zucchini in small saucepan with tight-fitting lid. Add ¼ cup water; bring to a boil over high heat. Reduce heat to medium. Cover; steam 4 minutes or until vegetables are crisp-tender. Transfer vegetables to colander; drain.

4. Remove skewers. Discard lemon and herbs from cavity of chicken. Remove skin from chicken. Cut chicken into pieces. Remove onions and garlic from pan with slotted spoon to medium serving bowl or plate. Add carrots and zucchini; mix well. Arrange vegetable mixture around chicken. Garnish with fresh rosemary and lemon, if desired.

Makes 6 servings

Nutrients per Serving

Calories	282
Total Fat	10 g
Cholesterol	120 mg
Sodium	133 mg

Roasted Rosemary-Lemon Chicken

Herbed Angel Hair Mushroom Wedge

4 cups cooked angel hair pasta
¾ cup cholesterol-free egg substitute
½ cup freshly grated Parmesan cheese
2 green onions including tops, chopped
1 tablespoon chopped fresh basil
1 tablespoon chopped fresh sage
1 tablespoon chopped fresh mint
⅛ teaspoon black pepper
1 tablespoon olive oil
2 cups sliced fresh mushrooms
1 cup Tomato-Sage Sauce (recipe follows)

1. Preheat oven to 375°F. Combine pasta, egg substitute, cheese, onions, basil, sage, mint and pepper in large bowl. Mix well. Set aside.

2. Heat oil in medium nonstick skillet over low heat. Add mushrooms; cook and stir 2 to 3 minutes or until tender. Add mushrooms to pasta mixture.

3. Spray 9-inch square baking pan with nonstick cooking spray. Pour pasta mixture into pan, pressing firmly until packed down. Bake 25 to 30 minutes or until crisp and lightly browned and center is firm to touch. Remove from oven; cool slightly.

4. Prepare Tomato-Sage Sauce; set aside. Loosen pasta mixture from edges and bottom with spatula. Invert to remove from pan. Cut into wedges. Serve with Tomato-Sage Sauce.

Makes 8 servings

Tomato-Sage Sauce

2 cans (10 ounces each) no-salt-added whole tomatoes, undrained
1 teaspoon olive oil
3 cloves garlic, minced
¼ cup chopped fresh parsley
2 tablespoons chopped fresh sage
2 teaspoons sugar
¼ teaspoon black pepper

1. Place tomatoes in food processor or blender; process until finely chopped. Set aside.

2. Heat oil in medium saucepan over low heat. Add tomatoes, garlic, parsley, sage, sugar and pepper. Cook over medium heat 30 minutes or until thickened.

Makes 8 (¼-cup) servings

Nutrients per Serving

Calories	136
Total Fat	4 g
Cholesterol	5 mg
Sodium	150 mg

Caribbean Pork Stew

1½ pounds lean boneless pork, cut into ¾-inch cubes
¼ cup all-purpose flour
½ to ¾ teaspoon ground red pepper
½ teaspoon salt
½ teaspoon paprika
3 tablespoons vegetable oil
2 cloves garlic, chopped
1 medium onion, coarsely chopped
1 can (16 ounces) crushed tomatoes, undrained
2 tablespoons white wine
½ teaspoon ground ginger
½ teaspoon ground allspice
¼ teaspoon ground nutmeg
1 cup sliced fresh mushrooms
1 green bell pepper, coarsely chopped
1 red bell pepper, coarsely chopped

1. Place pork in resealable plastic food storage bag. Combine flour, ground red pepper, salt and paprika in small dish; sprinkle over pork. Close bag; shake to coat.

2. Heat oil in 5-quart Dutch oven over medium-high heat. Add pork; brown, stirring frequently. Add garlic and onion; cook and stir 4 minutes or until onion is soft.

3. Add tomatoes, ¼ cup water, wine, ginger, allspice and nutmeg; bring to a boil over high heat. Reduce heat to low; simmer, uncovered, 30 minutes, stirring occasionally.

4. Stir in mushrooms and bell peppers. Simmer, uncovered, 12 minutes or until peppers are tender. Garnish with fresh sage leaves, if desired.

Makes 6 servings

Nutrients per Serving

Calories	311
Total Fat	14 g
Cholesterol	64 mg
Sodium	374 mg

Caribbean Pork Stew

➥ Garden-Vegetable Bulgur Stew

Garden-Vegetable Bulgur Stew

1 tablespoon vegetable oil
1 large onion, chopped
2 medium tomatoes, peeled and chopped
2 medium carrots, peeled and sliced
4 ounces fresh green beans, cut into 1-inch pieces
2 green onions, sliced
¾ cup canned garbanzo beans, drained
1 can (12 ounces) tomato juice (1½ cups)
⅓ cup uncooked bulgur
1 tablespoon dried mint leaves
1 teaspoon dried summer savory leaves
½ teaspoon salt
Dash black pepper
1 small zucchini, sliced

1. Heat oil in 5-quart Dutch oven over medium heat. Add onion; cook and stir until onion is tender.

2. Stir tomatoes, carrots, green beans, green onions, garbanzo beans, tomato juice, 1 cup water, bulgur, mint, savory, salt and pepper into Dutch oven. Bring to a boil over high heat. Reduce heat to medium-low; simmer, uncovered, about 20 minutes or until beans and carrots are slightly tender.

3. Add zucchini to vegetable mixture. Bring to a boil over high heat. Reduce heat to medium-low; simmer, uncovered, about 4 minutes or until zucchini is slightly tender. Serve in bowls and garnish with dollops of sour cream, if desired.   *Makes 4 servings*

Nutrients per Serving

Calories	174
Total Fat	5 g
Cholesterol	0 mg
Sodium	740 mg

Red Snapper with Brown Rice and Tomato Stuffing

1 can (14½ ounces) fat-free reduced-sodium chicken broth
1 cup uncooked brown rice
1½ tablespoons chopped fresh savory *or* 1½ teaspoons dried savory leaves
1 tablespoon chopped fresh oregano *or* ¾ teaspoon dried oregano leaves
⅛ teaspoon ground red pepper
¾ cup coarsely chopped yellow summer squash
⅓ cup sliced green onions
¼ cup chopped fresh parsley
1 cup chopped tomatoes
3 to 4 lime slices
Fresh savory sprigs (optional)
Fresh oregano sprigs (optional)
2 to 2½ pounds fresh or frozen red or yellow tail snapper, scaled and head removed

1. Bring broth and ⅓ cup water to a boil over high heat in medium saucepan. Stir in rice, chopped savory, chopped oregano and red pepper. Return to a boil. Reduce heat to medium-low. Cover; simmer 20 minutes.

2. Stir in squash, green onions and parsley. Cover; simmer 15 minutes or until rice is almost tender and liquid is absorbed. Stir in tomatoes. Spoon into ungreased 1½-quart casserole.

3. Preheat oven to 400°F. Spray shallow baking pan with nonstick cooking spray. Arrange lime slices, savory and/or oregano sprigs in fish cavity, if desired. Place fish in prepared pan.

4. Cover; bake fish and stuffing at the same time, 25 to 30 minutes or until fish flakes easily when tested with fork and stuffing is heated through. Spoon stuffing onto serving platter; arrange fish over stuffing. Garnish fish with green onions, if desired.   *Makes 4 servings*

Nutrients per Serving

Calories	430
Total Fat	5 g
Cholesterol	83 mg
Sodium	130 mg

Red Snapper with Brown Rice and Tomato Stuffing

Tarragon Chicken Salad Sandwiches

1¼ pounds boneless skinless chicken breasts, cooked
1 cup thinly sliced celery
1 cup seedless red or green grapes, cut into halves
½ cup raisins
½ cup plain nonfat yogurt
¼ cup reduced-fat mayonnaise or salad dressing
2 tablespoons finely chopped shallots or onion
2 tablespoons minced fresh tarragon *or* 1 teaspoon dried tarragon leaves
½ teaspoon salt
⅛ teaspoon ground white pepper
6 lettuce leaves
6 whole wheat buns, split

1. Cut chicken into ½-inch pieces. Combine chicken, celery, grapes and raisins in large bowl. Combine yogurt, mayonnaise, shallots, tarragon, salt and pepper in small bowl. Spoon over chicken mixture; mix lightly.

2. Place 1 lettuce leaf in each bun. Divide chicken mixture evenly; spoon into buns.

Makes 6 servings

Nutrients per Serving

Calories	353
Total Fat	7 g
Cholesterol	76 mg
Sodium	509 mg

 Tarragon Chicken Salad Sandwich

Crab Spinach Salad with Tarragon Dressing

12 ounces coarsely flaked cooked crabmeat *or* 2 packages (6 ounces each) frozen crabmeat, thawed and drained
1 cup chopped tomato
1 cup sliced cucumber
⅓ cup sliced red onion
¼ cup nonfat salad dressing or mayonnaise
¼ cup low-fat sour cream
¼ cup chopped fresh parsley
2 tablespoons skim milk
2 teaspoons chopped fresh tarragon *or* ½ teaspoon dried tarragon leaves
1 clove garlic, minced
¼ teaspoon hot pepper sauce
8 cups packed torn, stemmed, washed spinach

1. Combine crabmeat, tomato, cucumber and onion in medium bowl. Combine salad dressing, sour cream, parsley, milk, tarragon, garlic and pepper sauce in small bowl.

2. Line four salad plates with spinach; top with crabmeat mixture. Drizzle dressing over salad.

Makes 4 servings

Nutrients per Serving

Calories	170
Total Fat	4 g
Cholesterol	91 mg
Sodium	481 mg

🦀 *Crab Spinach Salad with Tarragon Dressing*

 *Beef Bourguignon*

Beef Bourguignon

1 boneless beef sirloin steak, ½ inch thick, trimmed, cut into ½-inch pieces (about 3 pounds)
½ cup all-purpose flour
4 slices uncooked bacon, diced
3 cups Burgundy wine or beef broth
2 medium carrots, diced
1 teaspoon dried marjoram leaves
½ teaspoon dried thyme leaves
½ teaspoon salt
  Black pepper
1 bay leaf
2 tablespoons vegetable oil
20 to 24 fresh pearl onions
8 small new red potatoes, quartered
8 to 10 mushrooms, sliced
3 cloves garlic, minced

1. Coat beef with flour, shaking off excess. Set aside.

2. Cook and stir bacon in 5-quart Dutch oven over medium-high heat until partially cooked. Add half of the beef to bacon; brown over medium-high heat. Remove with slotted spoon; set aside. Brown remaining beef. Pour off drippings. Return beef and bacon to Dutch oven.

3. Stir in wine, carrots, marjoram, thyme, salt, pepper to taste and bay leaf. Bring to a boil over high heat. Reduce heat to low. Cover; simmer 10 minutes.

4. Meanwhile, heat oil in large saucepan over medium-high heat. Cook and stir onions, potatoes, mushrooms and garlic about 10 minutes. Add to Dutch oven. Cover; simmer 50 minutes or until meat is fork-tender. Remove and discard bay leaf.
Makes 10 to 12 servings

Nutrients per Serving

Calories	429
Total Fat	10 g
Cholesterol	80 mg
Sodium	267 mg

Savory Seafood Soup

2½ cups water or chicken broth
1½ cups dry white wine
1 small onion, chopped
½ red bell pepper, chopped
½ green bell pepper, chopped
1 small clove garlic, minced
½ pound raw halibut, cut into 1-inch pieces
½ pound raw sea scallops, cut into halves
1 teaspoon dried thyme leaves
  Juice of ½ lime
  Dash of hot pepper sauce
  Salt and ground black pepper

1. Combine water, wine, onion, bell peppers and garlic in large saucepan. Bring to a boil. Reduce heat to medium. Cover; simmer 15 minutes or until peppers are tender, stirring occasionally.

2. Add halibut, scallops and thyme. Continue cooking 2 minutes or until halibut and scallops turn opaque. Stir in lime juice and pepper sauce. Season to taste with salt and black pepper.
Makes 4 servings

Nutrients per Serving

Calories	194
Total Fat	2 g
Cholesterol	42 mg
Sodium	156 mg

INDEX

A

Acid-alkaline balance, 24, 25
Angelica, 71, 96
Anise, 71, 96
Anthracnose, 64
Aphids, 61
Apricot-Glazed Beets, 109
Artichoke. *See also* Globe artichoke;
    Jerusalem artichoke.
    Pepper-Stuffed Artichokes, 107
Asparagus, 74
    Cold Asparagus with Lemon-Mustard
        Dressing, 107
    disease control, 65
    harvesting, 74
    planting and growing, 40, 42, 74
    Shanghai Chicken with Asparagus and
        Ham, 108
    varieties, 74
    winter protection for, 55, 74

B

Baked Acorn Squash with Apples and Raisins,
    155
Barbecued Pork Sandwiches, 126
Basil, 71, 96
    Basil-Pecan Shells with Smoked Salmon,
        165
    Chicken Breasts with Orange-Basil Pesto,
        165
Beans, 75. *See also specific types.*
    Bean & Mushroom Salad with Fresh Herb
        Dressing, 176
    harvesting, 75
    pest and disease control, 62, 63, 64, 65
    planting and growing, 42, 75
    trellis systems, 46, 47
    varieties, 75
Beef and Parsnip Stew, 136
Beef Barley Soup, 175
Beef Bourguignon, 188
Beet, 76
    Apricot-Glazed Beets, 109
    harvesting, 76
    pest and disease control, 63, 65
    planting and growing, 12, 15, 36, 42, 76
    varieties, 76
Beetles, 61
Black Bean and Tempeh Burritos with Sauce,
    170
Black-eye pea, 43, 87. *See also* Pea.
    Hoppin' John Salad, 137
Blights, 64
Borers, 62
Braised Oriental Cabbage, 118
Broad bean, 42. *See also* Beans.
Broccoli, 76
    Broccoli & Cauliflower with Mustard Sauce,
        115

Broccoli *(continued)*
    Broccoli Boutonnieres and Buttons, 111
    Broccoli Timbales, 110
    Cream of Broccoli Soup, 110
    harvesting, 76
    pest control, 62
    planting and growing, 15, 17, 32, 42, 76
    varieties, 76
    Vegetable Rings on Broccoli Spears, 111
Brussels sprouts, 17, 32, 42, 76
    Broth-Simmered Brussels Sprouts, 112
    Brussels Sprouts with Lemon-Dill Glaze,
        172
    Lemon Brussels Sprouts, 112
Bush bean. *See* Beans; Green bean; Lima
    bean.
Butternut Squash in Coconut Milk, 152

C

Cabbage, 77. *See also* Chinese cabbage.
    Cabbage Wedges with Tangy Hot Dressing,
        112
    harvesting, 77
    pest and disease control, 60, 62, 63, 65
    planting and growing, 12, 15, 17, 32, 42, 49,
        77
    varieties, 77
    Warm Blackened Tuna Salad, 114
Cabbage worms, 62
Cages, for tomatoes, 46, 47
Cajun-Style Chicken Soup, 132
Cajun-Style Corn with Crayfish, 120
California black-eye pea, 43, 87. *See also* Pea.
Cantaloupe (muskmelon), 17, 43, 85. *See also*
    Melons.
Cardoon, 42, 77
Caribbean Pork Stew, 182
Carrot, 77
    Carrot Cake, 115
    harvesting, 77
    Nutmeg & Honey Carrot Crescents, 114
    pest control, 62, 63, 64
    planting and growing, 12, 36, 42, 77
    Savory Matchstick Carrots, 114
    varieties, 77
Cauliflower, 78
    Broccoli & Cauliflower with Mustard Sauce,
        115
    harvesting, 78
    Indian-Style Vegetable Stir-Fry, 115
    pest control, 62
    planting and growing, 15, 17, 32, 42, 49, 78
    varieties, 78
Celeriac, 42, 78
Celery, 78
    Apricot and Ricotta Stuffed Celery, 116
    Celery Slaw with Cucumber-Mint Dressing,
        116
    Cioppino, 116
    harvesting, 78

Celery *(continued)*
    pest and disease control, 63, 65
    planting and growing, 32, 42, 78
    varieties, 78
Chard, 79. *See also* Swiss chard.
    harvesting, 79
    pest and disease control, 63, 65
    planting and growing, 15, 32, 42, 79
    varieties, 79
Chayote, 42, 55, 62
Chemical pesticides, 20, 21, 58, 61–65
Cherry Salsa, 170
Chervil, 71, 97
    Fruited Lamb Stew, 166
Chick pea, 42
Chicken Breasts with Orange-Basil Pesto,
    165
Chicken Chili, 143
Chicken Étouffée, 134
Chicken Fajitas, 144
Chicken Pot Pie, 138
Chicken, Tortellini and Roasted Vegetable
    Salad, 130
Chicory, 42, 79
    Orange and Green Salad, 117
Chile Verde, 155
Chilled Poached Salmon with Cucumber
    Sauce, 121
Chilly Vichyssoise with Cheese, 169
Chinese cabbage, 42, 79
    Braised Oriental Cabbage, 118
    Moo Shu Vegetables, 118
Chinese chives (Chinese leeks), 99
Chinese parsley (coriander), 71, 97
Chives, 71, 97
    Chilly Vichyssoise with Cheese, 169
    Chive Whole Wheat Drop Biscuits, 166
Chives, garlic (Chinese chives), 99
Chutney-Squash Circles, 154
Cilantro (coriander), 71, 97
    Cherry Salsa, 170
    Grilled Scallops and Vegetables with
        Cilantro Sauce, 169
Cioppino, 116
Citrus Salad with Bibb Lettuce, Watercress
    and Balsamic Dressing, 162
Climate, 12–13
Cloves, starting plants from, 40
Cob Corn in Barbecue Butter, 120
Cold Asparagus with Lemon-Mustard
    Dressing, 107
Coldframes, 12, 13, 34
Collards, 36, 42, 80
    Collard Green Medley, 120
Companion planting, 15
Compost, 28–29, 49, 50
Cool-season crops, defined, 12
Coriander, 71, 97
    Black Bean and Tempeh Burritos with
        Sauce, 170

Corriander (*continued*)
    Curried Cauliflower Rice & Vermicelli,
        170
Corn, 80
    Cajun-Style Corn with Crayfish, 120
    Cob Corn in Barbecue Butter, 120
    Corn and Tomatillo Salsa, 157
    harvesting, 80
    pest and disease control, 62, 65
    planting and growing, 15, 42, 80
    Roasted Corn & Wild Rice Salad, 121
    varieties, 80
Costmary, 71, 98
Country Green Beans with Ham, 108
Cover crops, 54, 55
Crab and Pasta Salad in Cantaloupe, 131
Crab Spinach Salad with Tarragon Dressing,
    186
Cream of Broccoli Soup, 110
Cress, 42, 95
Crisp Zucchini Ribbons, 152
Crop rotation, 17, 59
Crowns, starting plants from, 40
Cucumber, 81
    Chilled Poached Salmon with Cucumber
        Sauce, 121
    Cucumber Salad, 123
    harvesting, 81
    pest and disease control, 62, 63, 64, 65
    planting and growing, 12, 17, 32, 36, 42, 49,
        81
    Singapore Rice Salad, 123
    trellis systems, 16, 46, 47
    varieties, 81
Curried Cauliflower Rice & Vermicelli, 170
Curried Turkey Stew with Dumplings, 141
Cuttings, starting plants from, 40
Cutworms, 60, 62

D

Dandelion, 42, 81
    Italian Tomato and Dandelion Greens Soup,
        123
Design of gardens
    herb gardens, 68, 69, 70
    vegetable gardens, 16–17, 68
Dill, 71, 98
    Brussels Sprouts with Lemon-Dill Glaze, 172
    Dilled Tuna Sandwiches, 172
Direct-seeding, 36–39, 50
Disease control, 26, 59, 61, 64–65
Divisions, starting plants from, 40, 41
Dry bean, 42. *See also* Beans.
Drying, of herbs, 70

E

Earworms, 62
Eggplant, 82
    harvesting, 82
    Italian Eggplant with Millet and Peppers
        Stuffing, 124
    pest and disease control, 62, 63, 64
    planting and growing, 17, 32, 42, 49, 82
    Plum Rataouille, 123
    Roasted Eggplant Dip, 124
    varieties, 82
Endive, 42, 62, 82

F

Fall cleanup, 54, 55
Fennel, 71, 98
    Fennel with Parmesan Bread Crumbs,
        172
    Garden Greens with Fennel Dressing, 175
Fertilizing, 24, 25, 26–27. *See also* Compost.
Freezing of herbs, 70
French sorrel, 71, 91, 103
Frenched Beans with Celery, 109
Fresh Fruit with Creamy Lime Dipping
        Sauce, 163
Fresh Lima Beans in Onion Cream, 109
Fresh Tomato Pasta Soup, 157
Frost dates, 12, 14, 15, 32
Fruited Lamb Stew, 166
Fruitworms, 62
Fungi, diseases due to, 59, 64, 65

G

Garbanzo bean (chick pea), 42
Garden design. *See* Design of gardens.
Garden Greens with Fennel Dressing, 175
Garden sorrel, 43, 91
Garden-Vegetable Bulgur Stew, 185
Garlic, 40, 71, 83
    Garlicky Chicken Packets, 124
    Garlicky Mustard Greens, 131
    Roasted Garlic Hummus, 126
    Spicy Island Chicken, 126
Garlic chives, 99
Geraniums, scented, 71, 99
Globe artichoke, 40, 42, 55, 74
Greek Pasta and Vegetable Salad, 150
Green bean, 42, 75. *See also* Beans.
    Country Green Beans with Ham, 108
    Frenched Beans with Celery, 109
    Green Bean Bundles, 108
Green pea (shelling pea), 43, 87. *See also* Pea.
    Chicken Pot Pie, 138
    Green Pea and Potato Soup, 137
    Peas with Cukes 'n' Dill, 137
Grilled Flank Steak with Horseradish Sauce,
        127
Grilled Scallops and Vegetables with Cilantro
        Sauce, 169
Growing season, 12
Grubs, 62

H

Hardening off, 12, 34
Hardiness, defined, 12
Harvesting
    of herbs in general, 68, 70
    of specific vegetables, 74–95
Herbed Angel Hair Mushroom Wedge, 182
Herbed Duchess Turnips, 161
Herbicides, 28, 48, 49, 58
Herbs, 67–71, 96–105. *See also specific herbs.*
    encyclopedia of, 96–105
    garden design, 68, 69, 70
    harvesting, 68, 70
    planting and growing, 68, 71
    preserving, 70
Hoppin' John Salad, 137
Horehound, 71, 99
Hornworms, 64

Horseradish, 40, 42, 83
    Barbecued Pork Sandwiches, 126
    Grilled Flank Steak with Horseradish
        Sauce, 127
Hot Pepper
    Chicken Chili, 143
    Three Bean Chili, 143

I

Indian-Style Vegetable Stir-Fry, 115
Insecticides, 58
Insects, 26, 58–64
Inverted hills, 36, 38
Irish potato, 89
    harvesting, 89
    Low-Fat Cajun Wedges, 145
    pest and disease control, 60, 62, 64
    planting and growing, 17, 40, 43, 89
    Potato Pancakes, 146
    varieties, 89
    Zesty Lentil Stew, 145
Irrigation systems, 52, 53
Italian Eggplant with Millet and Peppers
        Stuffing, 124
Italian Tomato and Dandelion Greens Soup,
        123

J

Japanese Steak Salad, 147
Jerusalem artichoke, 40, 42, 74

K

Kale, 36, 42, 83
    Picante Pintos and Rice, 127
    Smoky Kale Chiffonade, 128
Kasha with Bow Tie Pasta with Mushrooms
        and Broccoli, 175
Kohlrabi, 17, 43, 84
    Kohlrabi with Red Peppers, 128

L

Leaf hoppers, 62
Leaf lettuce, 36, 84–85. *See also* Lettuce.
Leaf miners, 63
Leek, 43, 84
    Leek Cheese Pie, 128
Leeks, Chinese, 99
Lemon Brussels Sprouts, 112
Lettuce, 84–85
    Chicken, Tortellini and Roasted Vegetable
        Salad, 130
    harvesting, 85
    Mexican Hot Pot, 129
    pest control, 60, 62, 63, 64
    planting and growing, 12, 15, 32, 36, 43, 84
    Salad Primavera, 129
    varieties, 85
Light and shade requirements, 12, 13, 32
Lima bean, 42, 75. *See also* Beans.
    Fresh Lima Beans in Onion Cream, 109
Low-Fat Cajun Wedges, 145

M

Marjoram, 71, 100
    Beef Barley Soup, 175
    Kasha with Bow Tie Pasta with Mushrooms
        and Broccoli, 175

Mashed Rutabagas and Potatoes, 148
Mediterranean Sandwiches, 176
Melons. *See also* Watermelon.
   muskmelon (cantaloupe), 17, 43, 85
   pest and disease control, 62, 63, 64, 65
   planting and growing, 12, 17, 32, 43, 85, 95
Mexican Hot Pot, 129
Microwave Sweet Potato Chips, 146
Mildews, 65
Minted Melon Soup, 130
Mites, 63
Moo Shu Vegetables, 118
Mulches, 49–51, 54, 55
Muskmelon, 17, 43, 85. *See also* Melons.
   Crab and Pasta Salad in Cantaloupe, 131
   Minted Melon Soup, 130
Mustard, 36, 43, 85
   Garlicky Mustard Greens, 131

N

Nasturtium, 71, 100
Nematodes, 59
New Zealand spinach, 15, 43, 92
Nutmeg & Honey Carrot Crescents, 114

O

Okra, 43, 86
   Cajun-Style Chicken Soup, 132
   Shrimp Okra Gumbo, 132
Onion, 86
   Chicken Étouffée, 134
   harvesting, 86
   Onions Baked in Their Papers, 134
   pest and disease control, 63, 65
   planting and growing, 32, 40, 43, 86
   varieties, 86
Orange and Green Salad, 117
Oregano, 71, 100
   Bean & Mushroom Salad with Fresh Herb
      Dressing, 176
   Mediterranean Sandwiches, 176
   Pepperoni-Oregano Focaccia, 179
Oriental Chicken Kabobs, 144
Oyster plant (salsify), 43, 91

P

Pad Thai, 140
Parsley, 71, 101
   Pork and Vegetable Stew with Noodles, 179
   Spicy Parsley Sauce with Angel Hair Pasta,
      180
   Tabbouleh, 179
Parsnip, 43, 87
   Beef and Parsnip Stew, 136
   Parsnip Patties, 136
Pea, 87
   black-eye, 43, 87
   harvesting, 87
   Peas with Cukes 'n' Dill, 137
   pest and disease control, 63, 65
   planting and growing, 12, 43, 87
   shelling (green), 43, 87
   varieties, 87
Peach and Ricotta Filled Celery, 116
Peanut, 43, 88
   Curried Turkey Stew with Dumplings, 141
   Pad Thai, 140

Peasant Risotto, 117
Peppers, 88. *See also* Hot pepper; Sweet
      pepper.
   harvesting, 88
   Pepper-Stuffed Artichokes, 107
   pest and disease control, 60, 62, 63, 64
   planting and growing, 12, 15, 17, 32, 43, 49,
      88
   varieties, 88
Peppermint, 71, 101
Pepperoni-Oregano Focaccia, 179
Perennial crops, winter preparation for, 54, 55
Pest control, 26, 58–64
Pesticides, 20, 21, 58, 61–65. *See also*
      Herbicides.
pH, of soil, 24, 25
Picante Pintos and Rice, 127
Planning, of gardens. *See* Design of gardens.
Planting, 31–43. *See also* Transplanting.
   of cover crops, 55
   depth for, 37, 42–43
   direct-seeding in garden, 36–39, 50
   of herbs, 68
   inverted hills for, 36, 38
   mulches and, 50, 51
   rows for, 36–37
   scheduling of, 14, 15, 32
   spacing for, 36, 42–43
   starting seeds indoors, 32–33
   using plant parts for, 40–41
Plot plan, 16–17. *See also* Design of gardens.
Plum Rataouille, 123
Pole beans. *See* Beans; Green bean; Lima
      bean.
Pork and Vegetable Stew with Noodles, 179
Potatoes, 89. *See also* Irish potato; Sweet
      potato.
   harvesting, 89
   pest and disease control, 60, 62, 64, 65
   planting and growing, 17, 43, 89
   varieties, 89
Preservation
   of herbs in general, 70
   of specific herbs, 96–105
Propagation. *See also* Planting.
   from plant parts, 40–41
   of specific herbs, 96–105
   starting seeds indoors, 32–33
Protection
   of seedlings, 12, 13, 39, 62
   in winter, 54, 55, 74
Pumpkin, 89
   harvesting, 89
   pest and disease control, 62, 64, 65
   planting and growing, 17, 43, 49, 89
   varieties, 89

R

Radish, 90
   harvesting, 90
   Japanese Steak Salad, 147
   pest control, 63
   planting and growing, 12, 15, 36, 43, 90
   varieties, 90
Ragoût of Tuna, 158
Rain gauges, 53
Record keeping, 16

Red Snapper with Brown Rice and Tomato
      Stuffing, 185
Rhubarb, 90
   harvesting, 90
   planting and growing, 40, 41, 43, 90
   preparing for winter, 55
   Rhubarb and Strawberry Sauce, 146
   Rhubarb Chutney, 148
   varieties, 90
Roasted Corn & Wild Rice Salad, 121
Roasted Eggplant Dip, 124
Roasted Garlic Hummus, 126
Roasted Rosemary-Lemon Chicken, 180
Roasted Sweet Pepper Tapas, 143
Roman Spinach Soup, 150
Root maggots, 63
Rosemary, 71, 101
   Roasted Rosemary-Lemon Chicken, 180
Rotation, of crops, 17, 59
Rototillers and tilling, 16, 21, 54
Rows, for planting, 36–37
Rue, 71, 102
Rust, 65
Rutabaga, 17, 43, 90
   Mashed Rutabagas and Potatoes, 148
   Rutabaga "Fries," 148

S

Sage, 71, 102
   Caribbean Pork Stew, 182
   Herbed Angel Hair Mushroom Wedge, 182
Salad Primavera, 129
Salsify, 43, 91
Savory, summer, 71, 102
   Garden-Vegetable Bulgur Stew, 185
   Red Snapper with Brown Rice and Tomato
      Stuffing, 185
Savory Matchstick Carrots, 114
Savory Seafood Soup, 188
Seed, starting plants from
   cover crops, 55
   in garden, 36–39, 50
   indoors, 32–33
Seedlings
   indoor starting of, 32–33
   outdoor starting of, 36–39, 50
   protection of, 12, 13, 39, 62
   purchasing, 34
   thinning, 38
   transplanting to garden, 34, 35, 51
Sets, starting plants from, 40, 43
Shade requirements, 12
Shallot, 43, 91
   Snapper Fillets with Orange-Shallot Sauce,
      149
   Steak Frite, 148
Shanghai Chicken with Asparagus and Ham,
      108
Shrimp Okra Gumbo, 132
Sidedressing, 27
Singapore Rice Salad, 123
Size, of garden, 16
Slips, starting plants from, 40
Slugs, 60, 63
Smoky Kale Chiffonade, 128
Smuts, 65
Snails, 60, 63

191

Snap bean, 42, 75. *See also* Beans.
Snapper Fillets with Orange-Shallot Sauce, 149
Soil pH, 24, 25
Soil preparation, 23–29
    for coldframes, 12
    composting for, 28–29
    for cover crops, 55
    in fall, 54
    fertilizing for, 24, 25, 26–27
    soil testing for, 24–25
    tools for, 18–19, 21
    and watering, 52
Soil testing, 24–25
Sorrel, French, 71, 91, 103
Sorrel, garden, 43, 91
Southernwood, 71, 103
Soybean, 43
Spacing, 36, 42–43
Spearmint, 71, 103
Spicy Grapefruit Salad with Raspberry Dressing, 162
Spicy Island Chicken, 126
Spicy Parsley Sauce with Angel Hair Pasta, 180
Spicy Zucchini-Pepper Stew, 154
Spider mites, 63
Spinach, 92. *See also* New Zealand spinach.
    Greek Pasta and Vegetable Salad, 150
    harvesting, 92
    pest control, 63
    planting and growing, 12, 15, 36, 43, 92
    Roman Spinach Soup, 150
    varieties, 92
    Wilted Spinach Mandarin, 149
Squash, 92–93. *See also* Pumpkin; Summer squash; Winter squash.
    harvesting, 93
    pest and disease control, 62, 63, 64
    planting and growing, 15, 17, 32, 36, 43, 49, 92–93
    trellis systems, 46, 47
    varieties, 93
Staking, 46, 47
Starting plants. *See* Direct-seeding; Propagation.
Succession planting, 15
Suckers, starting plants with, 40
Summer savory, 71, 102
Summer squash, 17, 43, 92–93
    Crisp Zucchini Ribbons, 152
    Spicy Zucchini-Pepper Stew, 154
    Vegetable-Barley Pilaf, 150
Sun Country Chicken Salad, 162
Support, for plants, 46–47
Sweet pepper
    Chicken Fajitas, 144
    Oriental Chicken Kabobs, 144
    Roasted Sweet Pepper Tapas, 143

Sweet potato, 89
    harvesting, 89
    Microwave Sweet Potato Chips, 146
    pest and disease control, 64, 65
    planting and growing, 40, 43, 89
    Sweet Potato Bisque, 146
    Turkey, Corn and Sweet Potato Soup, 147
    varieties, 89
Sweet-Sour Turnip Green Salad, 161
Sweet woodruff, 71, 104
Swiss chard. *See also* Chard.
    Peasant Risotto, 117

T
Tabbouleh, 179
Tabbouleh in Tomato Cups, 158
Tansy, 71, 104
Tarragon, 71, 104
    Crab Spinach Salad with Tarragon Dressing, 186
    Tarragon Chicken Salad Sandwiches, 186
Three Bean Chili, 143
Temperature. *See also* Climate; Frost dates.
    for germination, 32
    for seedling growth, 34
Tenderness, defined, 12
Thinning, of seedlings, 38
Thrips, 63
Thyme, 71, 105
    Beef Bourguignon, 188
    Savory Seafood Soup, 188
Tillers and tilling, 16, 21, 54
Tomatillo, 94
    Chile Verde, 155
    Corn and Tomatillo Salsa, 157
Tomato, 94
    Fresh Tomato Pasta Soup, 157
    harvesting, 94
    pest and disease control, 60, 62, 63, 64, 65
    planting and growing, 12, 15, 17, 32, 35, 43, 49, 94
    Ragoût of Tuna, 158
    stakes and cages for, 46, 47
    starting new plants, 40, 94
    Tabbouleh in Tomato Cups, 158
    varieties, 94
Tools, 18–21
Transplanting. *See also* Seedlings.
    cutworm damage control, 60, 62
    of divided plants, 40, 41
    hardening off, 12, 34
    moving seedlings to garden, 34, 35, 51
    of suckers, 40
Trellis systems, 16, 46, 47
Tubers, starting plants from parts of, 40
Turkey, Corn and Sweet Potato Soup, 147
Turnip, 95
    harvesting, 95
    Herbed Duchess Turnips, 161

Turnips *(continued)*
    pest control, 63
    planting and growing, 12, 15, 17, 43, 95
    Sweet-Sour Turnip Green Salad, 161
    Turnip Shepherd's Pie, 161
    varieties, 95

V
Varieties, general consideration with, 14
Vegetable-Barley Pilaf, 150
Vegetable Rings on Broccoli Spears, 111
Viruses, 59, 65

W
Warm Blackened Tuna Salad, 114
Warm-season crops, defined, 12
Watercress, 95
    Citrus Salad with Bibb Lettuce, Watercress and Balsamic Dressing, 162
    Spicy Grapefruit Salad with Raspberry Dressing, 162
    Sun Country Chicken Salad, 162
Watering
    basic guidelines, 52, 53
    with coldframes, 12
    disease control and, 59
    irrigation systems, 52, 53
    mulches and, 49, 50, 51
    of seedlings, 32, 39
Watermelon, 95. *See also* Melons.
    disease control, 64
    harvesting, 95
    planting and growing, 17, 32, 43, 95
    varieties, 95
Wax bean, 75. *See also* Beans.
Weed control, 48
    herbicides for, 28, 48, 49, 58
    mulches for, 49–51, 54
    weeding for, 48
Weeds, list of, 48
White flies, 64
Wilt, 59, 65
Wilted Spinach Mandarin, 149
Winter preparation, 54–55, 74
Winter squash, 17, 43, 46, 93
    Baked Acorn Squash with Apples and Raisins, 155
    Butternut Squash in Coconut Milk, 152
    Chutney-Squash Circles, 154
Wireworms, 64
Woodruff, sweet, 71, 104
Wormwood, 71, 105

Y
Yellow bean, 75. *See also* Beans.

Z
Zesty Lentil Stew, 145